Mental Health and Work

Fit Mind, Fit Job

FROM EVIDENCE TO PRACTICE IN MENTAL HEALTH AND WORK

OECD
BETTER POLICIES FOR BETTER LIVES

This work is published under the responsibility of the Secretary-General of the OECD. The opinions expressed and arguments employed herein do not necessarily reflect the official views of OECD member countries.

This document and any map included herein are without prejudice to the status of or sovereignty over any territory, to the delimitation of international frontiers and boundaries and to the name of any territory, city or area.

Please cite this publication as:
OECD (2015), *Fit Mind, Fit Job: From Evidence to Practice in Mental Health and Work*, Mental Health and Work, OECD Publishing, Paris.
http://dx.doi.org/10.1787/9789264228283-en

ISBN 978-92-64-22091-1 (print)
ISBN 978-92-64-22828-3 (PDF)

Series: Mental Health and Work
ISSN 2225-7977 (print)
ISSN 2225-7985 (online)

The statistical data for Israel are supplied by and under the responsibility of the relevant Israeli authorities. The use of such data by the OECD is without prejudice to the status of the Golan Heights, East Jerusalem and Israeli settlements in the West Bank under the terms of international law.

Photo credits: Cover © boroboro/Shutterstock.com.

Corrigenda to OECD publications may be found on line at: *www.oecd.org/about/publishing/corrigenda.htm*.

Foreword

Mental ill-health is a key issue for labour market and social policies in OECD countries; an issue that has been long neglected also because of the widespread stigma and preconceptions. Yet mental ill-health exacts high costs on the people affected, businesses, and the economy as a whole. Things are beginning to change, however. OECD governments are increasingly coming to recognise that policy has a major role to play; it can help improve education outcomes and employment opportunities for people who suffer from mental ill-health; help those who are employed but struggling in their jobs; and prevent long-term sickness, unemployment and disability.

A first OECD report on this subject, *Sick on the Job? Myths and Realities about Mental Health and Work*, published in early 2012, identified the main knowledge gaps, broadened the evidence base, questioned some myths about the link between mental health and work, and painted a comprehensive picture of the underlying policy challenges. Nine reports in the series of *Mental Health and Work* country reviews (Australia, Austria, Belgium, Denmark, the Netherlands, Norway, Sweden, Switzerland and the United Kingdom) have then been published between early 2013 and mid-2015. They looked in depth into how selected OECD countries were tackling those policy challenges and drew detailed country-specific policy conclusions.

This new OECD report, *Fit Mind, Fit Job: From Evidence to Practice in Mental Health and Work*, provides a synthesis of the findings of the OECD's four-year review. It concludes that a transformation is required in policy thinking about mental health and work and sets out the key elements for an integrated policy approach to promoting better mental health and employment outcomes. The report also brings together a selection of concrete promising policy examples from the various areas of intervention that could help countries find their path for the future.

The synthesis report was launched and discussed at the High-Level Policy Forum hosted by the Dutch Government in March 2015, where its main conclusions were welcome by the Forum participants. The report provides a policy framework that can help to guide the reform process by OECD governments and main stakeholders. It provides useful insights for interventions across the policy areas of education, employment, health and welfare, which all need to work towards the same goal in a co-ordinated and integrated approach to generate the desired impact: better labour market inclusion of people with mental illness. Governments can also use the framework as a yardstick when evaluating the performance of the measures and policies they have taken.

The *Mental Health and Work* review was carried out by the Employment Analysis and Policy Division of OECD's Directorate for Employment, Labour and Social Affairs. This report was prepared by Iris Arends from the University Medical Center Groningen, Niklas Baer from the Psychiatric Services Basel-Landschaft, and Veerle Miranda, Christopher Prinz (project leader) and Shruti Singh from the OECD. The policy examples were compiled by Robin Risselada. Statistical work was carried out by Dana Blumin, with support from Maxime Ladaique. The report was edited by Ken Kincaid. Editorial assistance was provided by Marlène Mohier and project assistance by Natalie Corry. Valuable comments were provided by Bob Grove, Mark Keese, Mark Pearson and Stefano Scarpetta, and experts from some of the countries covered in the review.

Table of contents

Figures

Acronyms and abbreviations

ATAPS	Access to Allied Psychological Services
CBT	Cognitive Behavioural Therapy
CLB	Student Guidance Centres (*Centra voor Leerlingenbegeleiding*)
DSM	Diagnostic and Statistical Manual of Mental Disorders
EA	Employment Advisor
EAPs	Employee Assistance Programmes
EITC	Earned income tax credit
ESENER	European Survey of Enterprises on New and Emerging Risks
ESL	Early school leaving
EU	European Union
EUR	Euro
FFWS	Fit for Work Service
GBP	British pound sterling
GDP	Gross Domestic Product
GGZ Nederland	Dutch Association of Mental Health and Addiction Care
GP	General Practitioner
GPMHSC	General Practice Mental Health Standards Collaboration
GTB	Belgium specialised non-profit centre
HRM	Human Resource Management
IAPT	Increased Access to Psychological Therapies
ICD	International Statistical Classification of Diseases
IIZ	Inter-institutional co-operation
IPS	Individual Placement and Support
IWA	Inclusive Tripartite Workplace Agreement
JSCI	Job Seeker Classification Instrument
NEET	Not in Education, Employment or Training
NGO	Non-Governmental Organisation
NHS	National Health Service
NICE	National Institute for Health and Care Excellence
OP	Occupational Physician
PES	Public Employment Service
PHaMS	Personal Helpers and Mentors Programme
PHP	Practitioner Health Programme

POH-GGZ	Dutch abbreviation for Practice Support Professional for Mental Health Care
PPP	Purchasing Power Parity
PPS	Purchasing Power Standard
PVA	Austrian Disability Benefit Agency
PWE	Psychosocial work environment
SME	Small and Medium-sized Enterprises
UWV	Dutch Employee Insurance Agency
VDAB	Flemish Public Employment Service
WEA	Working Environment Authority
WHM-CIDI	World Mental Health Composite International Diagnostic Interview
WHO	World Health Organization
YLD	Years Lived with Disability
ZAT	Regional care and advice teams

Executive summary

Mental ill-health exacts a high price – on individuals, employers, and the economy. Apart from the distress they suffer individually, people with mental health problems also suffer economically through lower employment, higher unemployment and a high risk of poverty. Employers struggle with significant losses in productivity at work and high rates of sickness absence. And the economy at large bears the costs in the form of elevated social and health care expenditures.

These heavy costs are a direct consequence of the high prevalence of mental ill-health, especially of the mild-to-moderate kind. It affects one-fifth of the working-age population at any given moment, and one person in two will suffer a period of poor mental health during their lifetime. While there has been no long-term increase in prevalence, it is only recently that policy makers and society in general have begun to realise the scale of the economic, employment and social challenges that mental ill-health represents.

To address the high costs of mental ill-health it needs to become a priority for stakeholders in the workplace, in the health system, and in every branch of social policy, including unemployment and disability. Policy has been slow to react, however.

The big issues are clear:

- The early onset of mental ill-health that affects negatively education outcomes and the transition into employment;
- High levels of under-treatment and unmet health care needs;
- Significant stigma associated with mental ill-health which harms employment prospects of people affected;
- The high prevalence of mental ill-health among all working-age benefit claimants, including recipients of unemployment benefit.

OECD policy principles

Drawing on available evidence of the links between mental health and work in nine OECD countries, this report concludes that a policy transformation is needed in regard to **when** and **what** type of intervention is needed and **who** should carry it out. Currently intervention often comes too late, key stakeholders are left out, and different institutions and services tend to work in isolation. Changing the three parameters – when, what, who – could go a long way towards improving the labour market inclusion of people with mental ill-health.

- **When**
  The timing of intervention is critical. Interventions often come too late, once people have been out of the labour market for years. Even comprehensive measures have limited impact if delayed. Any action taken in school or the workplace will have a better, more lasting impact than waiting until people have dropped out of education or the labour market. Sickness and unemployment schemes also need to react quickly to help the excluded back into work.

- **What**
  Current policies are often delivered in silos. Health, employment, and education policies generally consider only their sectorial outcomes. Such isolated support is not good enough. People with mental ill-health struggling to keep, return to or find a job often have inter-linked social, health and employment problems which policy must address in an integrated way. Integrated service provision delivers significantly better, faster outcomes.

- **Who**
  Progress will not be made in meeting the challenge of mental ill-health if it is left to specialist mental health care workers and institutions. Mental ill-health is a mainstream issue that many stakeholders must address. Front-line actors outside the mental health sphere have a key role to play in securing better education and labour market outcomes for people with mental ill-health. Teachers, line managers, general practitioners, and employment service caseworkers are confronted with the effects of mental ill-health among their students, workers, patients, and customers on a daily basis. They are best placed to identify issues, to address impacts and implications, and to involve professionals as necessary.

None of the countries reviewed by the OECD has put in place an integrated approach across the different policy domains that successfully address mental health and work problems at an early stage. But plenty of promising examples can be found in different fields from which lessons can be drawn for a change in policy approach. Many of the examples, however, are short-lived pilot projects that have often not been rigorously evaluated. Better measurement and monitoring of policies and outcomes will allow better learning from promising examples.

A few universal policy elements are required to shift towards an integrated policy approach to promoting better mental health and employment outcomes:

- Key first-line actors, especially those outside the mental health field, need better competences to deal with mental ill-health; operational guidelines on how to identify mental health problems; and stronger tools and referral structures to tackle problems and their implications quickly when they arise.

- Responsibilities of the primary actors need to be spelled out more clearly. This is important for people concerned – employers, doctors and service providers – but equally for public actors such as benefit authorities, employment services, education authorities and the health care system.

- Financial incentives can provide an effective way to ensure that the interested parties live up to their responsibilities. Policy should seek to change systems so that all stakeholders are stimulated into or paid for doing the right thing. Incentives are needed to promote the early identification of mental ill-health, swift action to deal with it, and the integrated delivery of health care and employment services.

- Lastly, rigorous policy implementation is crucial. For instance, a number of guidelines and regulations already exist for employers, doctors, and other actors. But they will have little impact unless their use is systematically monitored and non-compliance sanctioned, which calls for much stronger leadership at both the political and managerial level.

The ultimate goal of policy should be to ensure that people receive quick and integrated support wherever and however they seek help, be it by seeing: a social worker or a teacher because of difficulties at home; a human resource professional to discuss trouble at work; a general practitioner to ask for a sickness certificate; a psychologist to look for help with a mood or anxiety problem; or an employment service counsellor to find a new job.

The OECD Mental Health and Work Policy Framework, consequently provides a series of general policy conclusions for all OECD countries under four headings:

- Help young people through mental health awareness and education policies.
- Strive for an employment-oriented mental health care system.
- Improve workplace policies and employer supports and incentives.
- Make benefits and employment services fit for people with mental ill-health.

Assessment and conclusions

The OECD mental health and work policy framework

Mental health is an important driver of labour market outcomes and thus affects economic growth and future development. In OECD countries, mental ill-health is responsible for between one-third and one-half of all long-term sickness and disability among the working-age population. It causes and exacerbates chronic physical illness, pushing up health care costs. And it lowers education outcomes – partly because those who are ill leave school early – so shutting off employment opportunities. Relatively to the mentally healthy, the employment rate of people who suffer from poor mental health is 15-30 percentage points lower and their unemployment rate is twice as high. They are also twice as likely to live in poor households. In the workplace, employees who suffer from mental ill-health tend to underperform and their low productivity is probably the single biggest cost factor, borne to a large extent by employers.

The prevalence of mental ill-health also accounts for it being a heavy economic burden. At any given moment, some 20% of the working-age population suffers from a mental illness, and one person in two will suffer a period of poor mental health during their lifetime. Most people with mental ill-health are affected by mild-to-moderate illness – predominantly mood and anxiety disorders, commonly referred to as "common mental illness".

If labour markets are to function well, it is important that policy makers address the interplay between mental health and work. They are slowly coming to recognise that they have long neglected an issue that is critical to people's well-being and for contributing to sustainable economic growth. The policy changes required are substantial and involve a large number of institutions and stakeholders working towards better co-ordinated policies and service delivery. Reform will therefore require strong political leadership. The consolidated set of social, education, health, and labour market policy responses that are needed to promote better mental health and employment outcomes are the focus of this report.

Rethinking mental health and work policy

In "Mental Health: The New Frontier for Labour Economics", Richard Layard wrote that improving mental health is vital to both economic growth and happiness and "could be the most important single step forwards [economically and socially] in the 21st century" (Layard, 2013). *Making Mental Health Count* (OECD, 2014d) stressed the vast economic and social costs of mental ill-health and high unmet need for appropriate care. *Sick on the Job?* (OECD, 2012) – identified the main challenges posed by the interplay between mental health and work and argued the case for a structural shift in policy.

The objective of this new OECD report, *Fit Mind, Fit Job*, is to identify the key elements of the policy transformation that are required to build a more mentally resilient workforce and improve the labour market inclusion of people who suffer from mental ill-health. There are three central components to that transformation:

- The first is a shift in **when** to intervene. Mental ill-health is often identified too late. Support and intervention at a time when people have been out of work for several years is often ineffective. Policy should focus on prevention, early identification, and early action.
- The second is a shift in **how** to intervene or **what** to do. Different institutions, especially in the health and employment areas, often operate in isolation in pursuit of their own objectives. And if there is such a dearth of integrated approaches, it is not least because incentives, obligations and procedures are scattered and contradictory.
- The third is a shift in **who** needs to intervene. Currently, the positive influence that front-line actors like teachers, managers, general practitioners and employment counsellors can have on education and labour market outcomes of people with mental ill-health is often poorly harnessed. These mainstream actors are best placed to help people early.

This report discusses why policy must make those changes and how it can achieve them. In doing so, it mainly draws on policy examples from nine OECD countries. The examples are rich in nature and, taken together, provide a promising and inspiring starting point. However, they cannot obscure the fact that there is a significant lack of data, knowledge, and rigorous evaluation of new policies and programmes, both generally and with regard to the policies advocated in this report. But this should not be a justification for inaction: policy makers cannot afford to wait until the evidence base is fuller. They need to act now and, at the same time, invest more in better evaluation of policies and programmes, especially those involving earlier, better integrated intervention which will yield longer-term returns on investment.

The report emphasises the need to take action across a range of policy arenas:

- Education policies to achieve optimal outcomes and robust school-to-work transitions;
- Health policies to deliver accessible treatment, which supports employment as a desirable outcome;
- Workplace policies to ensure high labour productivity and job retention;
- Benefit policies to promote a fast, sustainable return to work.

The policy principles developed in this report provide an integrated framework for guiding action in each country to promoting better mental health and greater labour market inclusion of people with mental illness.

When to intervene: Early identification and action

There is a large body of evidence showing that helping people stay in work is much more effective for sustainable employment than helping them return to a job after an absence. Similarly, the longer people are out of work – due to unemployment, sickness, or both – the more difficult it becomes to bring them back into the labour force and sustainable employment. These findings are even more valid for people who suffer from mental ill-health. Being out of work often has adverse effects on both their health condition and their workplace relationships (sick leave for mental illness being highly stigmatised), which triggers a vicious circle.

Helping people with mental ill-health back into employment is difficult when they have been out of work for a long period of time and reliant on social assistance or disability benefit. At that stage, their work motivation and self-confidence are so low that easing them back into sustainable employment is costly and fraught with uncertainty. Austrian data, for example, show that people are lost to the labour market once they are seeking to access disability benefit: even those who are denied such a benefit hardly ever walk the employment path again (OECD, 2015a).

The long-term inactive also need help, and every effort should be made to help them early. That thinking, for example, is behind the Swiss Disability Insurance, for example, which seeks to tackle conditions that are likely to result in disability benefit claims later in life. It promotes early notification of problems and offers a special low-threshold provision that focuses particularly on people with common mental illness (OECD, 2014a).

Acting at an early stage in the benefit system

Early action in the benefit system brings to the fore two policy tools critical to helping people back to work quickly and successfully: unemployment benefit and (where it exists) sickness benefit. Few unemployment systems are equipped to deal with mental ill-health despite its high and growing incidence. Indeed, prevalence is growing in many countries – as data from countries like Austria, Australia and the United Kingdom attest. The chief reason is that structural reforms to the disability system in many countries, which seek to restrict access only to those unable to work, have meant that more people with health problems and reduced work capacity are remaining in the unemployment system.

The standard approach taken in most countries' unemployment systems today is to exempt jobseekers with health problems from their participation and job-seeking requirements, and to hope that, and wait until, they return treated and cured. That is not the right approach for most jobseekers who suffer from mental ill-health, because most cannot be "healed" in the traditional sense of the word. Treatment and work reinforce each other: without treatment labour market participation is difficult to sustain and, without work, treatment is much less effective. Unemployment systems should therefore seek to identify jobseekers' underlying mental health problems, the obstacles those problems create to labour market reintegration, and the treatment needed to secure sustainable employment.

Among the countries reviewed by the OECD, Belgium has moved furthest in this direction: in the past years, 12% of the longer-term unemployed in Flanders were submitted to an in-depth screening (OECD, 2013a). In the United Kingdom, the *Employment and Wellbeing Toolkit* was introduced in 2014 to support employment coaches in identifying well-being needs for employment and appropriate interventions to enable job attainment among claimants with mental health problems.

When a front-line actor – e.g. an employment service caseworker – assesses a jobseeker's barriers to finding employment, questions on mental health status are essential. If need be, the jobseeker should be referred for in-depth assessment and targeted support, in addition to any appropriate mainstream employment support. The expectations and participation required of jobseekers with mental health conditions should be made clear to them in order to encourage or even, in some circumstances, compel them to take up any special services being provided. If mental illness goes unnoticed and unaddressed, the risk of long-term and/or repeat unemployment is high.

Sickness benefit systems should usually be able to respond more quickly than unemployment benefit systems because they are familiar with claimants' health problems but they are often passive payment schemes that deal only with benefit eligibility and not return-to-work management. However, in some OECD countries, such as Sweden and Norway, the sickness benefit system encourages partial sick leave to maintain the workplace connection and foster gradual return-to-work (e.g. OECD, 2013b). To ensure timely return-to-work, sickness benefit policies should have well-established procedures for ensuring regular contact between sick workers and employers though not ignoring issues of confidentiality. In a few countries this is being realised by including the treating doctors and the development of individual return-to-work plans, but even in these cases this policy is not always well implemented and monitored.

Early preventive action in the workplace

Return-to-work plans are critical for employees suffering from mental ill-health. They have to contend not only with their personal problems, but also with workplace difficulties and conflicts that can be solved only if employers and, in particular, line managers get involved. Good management is therefore important. Binding obligations on employers to manage sickness absences and the return-to-work transition properly can help bring it about. Such obligations change the behaviour of both employers and employees, especially if they are backed up with corresponding strong financial incentives, e.g. in the form of sickness benefit reductions and extended periods of employer-paid sick pay. Reforms in the Netherlands and, to a lesser degree, in some other countries go in that direction, despite the challenge of striking a balance between employment protection and employer incentives to strengthen job retention without jeopardising hiring (OECD, 2014b).

The need for better workplace sickness policies is clear in view of the growing share of absences attributable to mental ill-health. More daunting problems still, however, are poor performance and productivity losses due to poor mental health. Data show that many people with common mental illness struggle at work. For example, 69% of the people with moderate mental health complaints report having problems in job performance compared to 26% of the people without mental health complaints. There is a strong business case for addressing the issue, yet employers hold on to poor workplace practices. A first step in the right direction in many countries is the amendment of labour law to include obligatory and far-reaching psychosocial risk prevention. It would be especially effective if complemented with clear guidelines and concrete tools for employers and labour inspection authorities, as in Denmark (OECD, 2013c). In all of the reviewed countries, however, the implementation of psychosocial risk prevention is slow, as traditional issues continue to dominate health and safety policy and the widespread psychosocial issues remain neglected.

Employers therefore need more than general prevention on the one hand and support for managing sick employees' return to work on the other. They also need a strategy for how to deal with underperformance and workplace conflicts caused by or related to mental illness. None of the reviewed countries can yet claim to be particularly advanced in the development of such a strategy, even though some big companies have started to address it. Management and line managers need the right support and training to help their employees with mental health problems to be able to perform their work. There is a big role in this context for employer and employee representative bodies to help develop guidelines in this area in addition to any public guidelines or action.

Action to ensure a good school-to-work transition

More than one-half of all mental illnesses have their onset in childhood and adolescence. Education systems thus have a key role to play in ensuring good educational outcomes and successful labour market transitions for children with mental health problems. Schools should seek to foster mental health resilience and help students with their social and emotional problems, especially when families cannot provide the necessary support. To avoid stigmatisation of young people struggling with mental health issues, schools should, as far as possible, promote general mental well-being and offer help that is easily available to all students and teachers. Two good examples are the *KidsMatter* and *MindMatters* programmes developed in Australia with the aim of promoting mental health and well-being, preventing problems, and enabling early intervention within schools (OECD, 2015b). *KidsMatter* has been trialled in 101 schools and found to improve general mental health and well-being.

Irregular school attendance can often be a sign of mental illness and eventually turn into early school leaving. Policies should therefore reach out to truants and early school leavers. To guide and monitor such children, some countries have introduced very strong measures. Denmark's municipal *Youth Guidance Centres*, for example, are mandated to intervene very quickly upon truancy to prevent early school leaving (OECD, 2013c). Other countries have put in place freely accessible structures for general health promotion but with a special focus on mental health that teenagers can access easily without being labelled as mentally ill, such as *Youth Clinics* in Sweden which have been able to reach out to 1.3 million young people (OECD, 2013d). These facilities offer a range of support that includes mental health care and counselling from social workers.

Another critical moment is the transition from youth to adulthood and from school to work. A smooth transition to the labour market is important for building the confidence of all young people, particularly those with a mental illness. The move is much more difficult for those with low educational attainment among whom young people with mental ill-health are over-represented. Schools can do more to smooth the transition, for example by early involvement of employment professionals to ensure that strugglers are not lost from sight or left alone too long. In Flanders (Belgium), for example, 85% of all school leavers register with the public employment service, which focuses strongly on young people's first-job experience and monitors mental health issues regularly (OECD, 2013a).

Access to mental health treatment

Early action is also an issue for the health care system. Under-treatment is pervasive in most countries and the length of time between the onset of illness and first treatment tends, sadly, to be extremely long – more than ten years on average, according to some studies. Yet treatment is far more effective in the early stages of illness when people are still generally well integrated into their communities, schools, and jobs. Worryingly, in many OECD countries, it is among young people that rates of under-treatment are highest and waiting times for counselling or therapy are longest. Moreover, some countries have recently reported cuts to mental health services including for young people as a result of overall health spending cuts (in real terms) (OECD, 2014d). Improving access to mental health care must be a priority. Additionally, the provision of appropriate treatment is a point of concern, especially for people suffering from mild-to-moderate mental ill-health who often are only prescribed medication (such as antidepressants). Improving and expanding the care provided in primary care settings would be an important first step (OECD, 2014d). In that respect, recently taken measures in Australia and the United Kingdom to increase the provision of psychotherapeutic therapies for common mental health problems specifically have proven highly effective, albeit less so for children than for adults (OECD, 2015b; OECD, 2014c). For example, through the United Kingdom's *Increased Access to Psychological Therapies* programme, 1.1 million people with common mental disorders received treatment between 2010 and 2012 with 45% recovery rates.

Who needs to intervene: Involving and empowering mainstream actors

Mental illness was long considered a health issue only and the exclusive responsibility of the health care system. A better understanding of the close links between mental ill-health and educational, social, and employment-related status and outcomes has exposed the narrowness of that perspective. The high prevalence of common mental illness makes it a mainstream issue. People who deal with it daily and directly are best placed to identify problems early, address their impact and implications, and/or initiate early action by mental health care practitioners.

This report identifies four groups of front-line actors as particularly important to the sustainable labour market inclusion of people who suffer from mental ill-health: teachers, line managers, general practitioners (GPs), and employment service caseworkers. Policy should focus on three ways of empowering them:

1. Raise awareness of the problem and their key role in addressing it;
2. Develop their competence in dealing with mental health issues and ability to do the right thing at the right time;
3. Put in place an accessible support structure to which they can refer people with mental health problems – students, workers, patients, jobseekers – for swift and proper professional care.

Raising awareness among front-line actors

Mental health-related problems still go unnoticed for too long. And, when front-line actors eventually notice such problems, they are not always able to adequately address them. The fact is that front-line actors generally lack the knowledge and experience to help people with signs of mental ill-health and often find it difficult to talk about mental health issues. As a result, students, workers and jobseekers with mental health problems run the risk of failing at school, losing their job, or not finding one for a long time. When GPs, for example, write out a sickness certificate, they often do little to help workers with mental ill-health address their work problems and return to work. In the worst case, people end up on long-term benefits, such as disability benefit, just because their problems were never adequately addressed.

Raising awareness among front-line actors of the high prevalence of mental ill-health, and the key role they play in good outcomes for the people concerned is an important first step. Anti-stigma campaigns in many countries have successfully contributed to greater awareness by specifically targeting front-line actors (e.g. workplace campaigns such as *Business in Mind* in Australia and the *Mentally Healthy Workplace Programme* in the United Kingdom). Representative professional bodies (e.g. teachers' unions or general practitioners' associations) can also play a key part in building awareness, as can employers in their companies and human resource departments. Equally, managerial leadership is needed to helping employment services and line managers understand their role.

Better mental health competence for all actors

Developing mental health competence is the second main policy thrust. Line managers and employment service caseworkers need the proper training to be better able to signal employees and jobseekers struggling in work (or in finding work) due to poor mental health, understand the work and performance implications and impacts of mental ill-health, and know what to do when mental health-related problems with job performance surface. That knowledge will also make it easier for them to judge how much they can expect from a worker or a jobseeker with a mental health condition. Some countries already propose management tools specifically for helping front-line actors to identify critical situations and do the right thing at the right time.

For teachers and, in particular, GPs, changes should be made to their basic training curricula to give them a fuller grasp of mental illness and its impact. Discussions to that effect are on-going in countries such as Austria and the United Kingdom. Some countries – like Australia and Denmark – have recently invested significantly in mental health training courses for GPs. They also fund the mental health care provided by doctors who attend these courses (OECD, 2015b; OECD, 2013c). Training for GPs should be substantive because they are often the first port of call for people with mental health problems and often the only medical professional who ever treat them.

An important part of GP training should be the capacity to deal with work ability, workplace requirements, and sickness certification, especially in the case of mental ill-health. Indeed, more and more OECD countries now require doctors to draw up sickness certificates that include much more information on what a patient is still able to do. Examples are the *fit note*, as opposed to the sick note, that British doctors must fill in and the *work ability record* that Danish GPs are asked to complete in addition to the traditional sick note (OECD, 2014c; OECD, 2013c). Illness-specific sickness certification guidelines, like those developed in Sweden, also follow this purpose (OECD, 2013d).

Access to professional support

The third key element in empowering mainstream actors to deal with mental ill-health is an easily accessible support structure where people with mental health problems – students, workers, patients, jobseekers – get swift and proper professional attention. Schools in some countries have such support structures – e.g. external care teams in the Netherlands and Belgium's student guidance centres (OECD, 2013a; OECD, 2014b). However, they generally cater to young people with more severe mental health problems. Support, and even treatment for people with mild-to-moderate mental ill-health, is more forthcoming from front-line professionals – e.g. Austria's youth coaches and psychology-trained teachers for students with social and emotional difficulties, or Australia's *Youth Connections*, a programme that serves disaffected young people (OECD, 2015a; OECD, 2015b).

Employers and line managers rarely have access to professional support. Some countries, especially in Northern and Western Europe, have strong occupational health systems that support employers and, to some degree, employees. But occupational physicians, too, generally lack mental health knowledge, and very few countries call on occupational psychologists. In English-speaking countries, employee assistance programmes are common, and bigger companies in all OECD countries are increasingly building their own health units. Although these are all promising approaches, they suffer from low take-up by employees in need and do not exist in small and medium-sized companies (SMEs), where insufficient knowledge and resources preclude any spending on support services. This gap can potentially be filled by a bigger role for work councils and trade unions in those SMEs, in co-operation with the employer, with the support of public resources.

The degree to which employment service caseworkers have access to professional support also varies considerably. The employment services in a few countries (like Sweden) have some psychological expertise available, though not enough for caseworkers to get help quickly (OECD, 2013d). Belgium has a more elaborate support system for severe diagnosed disorders, not for common mental illness (OECD, 2013a). Other countries (like Denmark) call on psychologically-trained caseworkers who work with jobseekers suffering from common mental illness. Because their caseloads are very light they achieve excellent outcomes, but this reaches only a few clients (OECD, 2013c). Greater investment in support from professional practitioners requires making a stronger business case for the high returns for the unemployment system itself.

GPs, too, need quick access to professional support. Referring patients with mental illness to specialists, particularly psychiatrists, in the health care system is not sufficient or always appropriate. Not only do patients in most countries face considerable waiting times but not all need to see a specialist, and specialised care is generally costly. A complementary solution would be to have mental health care providers in primary care practices. Australia and the Netherlands have recently moved to provide funding to enable GPs to hire mental health nurses (OECD, 2015b; OECD, 2014b). In the Netherlands, 62% of the GPs now offer extra support by mental health nurses. In both countries, the move has led to improved access to treatment, better compliance, and closer working relationships with specialised mental health doctors.

How to intervene: achieving well-integrated policies and service delivery

One of the biggest problems in all of the reviewed countries is the mismatch between the needs of the people suffering from mental ill-health and the services that are provided. Many of those with poor mental health require both health *and* employment support. Generally, though, they get only one or the other – and sometimes neither. The mismatch – and shortfall – is worrying in view of the considerable evidence on how mental ill-health can be a barrier to employment and work can be an important element in recovery.

Typically, the mental health and employment sectors operate independently of each other, with different objectives and approaches, and often under different government authorities. Medical services aim to treat people with mental ill-health and improve symptoms and everyday well-being, often with scant regard for employment and workplace issues. Employment services seek to keep employees in work or bring people back into employment through training and activation (e.g. making benefit entitlement conditional on collaborating in return-to-work activities or active job seeking), but usually either fail to address employees' or jobseekers' frequent health issues or wait until they come back "cured" from treatment. This arrangement can meet only some of the needs of people with poor mental health, which leads to patchy social and employment outcomes.

Gradual development of more integrated approaches

Policy across the OECD is slowly responding in different ways through approaches that address employment *and* health needs (Arends et al., 2014). Several countries have been introducing whole-of-government mental health initiatives and action plans, with the emphasis increasingly on retaining and finding employment. The *Australian Ten-Year Roadmap for National Mental Health Reform* and, especially, the *Norwegian National Strategic Plan for Work and Mental Health* are two such instances (OECD, 2015b; OECD, 2013b). These moves in the right direction should be backed up by setting clear targets and measuring to what extent they have been met. The Outcomes Framework of England's National Health Service recently moved a step further towards supporting an integrated approach by using two employment-related outcome targets, on sickness absence rates and employment rates of people with disability and mental ill-health, in addition to a suite of more narrowly drawn "health" indicators. Monitoring of each actor's achievements is necessary to ensure that all actors engage fully with the shift in emphasis.

Some countries have taken a step closer to employment and health service integration. They have developed policies whereby sectors are transparent about the actions they take, share information and knowledge, and have found solutions to address confidentiality issues. Two examples are the systematic communication between the mental health sector and the public employment service in the Netherlands and between social security and the public employment service in Austria (OECD, 2014b; OECD, 2015a), both initiatives relevant for people with more severe mental illness at risk of becoming long-term unemployed or inactive.

Sweden has gone even further by making services from different stakeholders more coherent through financial co-ordination: resources of the social insurance authority, the public employment service and the municipal welfare sector are pooled in order to provide more integrated vocational rehabilitation services (OECD, 2013d). Switzerland has been trying something similar through *inter-institutional co-operation* though with much more diversity in approaches across the country (OECD, 2014a).

Policy makers in some countries have sought to provide the right services to clients through partnerships between different sectors, with one institution acting as a case manager co-ordinating the services they provide. One good example is a programme developed by the Flemish employment service in co-operation with the mental health and welfare sectors. It brings together a job coach from the employment service (who is also the case co-ordinator), a health coach from the mental health sector, and an empowerment coach from welfare (OECD, 2013a). A further example is Denmark's new vocational rehabilitation model designed to prevent disability benefit claims. It is co-ordinated by the municipal job centre and involves health services, social services, and the education sector (OECD, 2013c).

Promising examples of fully integrated service delivery

A few countries are in fact moving further towards delivering truly integrated mental health and employment (or education) services alongside each other. They come in two forms:

1. More integrated services delivered *within* a sector through the provision of employment support in the health system and health care in the employment system;
2. Services delivered by a *new entity* specialised in integrated service provision.

Good examples of integrated services within a sector are to be found in the health sector. *Individual Placement and Support* (IPS) for people with severe mental ill-health is the most widespread approach. This model uses an evidence-based fidelity scale to measure the level of implementation or the degree of adherence to the characteristics of the intervention. A key element of the model is the on-going support for both the employer and the employee to ensure on-the-job learning and prevent drop-out although sustaining employment remains the biggest challenge.

Another example of how mental health service providers cross sector boundaries to support people with common mental illness is the employment advisor working alongside a psychological therapy provider in the UK's *Improving Access to Psychological Therapy* initiative (OECD, 2014c). A pilot study of this initiative showed that through the support provided by the employment advisors, 63% of the patients on sick leave were able to return to work.

A good example of a new entity that provides integrated services is the Australian *headspace* programme. It delivers such services largely free of charge to 12-to-25 year-olds, mostly through self-referral, and often reaches young people with non-diagnosed mental illness – a recent evaluation of the programme participants showed that 17% had a sub-threshold mental health condition (OECD, 2015b).

Policy makers could develop all these approaches alongside each other in order to work towards better labour market outcomes for people with mental ill-health. Critical to success are: i) the alignment of policy objectives and financial incentives; ii) rigorous implementation; and iii) on-going evaluation. The first is particularly important for efforts to deliver simultaneous client-oriented support from different institutions and professionals across different sectors.

Aligning objectives and incentives

In principle, aligning sector-specific policy objectives should be evident because both the health and employment sectors aim to improve individuals' ability to function in society. That goal can be furthered by ensuring that all professionals properly understand the mutual links between mental health and employment and how actions in one impact and spill over into the other.

However, stakeholders and professionals also need better rewards and financial incentives if they are to push for and participate in integrated service delivery. There is too much focus in the health system on rewarding repeat use of health services, and too little on rewarding successful addressing of mental health needs, including through increased employment. Similarly, public employment services while trying to address client needs to succeed in work reintegration need more funding and better incentives for addressing their clients' mental health issues. Financial co-ordination and the pooling of resources between sectors go some way to addressing that problem.

Clearer obligations and guidelines are also desirable on when and how to use and invest in integrated service delivery. To the extent possible, rules and regulations should be binding on all stakeholders, as voluntary service integration cannot deliver high take-up and can therefore be detrimental to better outcomes on a macro level.

Good implementation and evaluation

Current policy initiatives often suffer from discrepancies between lofty ambition and modest efforts of implementation. Whole-of-government strategies, for example, aim to set the agenda for better policy across governments but often fail to clearly set out what each stakeholder should do to achieve the policy objectives. And implementation cannot be left to the discretion of stakeholders only. Strong leadership at both the political and the managerial level is necessary to change practices and foster understanding of the need for integrated services at all levels of an organisation and of the consequences of failing to deliver them. Roles need to be clearly assigned and newly implemented practices monitored continuously.

Policy evaluation, too, needs to be improved. Policy makers need better data and better knowledge on social, health and employment outcomes to decide which policies to continue and which new ones to trial. The stakeholders involved also need continuous feedback to assure improvement in the way policies and services are delivered. Rigorous evaluation of new intervention programmes or services requires methodologically sound (pilot) studies, ideally including a comparison group and random allocation, systematic data collection and – particularly important – the measurement of longer-term labour market outcomes for people with mental ill-health.

Future directions for better integrated services

Some people seek help through the health care system and others through the employment system. This should not matter. It should be the responsibility of each sector to deliver integrated services in line with client needs, which in turn requires a much better understanding in all sectors of the needs of clients with a mental illness. More integrated provision of services *within* each sector – e.g. through employment advice in the mental health system and psychological expertise in employment services – appears to be the easiest and most cost-effective approach because it requires less harmonisation of the objectives and incentives of the professionals involved.

Integrated mental health and employment services can improve labour market outcomes for people with mental ill-health if implemented rigorously. However, some of the gains will be realised in sectors other than those where investment has been made, and not every sector will see its costs reduced – or not, at least, to the same degree or in the short run. It is important to state the business case for each sector (e.g. the health and social protection systems), for each entity within a sector (e.g. the unemployment and disability systems) and for the economy as a whole.

Moving towards better policy: The OECD mental health and work policy framework

Strengthening mental health and work policy in order to improve the labour market and social outcomes of people with mental ill-health and generally bolster mental health resilience needs concerted action in a range of policy fields. Action has to be synchronized across them, following the same objectives and using the same policy framework.

Helping young people through mental health awareness and education policies

Develop mental health competence among teachers and education authorities:

- Include mental health competence in the teacher-training curriculum;
- Invest in preventive mental health programmes in schools (coping skills, emotional learning, etc.);
- Assure an adequate number of professionals with psychological training in schools.

Assure students' timely access to co-ordinated support for mental ill-health:

- Ensure waiting times are short in the mental health care sector for children and adolescents;
- Have in place a support structure linked to schools and other youth services that offers integrated services free of charge to all young people and has a special focus on common mental illness.

Invest in the prevention of early school leaving and support for school leavers, with mental health problems:

- Provide a solid evidence base on the link between school leaving and mental ill-health;
- Monitor early school leaving, watch for signs of mental health problems among early school leavers and provide support in all such cases.

Provide effective support for the transition from school to work:

- Ensure proper higher education and work transitions for people with common mental illness through career advice and access to treatment;
- Involve the PES as early as possible, e.g. by requiring all school leavers to register with the local PES office, build PES capacity to deal with youth with mental health issues and reinforce the links between schools and the PES;
- Prevent young people with mental health issues from becoming permanently dependant on disability benefit through effective and well-resourced multidisciplinary rehabilitation.

Towards an employment-oriented mental health care system

Assure timely access to recommended effective treatment of mental health problems:

- Increase the mental health system's capacity through a shift away from expensive specialist care and greater mental health treatment capacity for common mental ill-health in primary care;
- Investigate the use of on-line psychological therapies with solid treatment compliance.

Provide training and supports to GPs to treat mental illness:

- Expand the GP curriculum to include mental health training;
- Remunerate GPs for talking therapy time with their patients with mental health problems;
- Provide funding to GPs to incorporate mental health nurses and psychologists in their practices.

Improve incentives and tools for GPs to address work and sickness issues:

- Modify absence certification practices to focus on ability to work ("fit notes");
- Develop illness-specific guidelines for GPs on sickness certification and return-to-work practices;
- Provide funding for employment specialists who support GPs in their practices.

Strengthen the employment focus of the mental health system:

- Introduce employment outcomes in the quality and outcome frameworks of the mental health system;
- Integrate employment support into the treatment plan for people with common mental illness;
- Develop supported employment programmes for people with common mental ill-health.

Moving towards better policy: The OECD mental health and work policy framework (*cont.*)

Better workplace policies and employer-support mechanisms and incentives

Enforce legislation for psychosocial risk prevention:

- Specify employer obligations in regard to psychosocial risk assessment and risk prevention;
- Provide tools and supports to enable employers to adjust the psychosocial work environment;
- Shift the resources of labour inspectorates and occupational health services (where they exist) as necessary to adequately reflect the incidence and impact of psychosocial health issues.

Improve (line) managers' response to workers' mental health issues:

- Provide mental health training for (line) managers and co-workers;
- Offer toolkits to line managers on how best to deal with a worker's mental health problem;
- Develop mental health knowledge in HR departments to support and monitor line managers;
- Promote employee mental health screening and paying for short-term intervention.

Design an effective return-to-work management process:

- Establish publicly funded fit-for-work counselling services with mental health competence to help sick-listed workers at an early stage;
- Promote a gradual return to work, which is also a means of helping to rebuild full work capacity;
- Strengthen the role of occupational physicians and occupational psychologists.

Strengthen incentives and obligations for employers to prevent and address sick leave:

- Increase employer responsibility for return-to-work planning for sick employees;
- Promote meetings between employers, employees with mental ill-health and treating doctors;
- Extend the sick-pay obligation as an incentive to prevent absences and support return-to-work.

Making benefits and employment services fit for claimants with mental ill-health

Prevent disability benefit claims for mental illness:

- Focus on early intervention and identification of people in need of support, with medical and vocational rehabilitation measures targeted at people suffering from mental ill-health;
- Better recognise the work capacity of people with mental illness and limit disability benefit to people permanently unable to work.

Identify and support jobseekers with mental health problems:

- Use adequate tools to identify jobseekers' mental health problems and the resulting labour market barriers;
- Implement clear guidelines for caseworkers on what to do when mental health problems surface;
- Ensure access to mainstream or special services for jobseekers with poor mental health, while avoiding exemptions from participation requirements as much as possible;
- Adjust the performance management process of the employment service to secure sufficient attention to jobseekers suffering from mental ill-health.

Invest in mental health competence for all benefit actors:

- Provide mental health training for caseworkers, welfare counsellors, and social workers;
- Put in place an easily accessible psychological coaching capacity in employment services and welfare offices.

Develop integrated health and work services in the employment sector:

- Pool resources with health authorities or purchase services from the health sector in order to deliver integrated multidisciplinary rehabilitation services;
- Develop programmes targeted at jobseekers and welfare clients with common mental illness which combine psychological advice with job-placement services or work experience programmes.

REFERENCES

Arends, I., N. Baer, V. Miranda, C. Prinz and S. Singh (2014), "Mental Health and Work: Achieving Well-Integrated Policies and Service Delivery", *OECD Social, Employment and Migration Working Papers No. 161*, OECD Publishing, Paris, http://dx/doi/org/10.1787/5jxsvvn6pq6g-en.

Layard, R. (2013), "Mental Health: The New Frontier for Labour Economics", *IZA Journal of Labor Policy*, Vol. 2:2.

OECD (forthcoming 2015a), *Mental Health and Work: Austria*, OECD Publishing, Paris.

OECD (forthcoming 2015b), *Mental Health and Work: Australia*, OECD Publishing, Paris.OECD (2014a), *Mental Health and Work: Switzerland*, OECD Publishing, Paris, http://dx.doi.org/10.1787/9789264204973-en.

OECD (2014b), *Mental Health and Work: Netherlands*, OECD Publishing, Paris, http://dx.doi.org/10.1787/9789264223301-en.

OECD (2014c), *Mental Health and Work: United Kingdom*, OECD Publishing, Paris, http://dx.doi.org/10.1787/9789264204997-en.

OECD (2014d), *Making Mental Health Count: The Social and Economic Costs of Neglecting Mental Health Care*, OECD Publishing, Paris, http://dx/doi/org/10.1787/9789264208445-en.

OECD (2013a), *Mental Health and Work: Belgium*, OECD Publishing, Paris. http://dx.doi.org/10.1787/9789264187566-en.

OECD (2013b), *Mental Health and Work: Norway*, OECD Publishing, Paris, http://dx/doi/org/10.1787/9789264178984-en.

OECD (2013c), *Mental Health and Work: Denmark*, OECD Publishing, Paris, http://dx/doi/org/10.1787/9789264188631-en.

OECD (2013d), *Mental Health and Work: Sweden,* OECD Publishing, Paris, http://dx.doi.org/10.1787/9789264188730-en.

OECD (2012), *Sick on the Job? Myths and Realities about Mental Health and Work*, OECD Publishing, Paris, http://dx.doi.org/10.1787/9789264124523-en.

Chapter 1

Mental health and work: The case for a stronger policy response

Mental health is costly for individuals concerned, for employers, for the labour market, for the social protection system and for the economy as a whole. This is explained by the high prevalence of mental ill-health, the early onset of mental illness that affects education and the labour market transition, high levels of under-treatment and unmet health care needs, and significant stigma associated with mental ill-health especially in the workplace.

The resulting main mental health and work outcomes include:

- *A large employment gap and high rates of unemployment for people with mental ill-health.*
- *High rates of underperformance among workers with mental health problems.*
- *A high prevalence of mental ill-health in all working-age benefit systems.*
- *Much higher income poverty risks for people with mental ill-health.*

Mental health is a key variable both in people's lives and in economic growth and development. It is closely bound up with well-being and quality of life and – when it is poor – affects education, employability, and performance at work. Mental ill-health, especially of the mild-to-moderate kind, affects as much as 20% of the working-age population at any given moment – further evidence of its economic relevance. The widespread costs and gains associated with mental health make it a key issue not only in OECD countries' health policies, but in their labour market and social policies, too.

Defining and measuring mental ill-health

Definition of mental ill-health

This report defines "mental ill-health" as any condition that meets clinically diagnosed threshold criteria. It is a definition that draws on the tenth edition of the *International Statistical Classification of Diseases and Related Health Problems* (ICD-10) and the *Diagnostic and Statistical Manual of Mental Disorders, 5th Edition* (DSM-5).

The report chiefly considers the mild-to-moderate end of the mental ill-health spectrum, where most disorders are mood or anxiety-related. It refers to them interchangeably as "common mental illnesses", "mental ill-health", "mental illness", "mental disorders", "mental health complaints", and "mental health problems".

Measuring the social and labour market outcomes of mental ill-health

Identifying and measuring mental ill-health is anything but straightforward. Administrative data often include the ICD or DSM codes that a medical assessment assigns to, say, a patient or a recipient of disability benefit. But they are not very helpful when it comes to measuring the social and labour market outcomes of people suffering from mental ill-health. To measure those outcomes, this report takes data from national health surveys. They combine labour market information with respondents' self-assessments of their mental health measured by validated mental health instruments (e.g. the Kessler Psychological Distress Scale – K10). Such instruments have shown they are good proxies for in-depth clinical interviews.

Comparing the social and labour outcomes of mental ill-health

This report seeks to measure and compare not the incidence of poor mental health in countries' working-age populations, but their social and labour market outcomes. To that end, the prevalence of mental ill-health across the OECD is assumed to be 20% – the stable, long-term rate that consistently emerges in countries' epidemiological studies. It allows comparison of outcomes between culturally different countries and also over time between different mental health instruments. A more detailed examination of this approach and its possible implications and the sensitivity of the assumptions for the resulting outcomes are found in the OECD report *Sick on the Job?* (OECD, 2012).

Key outcomes and challenges

A growing body of literature demonstrates the immense epidemiological burden of mental ill-health. According to the Global Burden of Diseases Study 2010, for example, mental disorders and substance abuse were the chief causes of years lived with disability (YLD) – 175 million years worldwide in 2010 (Whiteford et al., 2013). The resulting economic burden is also heavy, with mental ill-health costing individuals and the economy very dear.

Mental ill-health exacts a high price on OECD economies

There are significant gaps in information on the total costs of mental illness. Such costs are of different kinds: direct (especially for health care systems), indirect (especially for benefit systems) and intangible (especially losses in labour productivity). In the European Union, a large-scale project run on a country-by-country and disease-by-disease basis estimated the total costs of mental illness at around 3.5% of GDP in 2010, (Figure 1.1, Panel A). Estimates for non-European countries such as Australia and the United States yield similar results. The European study found that indirect and intangible costs – higher benefit expenditure and falls in productivity – accounted for more than 50% of the estimated total (Gustavsson et al., 2011).

Figure 1.1. **The costs of mental ill-health for the economy as a whole are high**

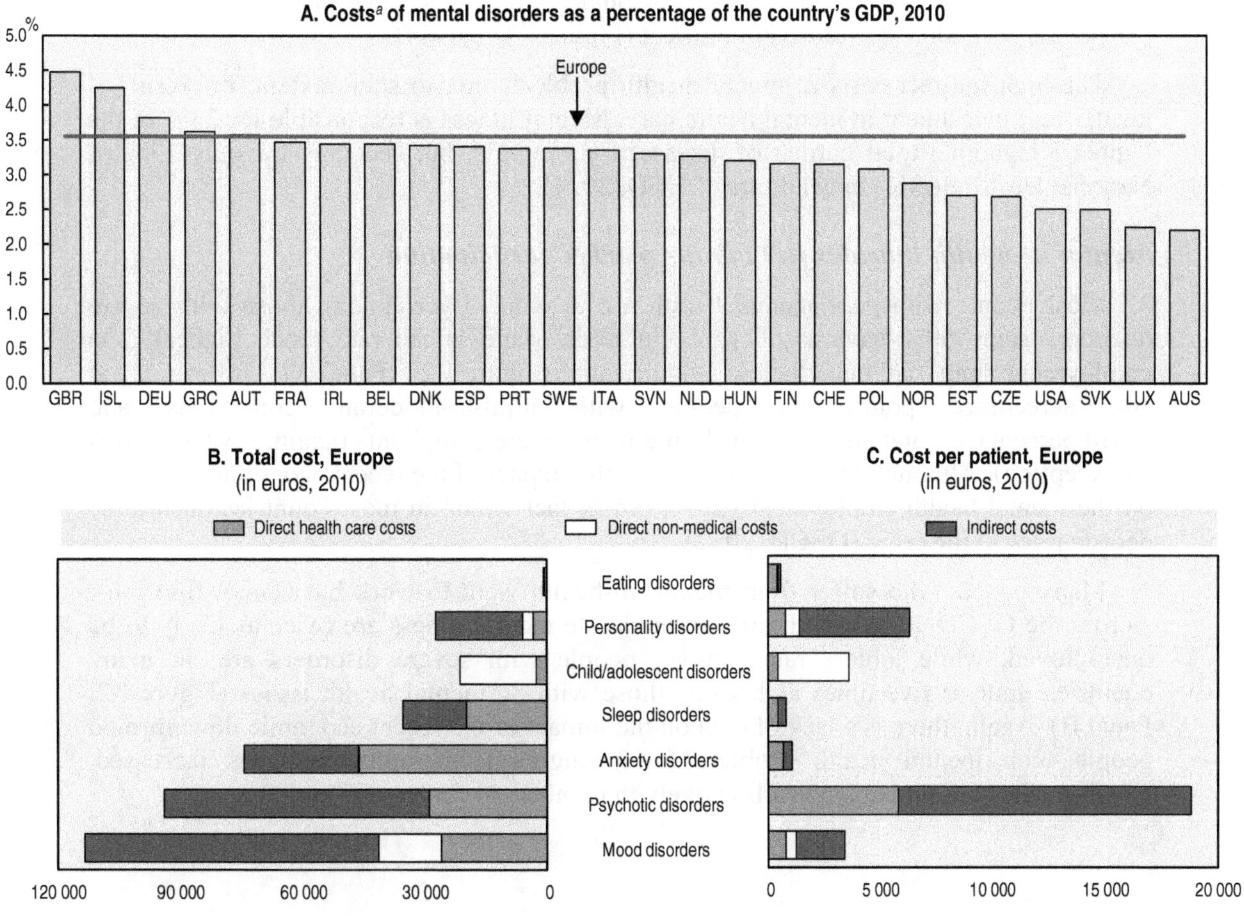

Note: "Costs" in Panel A are percentages of GDP expressed as millions of Purchasing Power Standard (PPS) for European countries. For Australia and the United States costs are expressed as percentages of GDP in current prices. Data for the United States are from 2005.

a. Cost estimates were prepared on a disease-by-disease basis, covering all major mental and brain disorders. This chart includes mental disorders only.

Source: OECD compilation based on: Gustavsson, A. et al. (2011), "Cost of Disorders of the Brain in Europe 2010", *European Neuropsychopharmacology*, No. 21, pp. 718-779 for European countries; Medibank Private Limited and Nous Group (2013), *The Case for Mental Health Reform in Australia: A Review of Expenditure and System Design* for Australia; and Bayer, R. (2005), *The Hidden Costs of Mental Illness*, Upper Bay Counselling and Support Services for the United States.

StatLink http://dx.doi.org/10.1787/888933184009

Although the study's estimate of 3.5% of GDP is considerable, it is still on the conservative side for two main reasons. First, it did not include disorders related to substance abuse. Second, the only indirect costs it covered were sickness and disability benefit spending. It did not consider expenditure generated by mental illness in other benefit systems not related to health. Similarly, it counted the productivity losses only of workers actually suffering from poor mental health, not the effect they had on the productivity of their co-workers.

The European study also illustrated the shares of different mental illnesses in total costs. The biggest drivers are mood, psychotic, and anxiety disorders. Psychotic disorders show a high per-person cost, while the sheer prevalence of mood and anxiety disorders account for their high costs. The per-person costs of mood complaints are only about one-sixth of those associated with psychotic conditions, and per-person costs are even lower for anxiety-related problems. Personality disorders have the second highest per-person cost, almost exclusively indirect (Figure 1.1, Panel B).

The high indirect costs of mental health problems are, to some extent, the result of insufficient investment in mental health care. Mental illness is responsible for 23% of the United Kingdom's total burden of disease, for example, but accounts for only 13% of National Health Service expenditure (OECD, 2014).

Mental ill-health impedes full labour market participation

Most people with poor mental health are in work. Even among those with severe disorders some 50% have a job (only in Switzerland is the rate much higher). The employment gap is nevertheless significant (Figure 1.2, Panel A). It stands at 10-15 percentage points for people with mild-to-moderate complaints and 25-30 percentage points for those suffering from severe complaints (again, Switzerland is an exception). Although little is known about the impact of the recent economic downturn on the mental health employment gap, it did in fact widen in most countries during the decade prior to the crisis (OECD, 2012).

Many people who suffer from mental ill-health want to work but cannot find jobs. Across the OECD, people with mild-to-moderate mental illness are twice as likely to be unemployed, while jobless rates among people with severe disorders are, in many countries, four or five times as high as those with no mental health issues (Figure 1.2, Panel B). Again, there is a lack of data on the impact of the recent economic downturn on people with mental health problems. As long-term unemployment has increased, however, they are probably even less likely than others to find a new job.

Figure 1.2. **Employment and unemployment gaps are considerable for people with mental ill-health**

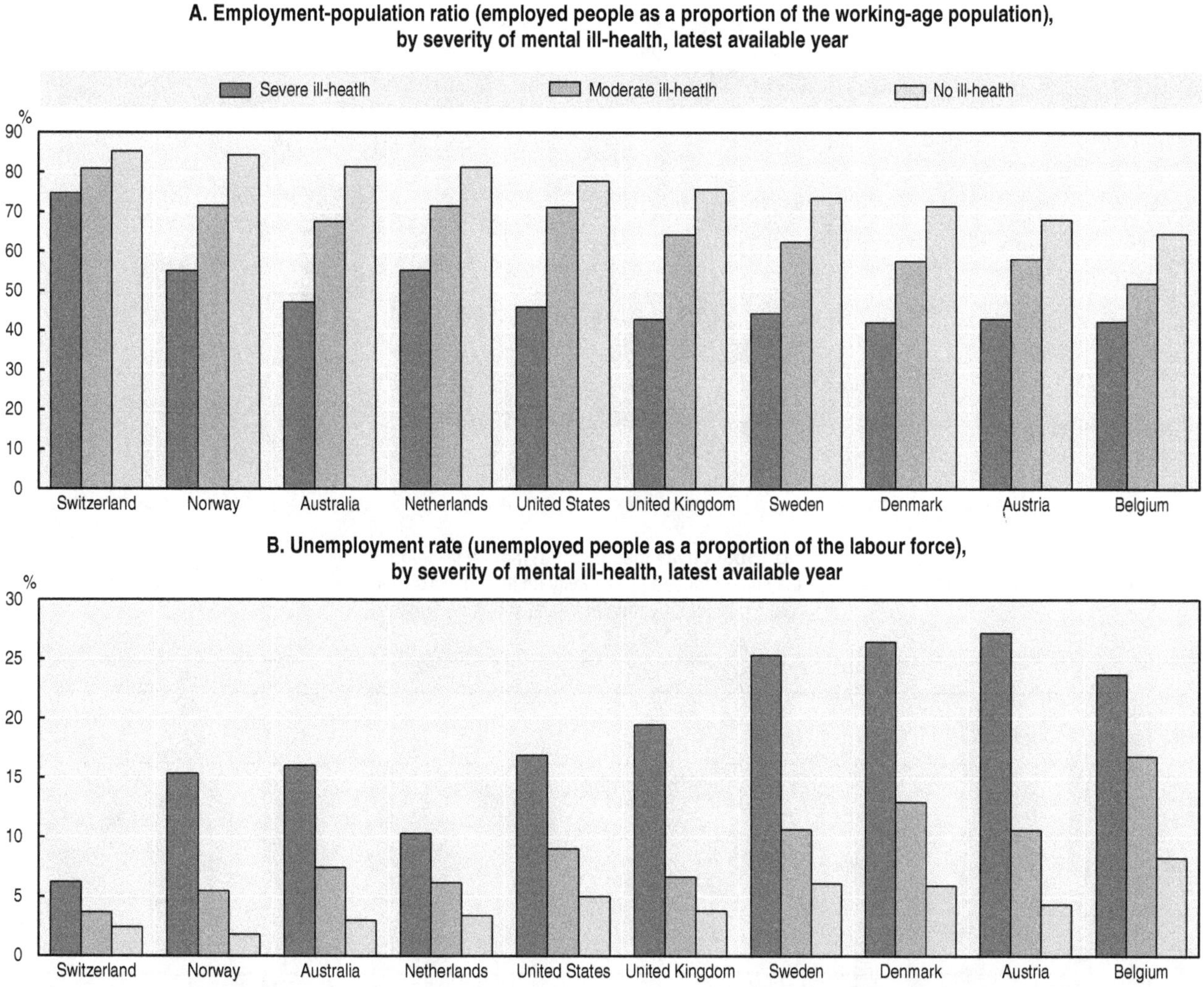

Source: National health surveys. Australia: National Health Survey 2011-12; Austria: Health Interview Survey 2006-07; Belgium: Health Interview Survey 2008; Denmark: Danish National Health Survey 2010; Netherlands: POLS Health Survey 2007/09; Norway: Level of Living and Health Survey 2008; Sweden: Living Conditions Survey 2009-10; Switzerland: Health Survey 2012; United Kingdom: Adult Psychiatric Morbidity Survey 2007; United States: National Health Interview Survey and 2008.

StatLink http://dx.doi.org/10.1787/888933184017

Employers also pay a high price for mental ill-health

Although most people with mental health problems have a job, many of them struggle to perform well – at a considerable, and increasingly acknowledged, cost for employers. Measuring performance problems and productivity losses is difficult, however.

Indirect measures based on employee responses suggest that productivity losses at work are substantial and the incidence of "presenteeism", i.e. being at work despite illness, is high. According to Eurobarometer 2010, three in four workers who have not taken sick leave despite their mental ill-health report having accomplished less than they would have wished. The ratio is only one in four among their peers with no such health problems (Figure 1.3, Panel A). The disparity is consistent across European OECD countries (Figure 1.3, Panel D).

Figure 1.3. **Workers suffering from mental ill-health who attend work show less productivity**

Average incidence over a selection of European countries, 2010

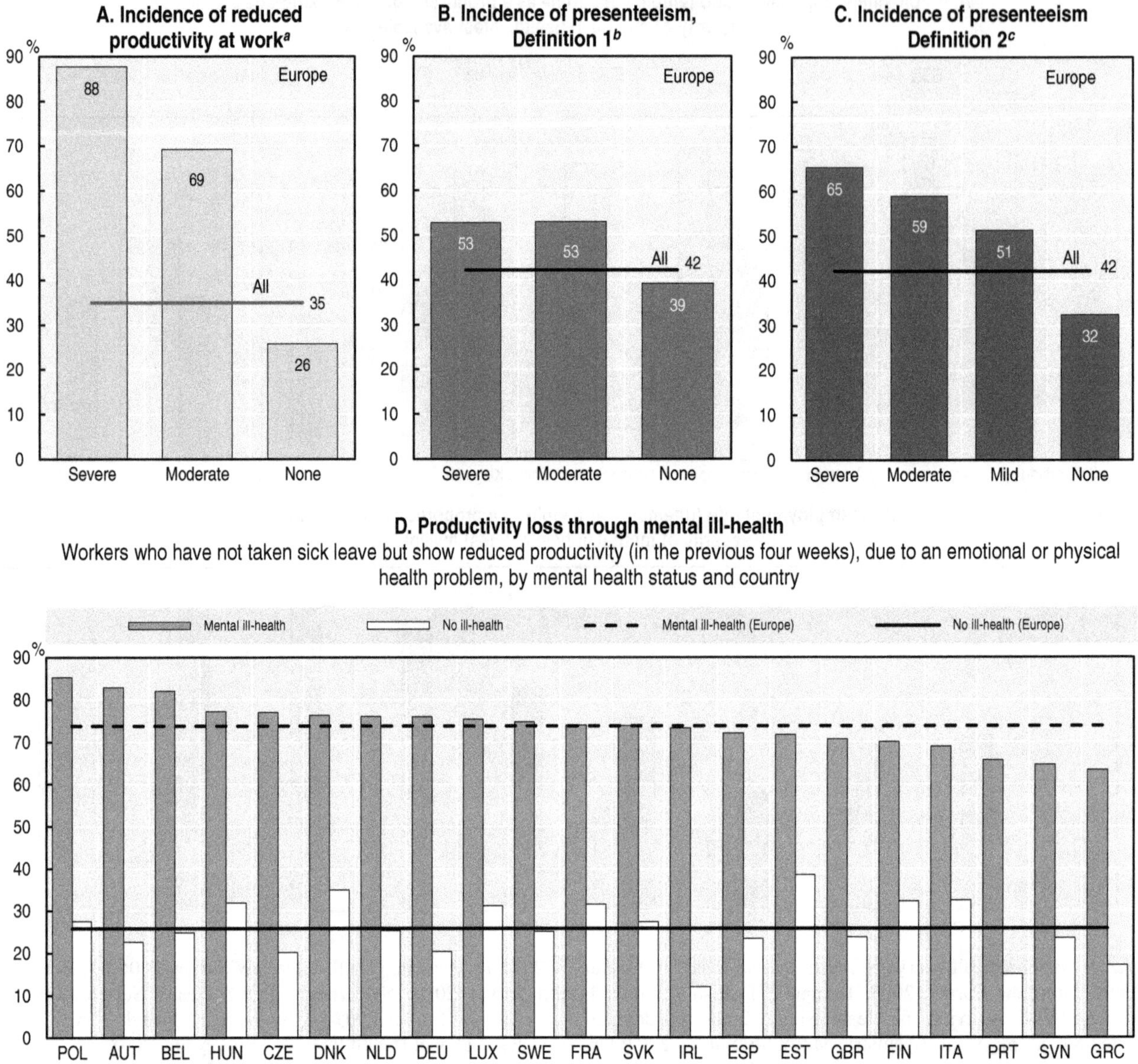

a. Percentage of workers not absent in the previous four weeks but who accomplished less than they would have liked as a result of an emotional or physical health problem. The data are an average of the 21 countries in the 2010 Eurobarometer.

b. Definition 1: The mental disorder variable is based on a set of five items: feeling cheerful; feeling calm; feeling active; waking up fresh and rested; feeling fulfilled. The data are an average of the 24 countries in the 2010 European Working Conditions Survey.

c. Definition 2: This mental disorder variable is based on three answers to the question, "Over the past 12 months, did you suffer from any of the following problems: depression or anxiety; overall fatigue; insomnia or general sleep difficulties?" The data are an average of the 24 countries in the 2010 European Working Conditions Survey.

Source: OECD estimates based on the Eurobarometer 2010 for Panels A and D, and the European Working Conditions Survey 2010 for Panels B and C.

StatLink http://dx.doi.org/10.1787/888933184026

Similarly, data from the European Working Conditions Survey suggest that workers who suffer from poor mental health are more likely than not to attend work despite being sick (Figure 1.3, Panels B and C).

Substantial costs are incurred by social protection systems

Because workers with mental health problems tend to be more disconnected from the labour market than their mentally healthy peers, it is not surprising that social protection systems bear the brunt of the indirect costs of mental ill-health. In all OECD countries, people diagnosed with a mental disorder account for 30%-40% of disability benefit caseloads (Figure 1.4, Panel A). Total disability benefit expenditure stands at around 2% of GDP on average (OECD, 2010), with mental ill-health alone therefore accounting for around 0.7%. The significant rise of mental ill-health in benefit caseload OECD-wide over the past decade is attributable predominately to the growing recognition of mental illness.

Figure 1.4. **The costs of mental ill-health for benefit systems are high**

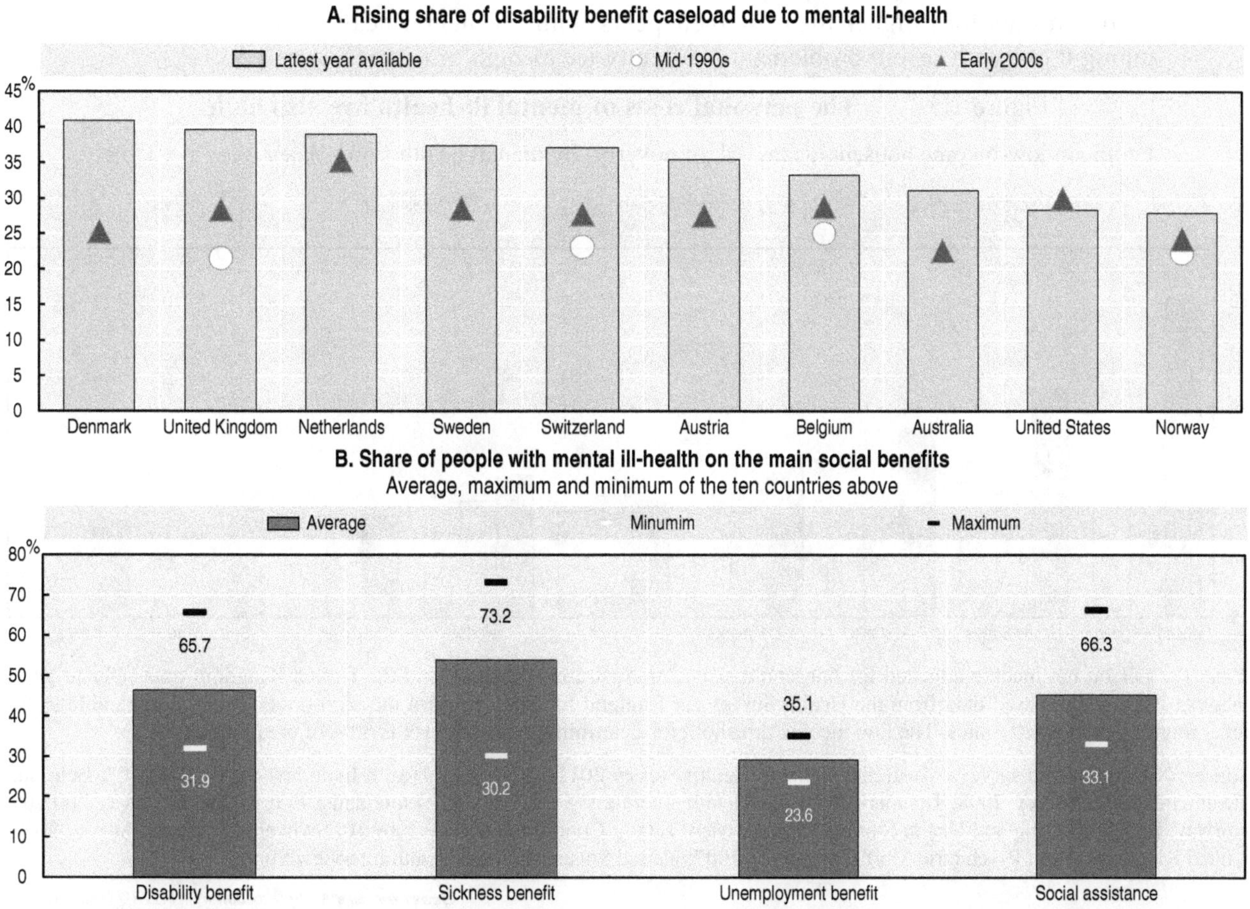

Note: Data in Panel A refer to new claims for Denmark and the United States (caseload data are unavailable). They exclude the temporary benefit in Norway and the special benefit for people with congenital or adolescent disability in the Netherlands.

Source: Panel A: OECD questionnaire on mental health; Panel B: national health surveys. Australia: National Health Survey 2011-12; Austria: Health Interview Survey 2006/07; Belgium: Health Interview Survey 2008; Denmark: Danish National Health Survey 2010; Netherlands: POLS Health Survey 2007-09; Norway: Level of Living and Health Survey 2008; Sweden: Living Conditions Survey 2009/10; Switzerland: Health Survey 2012; United Kingdom: Adult Psychiatric Morbidity Survey 2007; United States: National Health Interview Survey 2008.

StatLink http://dx.doi.org/10.1787/888933184038

Mental illness does not put a great strain on the disability benefit system alone. It costs sickness benefit regimes and social assistance as much, if not more. Data from national health surveys across a number of countries reveal that some 45%-50% of all beneficiaries of such systems suffer from mental illness (Figure 1.4, Panel B). What's more, around one-third of unemployment benefit recipients suffer from mental ill-health – a share that is much higher among the long-term unemployed. People often suffer from illnesses that have not been formally diagnosed or assessed, but which are nevertheless a considerable impediment to successfully returning to the labour market.

Mental ill-health can push individuals closer to poverty and into poor quality jobs

The personal costs of mental ill-health are also high. They include, for example, material deprivation due not only to no or low income from work, but to benefit payments that cannot fully offset lost earnings. Data that consider individuals' revenues from work, benefits, and sources like private capital, and those of household members, tell a stark story. People suffering from mental ill-health run a significantly higher risk of living in low-income households. For people whose mental ill-health is mild-to-moderate the risk is around one-third higher than for their peers with no mental health complaints, while among those with severe problems it is often twice as high or more (Figure 1.5).

Figure 1.5. **The personal costs of mental ill-health are also high**

People in low-income households (at risk of poverty) by mental health status, latest year available

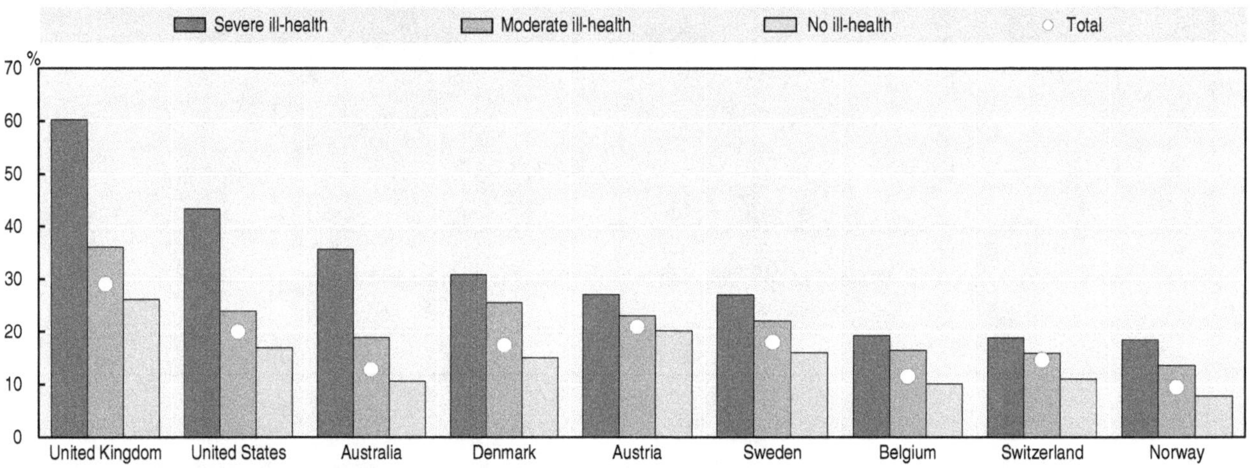

Note: Per person net income adjusted for household size. For Australia, Denmark and the United Kingdom data refer to gross income. Net-income based data from the Health Survey for England for 2006 confirm the high poverty risk, comparable to the level found in the United States. The low-income threshold for determining poverty risk is 60% of median income.

Source: National health surveys. Australia: National Health Survey 2011-12; Austria: Health Interview Survey 2006-07; Belgium: Health Interview Survey 2008; Denmark: National Health Interview Survey 2005; Netherlands: POLS Health Survey 2007/09; Norway: Level of Living and Health Survey 2008; Sweden: Living Conditions Survey 2009 10; Switzerland: Health Survey 2012; United Kingdom: Adult Psychiatric Morbidity Survey 2007; United States: National Health Interview Survey 2008.

StatLink *http://dx.doi.org/10.1787/888933184044*

There is a clear link between mental health problems and poor job quality. Figure 1.6 shows that people with mental health issues earn less per hour (Panel B), have less secure jobs (Panel C), are less satisfied with their jobs (Panel D), report strain more often (Panel E), and enjoy less respect or recognition for their work (Panel F). People with mild-to-moderate disorders seem to work the most (which may cause stress and dissatisfaction), while those with severe problems work the shortest hours (Panel A).

Figure 1.6. **Workers with mental ill-health work in jobs of poorer quality**

Average outcomes over a selection of European countries, 2010

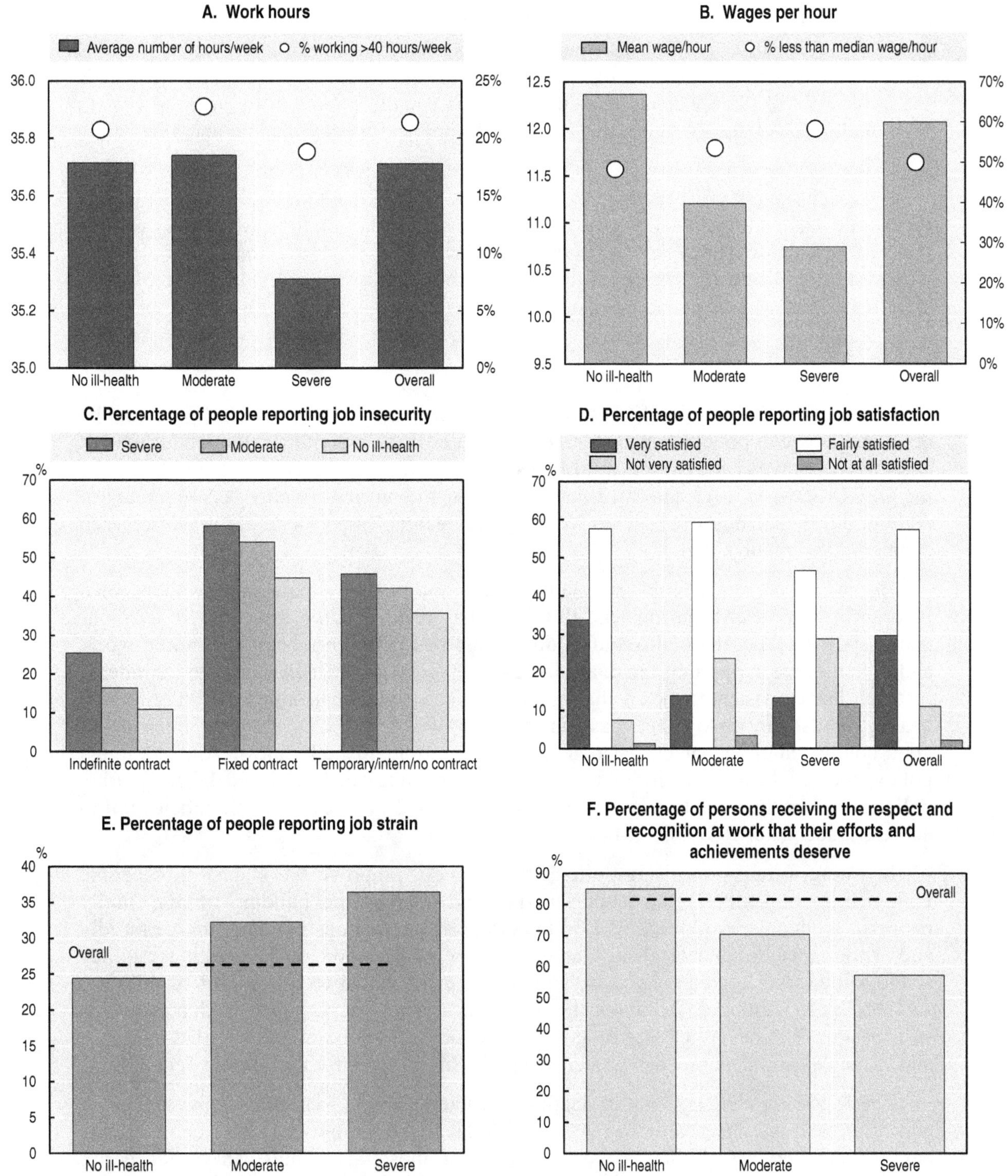

Note: Data refer to the country averages established by Eurobarometer and the European Working Conditions Survey.

Source: OECD calculations based on Eurobarometer 2010 (Panels A, E and F) and the European Working Conditions Survey 2010 (Panels B, C and D).

StatLink http://dx.doi.org/10.1787/888933184058

Overall, then, the working conditions and job quality of people with mental health problems appear only somewhat worse. Still, for some workers they may be large enough to contribute to a further worsening of their condition and heighten the risk of job loss, so neutralising any of the positive effects of employment. Differences in job satisfaction, however, are relatively wide, with people who suffer from mild-to-moderate illness as broadly dissatisfied as those with severe disorders. Thus, while boosting employment is the only way to square income discrepancies, it is equally important to ensure access to high-quality jobs that offer good working conditions and are sustainable and adequately paid.

Evidence suggests that there are two problems: employment and unemployment gaps on the one hand, and job quality and work performance issues on the other. Policy makers must address both if they are to increase productive employment among people with mental health problems, thereby lowering the price paid by individuals, employers, benefit systems, and the economy as a whole.

Policy can make a difference

Outcomes and policy challenges are very similar in all OECD countries. What can be done and how can policy change to ease the high costs to individuals, the labour market and the economy arising from mental illness? The series of country reports published by the OECD between 2013 and 2015 demonstrate that countries are only just beginning to address those challenges (as shown by the policy examples provided at the end of each chapter of this report).

Because of the considerable stigma that attaches to mental illness and the widespread ignorance of its economic impacts, this issue has received little attention from labour market policies. Yet the multi- and bi-directional ties between mental health and work, and the evidence supporting them, are increasingly clear and widely understood. Indeed, research has consistently shown that employment is good for health, especially mental health, whilst unemployment has an adverse effect (OECD, 2008). Importantly, good-quality employment can also help recovery from mental illness. And, although policy, too, could make a difference, it is not yet doing so. Social and labour market policies neglect the issue to a large extent (OECD, 2012), and even health policies fail to address it adequately (OECD, 2014).

Investing in and prioritising policies that strive to improve the inclusion of people with mental ill-health in the labour market and support the building of a mentally resilient, productive workforce will be important as populations continue to age rapidly and working environments change at ever faster rates. Good policy making requires sound knowledge, high-quality data, and strong evidence as to the impact of policies, services, and institutions. Although the mental health and work policy evidence base is still meagre, it is nevertheless growing. This report seeks to contribute to that evidence and to the development of a comprehensive policy framework for the coming decades.

The following chapters look in depth at the challenges in four main policy domains: education and youth, health care, the workplace and employers, and benefits and employment services. Policy makers in each of those areas must strive for early, integrated action which involves front-line actors.

REFERENCES

Bayer, R. (2005), *The Hidden Costs of Mental Illness*, Upper Bay Counselling and Support Services.

Gustavsson, A. et al. (2011), "Cost of Disorders of the Brain in Europe 2010", *European Neuropsychopharmacology*, No. 21, pp. 718-779.

Medibank Private Limited and Nous Group (2013), *The Case for Mental Health Reform in Australia: A Review of Expenditure and System Design*.

OECD (2014), *Making Mental Health Count: The Social and Economic Costs of Neglecting Mental Health Care*, OECD Publishing, Paris, http://dx/doi/org/10.1787/9789264208445-en.

OECD (2012), *Sick on the Job? Myths and Realities about Mental Health and Work*, OECD Publishing, Paris, http://dx.doi.org/10.1787/9789264124523-en.

OECD (2010), *Sickness, Disability and Work: Breaking the Barriers*, OECD Publishing, Paris, http://dx.doi.org/10.1787/9789264090606-en.

OECD (2008), *OECD Employment Outlook 2008*, Chapter 4 "Are All Jobs Good for Your Health? The Impact of Work Status and Working Conditions on Mental Health", OECD Publishing, Paris, http://dx.doi.org/10.1787/empl_outlook-2008-en.

Whiteford, H. et al. (2013), "Global Burden of Disease Attributable to Mental and Substance Use Disorders: Findings from the Global Burden of Disease Study 2010", *The Lancet*, Vol. 382, No. 9904, pp. 1575-1586.

Chapter 2

Ensuring educational attainment and school-to-work transition for young people with mental ill-health

Childhood and adolescence are crucial periods for promoting good mental health. Every second mental illness has its onset before the age of 14. Those suffering from mental ill-health are more likely to leave school early with poorer education outcomes and consequently have greater difficulty accessing the labour market. Education systems have a key role to play in identifying and supporting children with mental health issues at an early stage. Policies to prevent early school leaving and enable smooth transitions from school to work are essential if young people's education outcomes and adult working lives are not to be adversely affected.

Policy conclusions:

- *Develop mental health competencies among teachers and education authorities.*
- *Ensure timely access to co-ordinated support for students suffering from mental ill-health.*
- *Invest in the prevention of early school leaving and early action for school leavers.*
- *Provide effective support for the transition from school to work.*

Preparing people affected by mental ill-health for the labour market has to start early, long before they actually start looking for work. The foundations for employment opportunities in adult life are, to a great extent, laid during childhood, adolescence and early adulthood through good education. The educational attainments of young people with mental health problems are often poor, and many do not finish school at all. Getting off to such a disadvantaged start considerably heightens the risk of poor work outcomes like unemployment and work disability in later life.

The education system is the ideal setting for investing in ways to prevent adverse outcomes related to poor mental health, as 50% of all mental illnesses begin before the age of 14. Only mood disorders tend to start later in life (Figure 2.1). As affected people do not generally seek treatment for, on average, twelve years after the onset of their illness (Kessler and Wang, 2008), few young people come into contact with mental health care services. Strong support within the education system is therefore crucial.

Enabling young people with mental health complaints to attain high levels of education and prepare for a successful labour market career requires: i) mental health literacy among teachers and students; ii) timely access to co-ordinated, multidisciplinary support; iii) prevention and early action when students leave school early; and iv) effective support for the transition from school to work.

Figure 2.1. **Most mental illness has its onset in childhood or adolescence**

Median age of the onset of mental illness in the United States, 2001-03

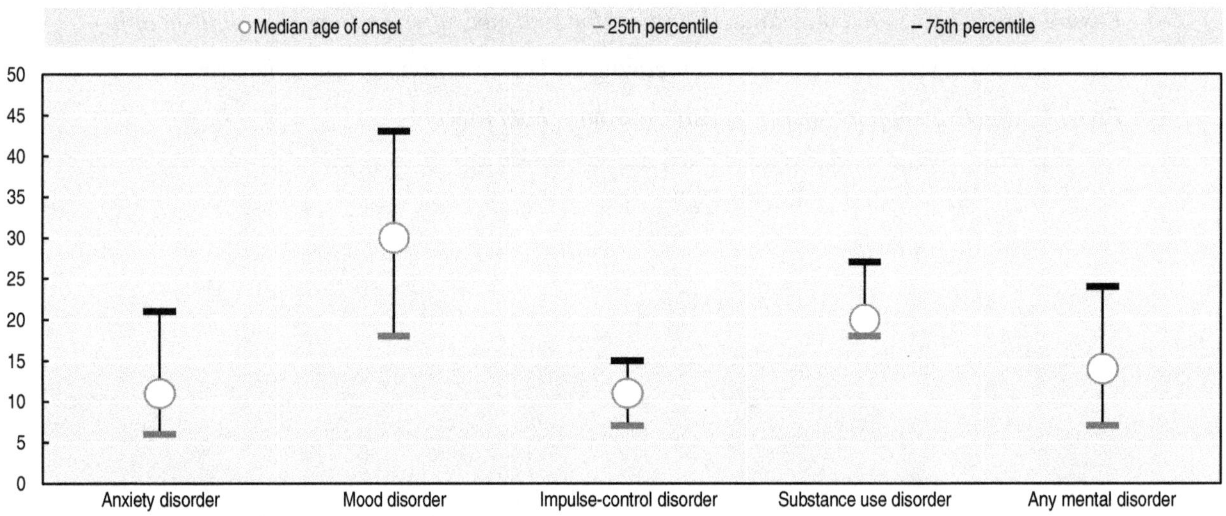

Source: OECD compilation based on Kessler, R. et al. (2005), "Lifetime Prevalence and Age-of-Onset Distributions of DSM-IV Disorders in the National Comorbidity Survey Replication", *Archives of General Psychiatry*, No. 62, pp. 593-603.

StatLink *http://dx.doi.org/10.1787/888933184060*

Mental health literacy and training for teachers and students

The few epidemiological studies on mental illness among young people show that the prevalence of diagnosed mental disorders is the same as or slightly higher than among adults. Between 20% and 30% of all young people experience a mental disorder at any given time with lifetime prevalence by age 20 sometimes reaching 50% (Merikangas et al., 2010; Ormel et al., 2014; Philip et al., 2014). Importantly, prevalence is particularly high among disadvantaged young people, i.e. those with little schooling (OECD, 2012).

Disadvantages early in life have long-term implications

Negative childhood experiences greatly affect mental health in adult life (Figure 2.2, Panel A). Indeed, most people who experience a mental disorder in adulthood have had mental health problems in childhood or adolescence already (Kim-Cohen et al., 2003). For the most prevalent mental illness among young people, anxiety disorder, the median age of onset is as low as 8-11 years of age (Kessler et al., 2005).

Young people with mental ill-health are more likely to show poor educational attainment and leave school earlier than their healthy peers (McLeod and Fettes, 2007; Veldman et al., 2014). Consequently, they are often to be found among those who are not in education, employment or training (NEETs) (OECD, 2013d). The share of early school leavers (17%) and NEETs (13%) is high in many OECD countries (Figure 2.2, Panel B) – and there is strong evidence that those groups face significant labour market disadvantages. Data for Austria, for example, reveal that many early school leavers and, especially, NEETs remain inactive for very long periods (Figure 2.2, Panel C).

Teachers play a crucial role in providing the support that can prevent negative educational outcomes. Generally, however, they are not trained to spot signs of mental illness. They find it particularly hard to detect internalising symptoms (e.g. anxiety and depressed moods) as opposed to such visible symptoms as disruptive or aggressive behaviour and disobedience. Nor do they have the means or the time to provide the extra support needed.

Yet school provides an ideal setting for building mental health resilience and easing the stigma that weighs so heavily on mental illness. As many students will either experience some form of mental ill-health themselves or know a peer with such problems, greater mental health literacy among school-goers could help strengthen support for and inclusion of young people with mental health problems.

Developing general mental health competencies in the school system

Although many countries have developed preventive mental health programmes, only a few have rolled them out in their schools on a national scale. In Norway, the *Mental Health in Schools* co-operative project, which ran from 2004 to 2011, comprised mental health training directed specifically at teachers and their students. They were designed to improve mental health literacy, so enabling teachers to better identify mental health problems and understand and support their students (Factsheet 2.1).

Similarly, the Australian Government funds two programmes to promote mental health: *KidsMatter* for use in primary schools and *MindMatters* for secondary establishments (Factsheet 2.2). Both take a "whole-school" approach. They provide training in fostering mental health and use a structured approach to help schools identify their strengths and weaknesses with regard to mental health promotion.

Figure 2.2. **Young people at risk need more attention earlier to prevent poor outcomes later**

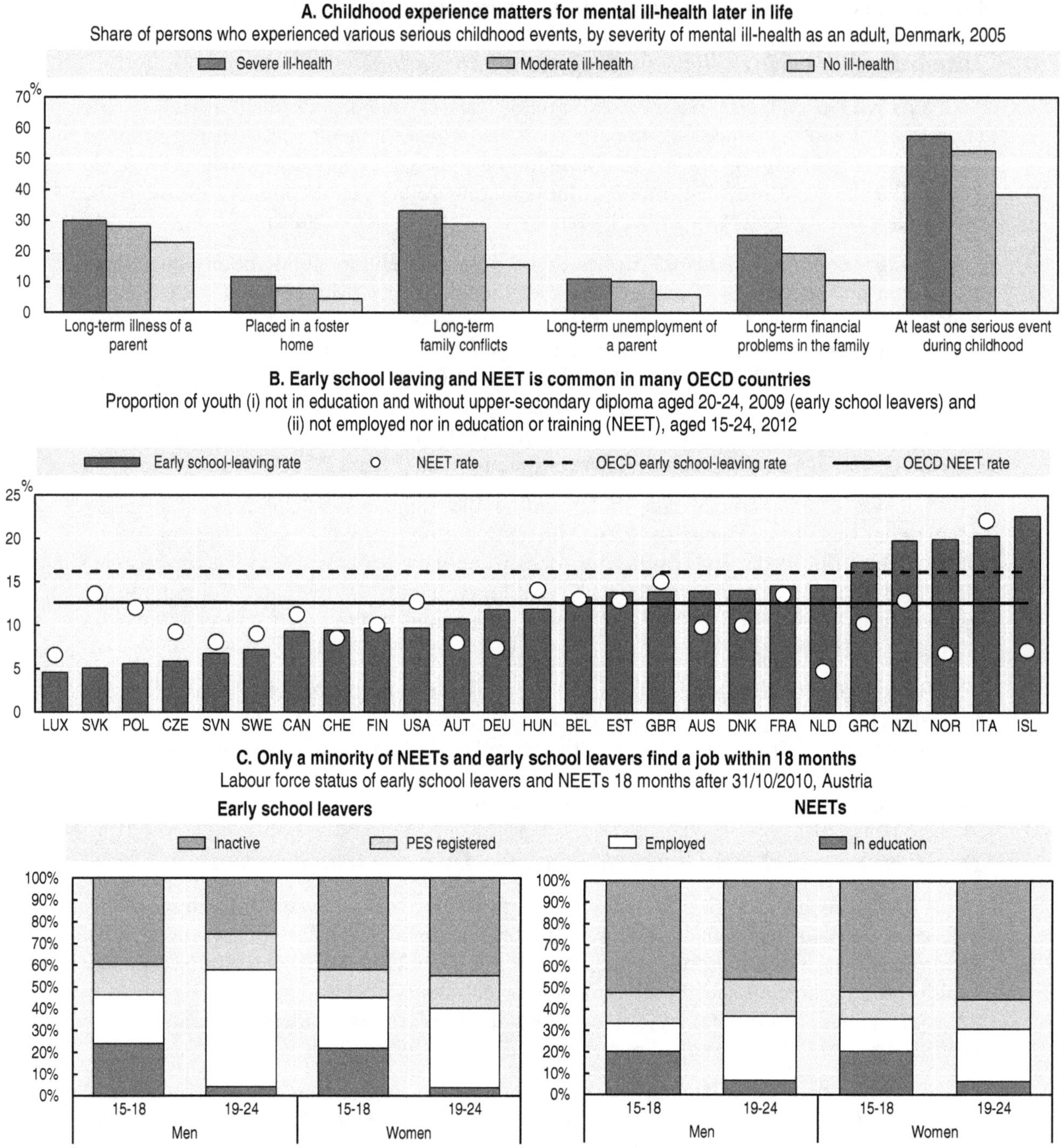

NEET: Neither in employment nor in education or training.

Note: OECD total includes all 34 member countries. "Inactive" refers to all persons who are not classified as employed or unemployed.

Source: Panel A: National Health Interview Survey, 2005; Panel B: *OECD Education Database*; Panel C – Statistik Austria, Bildungsmonitoring,
www.statistik.at/web_de/statistiken/bildung_und_kultur/bildungsbezogenes_erwerbskarrierenmonitoring_biber/index.html.

StatLink http://dx.doi.org/10.1787/888933184079

KidsMatter and *MindMatters* also seek to stimulate collaboration between teachers, parents, students and the wider school community and guide schools in choosing the right course of action in four areas: i) positive school community; ii) student skills for resilience; iii) parents and families; and iv) support for students experiencing mental health difficulties (Wyn et al., 2000; MindMatters, 2014).

School-based mental health promotion programmes are difficult to evaluate rigorously, but studies have shown that they can be effective in sharpening teachers' and students' ability to spot mental health problems and in improving both students' mental health and educational performance (Slee et al., 2009; Langeveld et al., 2011; Weare and Nind, 2011; Skre et al., 2013). Qualitative research suggests that programmes are appreciated by schools and teachers and that they can change a school's culture in getting it to communicate openly about mental ill-health (Slee et al., 2009).

However, schools seldom implement full-scale mental health programmes. One alternative would be for the educational authorities to choose any particularly effective components of such programmes and incorporate them into the general teaching curriculum. To date, there appear to be no instances of compulsory training for teachers in how to spot mental ill-health or teach resilience skills. This is a missed opportunity given that the positive effects of mental health promotion programmes could carry over effectively into general teaching practices.

Key messages

The prevention of poor mental health and related schooling problems does not receive proper attention in the education sector. School-based mental health promotion programmes are not used widely, even though they foster a non-stigmatising school climate and help develop emotional skills, such as resilience and coping, among both students and teachers. Such programmes contribute to better mental health and school performance in the short term, which suggests that it would be worthwhile to invest in large-scale longitudinal studies to investigate whether they will also pay off in the long run through the greater participation in the labour market of young people with mental ill-health.

There are two core conclusions for improving mental health literacy among teachers and students:

- Invest in preventive mental health programmes in schools to develop resilience, coping skills and emotional learning more generally.
- Incorporate mental health competence training in the teacher-training curriculum.

Timely access to support for young people with mental ill-health is critical

Providing timely treatment and support to young people with poor mental health is challenging. Treatment rates are at their lowest and waiting lists at their longest among young people, many of whom are reluctant to seek professional help (OECD, 2012). General preventive health checks for school-aged children are a widespread practice, but they are so broad in range and last such a short time that they are unlikely to spot any signs of incipient mental illness. School doctors, like general practitioners, lack mental health expertise.

School-based mental health support is insufficient

In many of the countries reviewed by the OECD, schools have developed in-house mental health services as a primary form of support. In some cases, teachers are trained to take up part-time roles as student advisors or student counsellors (OECD, 2015; OECD, 2014b), while in other cases school social workers, educationalists and psychologists form internal care teams, as in Belgium (Factsheet 2.3). The greatest advantage of school-based services is their low entry threshold, which enables teachers to refer students to them and students to access them at an early stage.

However, school-based mental health services generally have limited capacity. As shown in Figure 2.3 (Panel A), levels of teaching support staff in schools are low, resulting in heavy caseloads and long waiting lists. In Sweden, for example, school psychologists are responsible for around 2 000 students and waiting times of 16 weeks have been reported (Figure 2.3, Panels B and C). Similarly, in the Netherlands, the average caseload of a social worker in vocational education is 2 600 students (OECD, 2014b).

Figure 2.3. **Access to professional support in schools is limited in most countries**

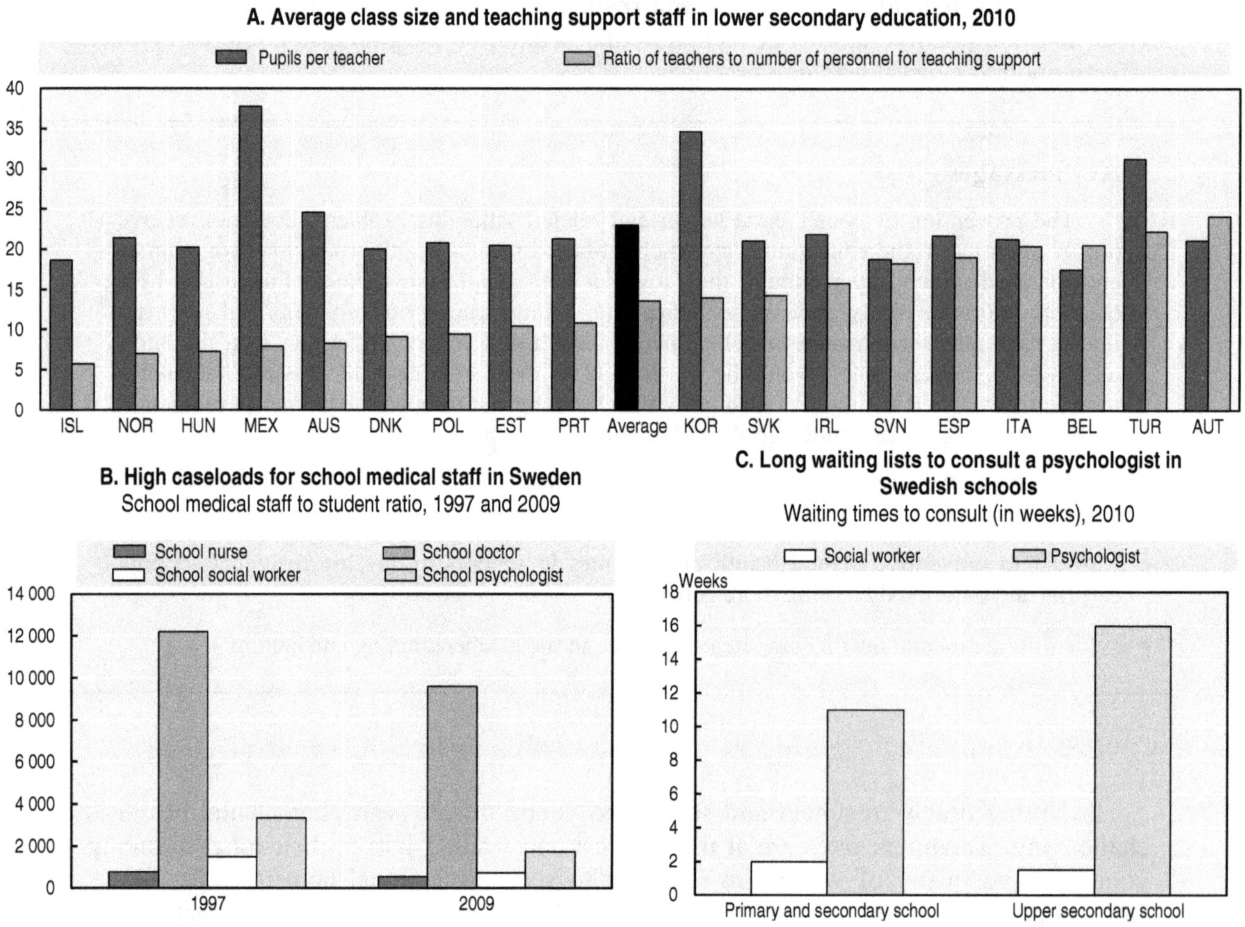

Note: Data for Belgium refer to Flanders only.

Source: Panel A: OECD (2010), *Creating Effective Teaching and Learning Environments: First Results from TALIS,* OECD Publishing, Paris; Panel B: Administrative data provided by Ministry of Education; and Panel C: Socialstyrelsen paper, Survey on Children's Health in School.

StatLink *http://dx.doi.org/10.1787/888933184081*

Further strain on the capacity to provide timely support comes from the lack of collaboration between schools and primary, specialised, and community mental health care services. When poor mental health deteriorates and problems transcend the school environment (and are family-related, for example), schools need to be able to refer to and work closely with other services. Yet, establishing collaborative networks to support young people has proven problematic. To look at the example of Sweden again, only 25% of schools work with other youth services (OECD, 2013d).

One reason for such poor collaboration is that it is neither compulsory nor backed by financial incentives. Another factor is that many of the reviewed countries have different youth services all operating independently, which makes it hard for parents, children, and schools to pick their way through to the most suitable care provider (OECD, 2014b).

Low threshold services and collaborative networks as policy response

To provide more timely, better co-ordinated treatment for young people with poor mental health, some countries have put in place multidisciplinary services outside schools. They have low thresholds so that young people can access them easily. Two different models can be distinguished: one has a preventive, general health approach and is open to all, while the other is geared to students who have been identified with mental health problems and accessed through school referrals.

Examples of preventive, open-to-all external services are Sweden's *Youth Clinics* (Factsheet 2.4) and the *headspace* centres in Australia (Factsheet 2.5), both of which are government funded. Although they are low-threshold, general-purpose services, they do have a special focus on promoting mental health, as reflected in their staff composition – psychologists, social workers, and health care professionals like general practitioners (GPs). Not only do they provide information and advice on mental health, they offer treatment to young people with mental health problems and, in the event of referrals, their multidisciplinary teams can call upon their close connections with a range of other health care services. The *headspace* centres in Australia go one step further in that they also provide vocational support and collaborate closely with public employment services as a matter of course.

Examples of the model that uses referrals from schools are the *Student Guidance Centres* in Flanders, Belgium (Factsheet 2.6), and the *Care and Advice Teams* in the Netherlands (Factsheet 2.7). Their core focus is the provision of individual, multidisciplinary support for students with behavioural, emotional, and/or social problems. Students' problems are discussed in multidisciplinary teams that bring together GPs, psychologists, social workers, and educationalists. The Dutch structure also includes school representatives. Treatment is part of the support that the Belgian and Dutch centres provide. Another strength lies in co-ordinating health care through referral to other providers and in informing and guiding schools, parents and teachers through the health and community care system.

Both models have their strengths. With their preventive, general approach, the *Youth Clinics* and *headspace* avoid labelling young people who come to them with a "problem" and in this way avoid immediate medicalisation of mental health issues. Accordingly, they are very low-threshold and anyone can make use of their facilities. The open-to-all approach increases the chances of encountering young people with the first signs or sub-threshold symptoms of non-diagnosed mental ill-health. Close connection with the school system is the major strength of the referral-based *Student Guidance Centres* and *Care and Advice Teams*. These ensure that children identified by schools as having social, emotional or behavioural problems or needs, can be referred swiftly for support, guidance, and suitable care.

Restricted capacity hampers the proper implementation of both kinds of care. The Flemish *Student Guidance Centres* have difficulty coping with the growing demand, while the Dutch *Care and Advice Teams* are able to cater for only 1% of the primary and 4% of the secondary school populations. Those figures are very low given that 20-30% of young people experience mental ill-health. In practice only those with severe problems receive support. What's more, close collaboration between multidisciplinary teams and specialised mental health care professionals is rendered useless in case of long waiting lists for psychologists and psychiatrists.

The reviewed countries have not yet responded to the shortages of mental health staff in schools or to the insufficient capacity of child and adolescent mental health care systems as a whole. Governmental influence does not reach far into schools in a number of countries where schools enjoy considerable degrees of autonomy. Nevertheless, where schools do receive state funding, governments could consider earmarking a certain amount for investment in school-based mental health support.

Key messages

Although in-school mental health services are common in OECD countries, they lack the capacity to provide timely support to all students in need. To ensure that young people – even those with mild-to-moderate mental health problems – receive attention, the public provision of freely accessible general health care services with a focus on mental health would be a valuable addition in many countries. There is a need for multidisciplinary facilities that bring together front-line social assistance, general and mental health services, and employment support. These actors should work closely with schools and specialised professionals in a coherent, co-ordinated manner.

The following strategies would go some way to ensuring that young people have timely access to support and treatment:

- Increase the number of psychologically-trained professionals available in schools.
- Ensure waiting times are short in the mental health care sector for children and adolescents.
- Set up a special support structure (possibly a special agency) linked to schools and other youth services. It should offer integrated services free of charge to all young people with a focus on common mental illnesses.

Preventing early school leaving

Young people who leave school early with no qualifications have low job prospects. In the Netherlands, for example, they have been found to be twice as likely to be unemployed than those who complete school (OECD, 2014b). There is also a much higher probability that they will have to rely on financial assistance such as social security benefits (OECD, 2013d).

Early school leaving is more frequent among young people with mental ill-health

Leaving school early is more prevalent among young people who have moderate to severe mental health problems. Among young people with no mental health issues an average of 14% leave school early, compared to 20% among those who suffer from moderate mental illness and 26% among those with severe mental illness (Figure 2.4, Panel A). The EU 2020 Strategy for Education and Training has set a target for reducing the percentage of early school leavers to 10%; meeting that target will be especially challenging when it comes to young people who suffer from mental ill-health. The problem, however, is not restricted to the EU area. In Australia and the United States, too, there are high numbers of early school leavers among young people with poor mental health (Figure 2.4, Panel B).

Figure 2.4. **Leaving school early lowers educational attainment and job prospects**

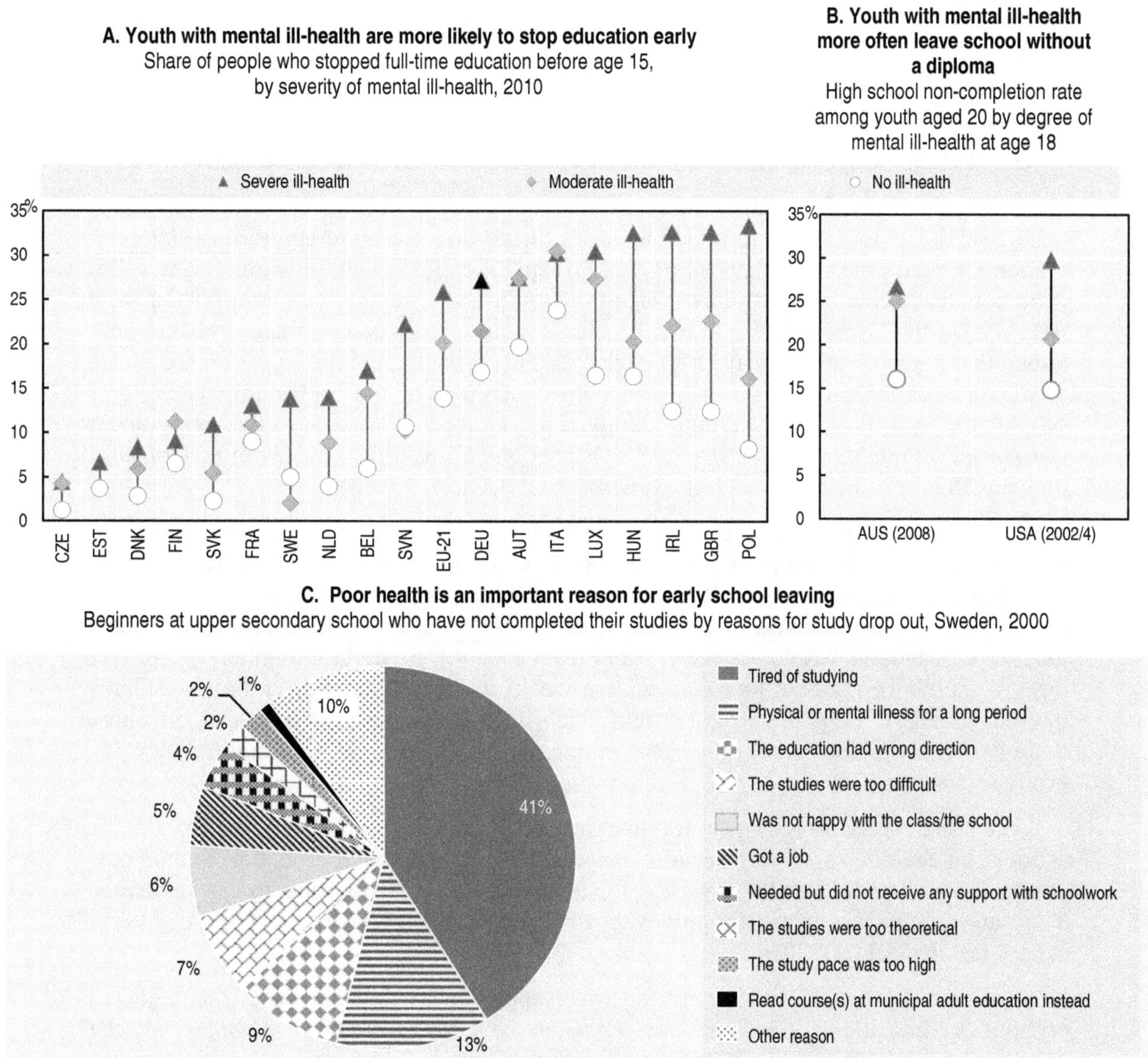

Source: Panel A: OECD compilation based on Eurobarometer 2010; Panel B: OECD estimates based on Youth in Focus (Australia) and the National Longitudinal Survey of Youth 1997 (United States); and Panel C: Statistics Sweden.

StatLink http://dx.doi.org/10.1787/888933184091

Unique data from Sweden on reasons for leaving school early show that poor health is an important factor for many school leavers (Figure 2.4, Panel C). The inference is that mainstream policy to curb early school leaving needs to go beyond motivational issues and address how (mental) health problems hamper school attendance among young drop-outs. This is also supported by the finding that young people who visit mental health services more frequently have been found to be more than two times more likely to leave school early five years later (Homlong et al., 2013).

Good policy on early school leaving, but no focus on the role of mental ill-health

Many of the reviewed countries have taken measures to improve support for early school leavers and help them either go back to school or transition into work. Three approaches can be distinguished (although they are sometimes implemented in combination):

1. Rising the compulsory school attendance age.
2. Organising a central register for early school leaving.
3. Setting up special centres for the case management of early school leavers.

Rising the compulsory attendance age is one strategy to curb early school leaving. It makes schools and parents responsible for ensuring that the children attend school for longer, so increasing their chances of securing qualifications. School leaving ages differ from country to country – 16 years of age in Norway and Sweden, for example, and 18 in Belgium. In the Netherlands, children can leave school at 16 years of age, by when it is hoped that they will at least have obtained a secondary vocational qualification and go on to higher vocational education. However, in recognition of the high numbers of early school leavers – particularly among pupils in vocational education – the government introduced a "qualification obligation", whereby pupils have to stay on at school until they are 18 unless they obtain a basic qualification (OECD, 2014b).

To be able to act fast to curb early school leaving, a good registration system is fundamental. Several countries have put in place central registers to identify and track potential early school leavers. Registration may be centralised at different levels; e.g. municipally, as in Denmark, or nationally, as in the Netherlands. In both cases, schools must report students who have been absent from school for a certain number of hours or days, e.g. after 16 hours in four consecutive weeks in the Netherlands and after 20 half-days in Flanders, Belgium. In countries which do not have central registers, or where there is no obligation to report absent children (e.g. Sweden and Australia), they are easily lost from sight.

A central registration system for tracking early leaving may also serve to monitor schools on their rates of early school leavers. That is the practice in the Netherlands where schools are financially rewarded for lowering early leaving rates to certain levels. They are required to invest the money in further initiatives for the prevention of early school leaving (OECD, 2014b).

Several countries use a case management approach for students who leave school without qualification. The regional *Register and Co-ordination Centres* in the Netherlands (Factsheet 2.8), Australia's *Youth Connections* programme (Factsheet 2.9), and Austria's *Youth Coaches* (Factsheet 2.10) are all designed to help pupils who have left school or risk doing so to resume schooling or transition swiftly to higher or vocational education and employment. In the Netherlands and Australia, the centres have close links with other service providers, e.g. those that offer employment support.

A more prevention-oriented approach to early school leaving comes in the shape of Denmark's municipal *Youth Guidance Services* (Factsheet 2.11). Guidance counsellors follow all students and develop educational plans with them and their parents. They monitor students' transitions from lower secondary to upper secondary education and, should they fail to attend school, counsellors would get in touch very quickly and – if necessary – refer them to other support services.

Key messages

Notwithstanding the fine initiatives to tackle early school leaving, the high share of young people with mental ill-health among early school leavers is an issue that remains unaddressed. Most countries do not record reasons for early school leaving and consequently have no overall idea of how many early leavers struggle with mental ill-health. Countries that operate the case management approach should train case managers to identify and address mental health problems among early school leavers. They would thus be able to factor mental health issues into their return-to-school efforts. They could also initiate mental health treatment and support to prevent long-term absence from school.

To prevent early school leaving and enable quick action when it happens, countries should:

- Develop a central registry system for early school leaving (where this does not exist).
- Have a strong system in place for the case management of early school leavers, with particular emphasis on school leavers with mental illness.
- Build an evidence base on the link between school leaving and mental ill-health.

Effective support for the transition from school to work

Youth unemployment rates that are much higher than for the rest of the population and the disproportionate effect on young people of the massive jobs crisis of recent years underscore how difficult the transition from school to work has become (OECD, 2014c).

The transition to work is difficult for disadvantaged youth

Jobless rates among young people who suffer from poor mental health are worse than those of their mentally healthy peers. Longitudinal data from some countries paint an even gloomier picture: fewer such young people go on to higher education, which makes their chances of a successful transition into work even slimmer (Figure 2.5, Panel A). Young people with low educational attainment are at a great disadvantage when seeking their first job. Recent data for Austria confirm that young people who have merely completed compulsory schooling (nine years in Austria) take much longer to find work. They spend an average of 40 months job hunting, compared to ten months for those who complete high school and five months for those who go to university or a vocational school (Figure 2.5, Panel B). And, as young people with mental ill-health are overrepresented among pupils who leave school when compulsory schooling comes to an end, there is every chance that their first job experience will be disappointing – which will further contribute to falling self-esteem.

Figure 2.5. **The transition to higher education and employment is more difficult for young people who suffer from mental ill-health**

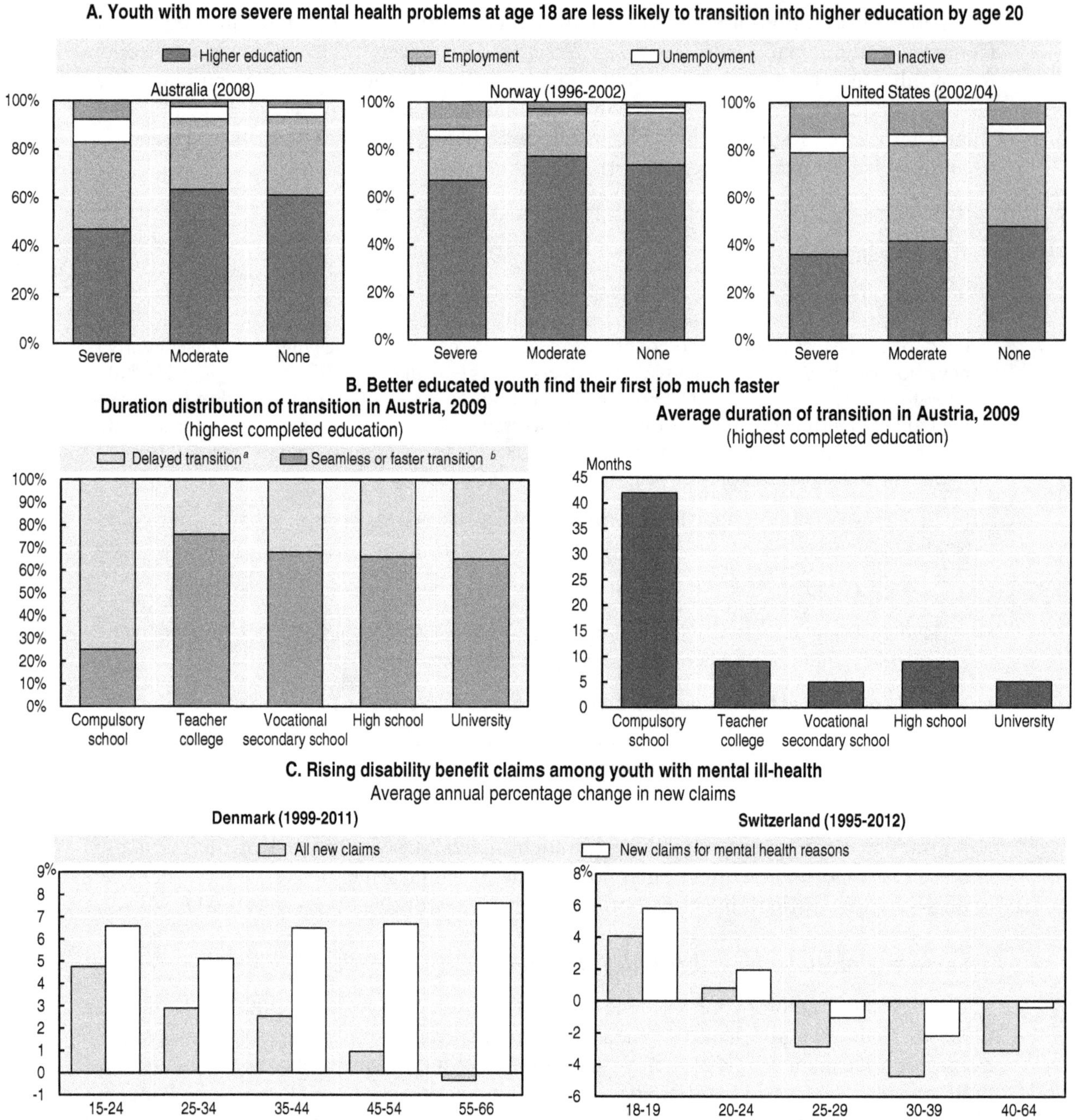

a. Persons between 15 and 34 years of age who have already completed their training and are living in private households.

b. Transition duration education/profession of more than three months (excluding persons who reported during the transition Präsenz-/Zivildienst as main activity).

Source: Panel A: OECD estimates based on Youth in Focus (Australia), Young HUNT (Norway), and the National Longitudinal Survey of Youth 1997 (United States); Panel B: Statistik Austria, LFS 2009 ad hoc module "Eintritt junger Menschen in den Arbeitsmarkt" (taken from Nationaler Bildungsbericht Österreich 2012, Band 1); and Panel C: OECD questionnaire on mental health.

StatLink http://dx.doi.org/10.1787/888933184104

In the past one or two decades, many OECD countries have seen a sharp rise in the number of young people aged 15 to 24 filing new disability benefit claims with a mental disorder. The increase has been much faster than in other age groups (Figure 2.5, Panel C), even in countries where disability benefit reform has led to a decline in new claims in all other age brackets (OECD, 2012). Swedish data also point to a close link between youth unemployment and disability claims: regions with higher youth jobless rates also show higher disability recipiency rates (OECD, 2013d).

Support for job seeking and work experience comes too late

In response to very high (and rising) unemployment rates among the young, countries have invested in activation programmes steered by the public employment service (PES). Under Sweden's *Youth Job Guarantee Scheme* (OECD, 2013d), for example, or the *Apprenticeship Guarantee* in Austria (OECD, 2015), unemployed young people who are registered at the local job centre attend programmes, often lasting several months, where they receive intensive job-search support or get their first work experience through apprenticeship arrangements. Denmark has also started to up-skill young registered jobseekers with no upper secondary education by enrolling them in mandatory education programmes (OECD, 2013c). Sweden has put in place special so-called *Navigator Centres* for unemployed young people who are estranged from the labour market because of mental ill-health, for example, or because they have never worked. The centres provide education, health care, and employment support and work closely with industry (Factsheet 2.12).

Most countries, however, have little inkling of the greater vulnerability of unemployed young people who suffer from poor mental health. The upshot is that they fail to address mental ill-health at all or consider it grounds for ineligibility for job support. Such stances are deeply damaging. While work can help improve poor mental health, the distance from the labour market widens the longer unemployment lasts, and unemployment grows worse (Strandh et al., 2014; OECD, 2013c; OECD, 2012; Mroz and Savage, 2006).

Despite the good intentions behind PES-administered youth activation programmes, there are two important shortcomings. First, rolling out such programmes is a reactive approach – i.e. taking action only after the fact, once young people have become unemployed. Governments should seek to bolster labour market integration programmes through earlier career support in mainstream education. However, job coaches in secondary or higher education are uncommon in the countries reviewed by the OECD. And although they are more common in special and vocational education, they have no training in spotting mental ill-health or addressing any of the attendant issues that may arise during first-time work experience (OECD, 2014a; OECD, 2014b). That such knowledge would be highly valuable is stressed by results from a Survey on Mental Wellbeing in Higher Education in the United Kingdom, showing that 80% of 56 higher education institutions reported a significant increase in the number of students approaching student services because of mental health needs (Royal College of Psychiatrists, 2011).

Second, only those young people who manage to sign on at their local employment offices may benefit from the activation programmes. So far, none of the reviewed countries has experimented with requiring school leavers to register with the PES so as to monitor those who have trouble finding work. Only in Belgium, where 85% of all school leavers sign on, is it common practice (OECD, 2013a).

Many OECD countries are also struggling with the rising numbers of disability benefit claims of young people, mostly on the grounds of mental ill-health. To prevent allowances being granted too early in life, a number of countries have tightened access to permanent disability benefit and instead pay temporary benefits. They have become a popular alternative. In Austria, for example, almost all allowances paid to young people are temporary at the outset (OECD, 2015). However, such a change of tack is not enough in itself, because countries do little to reactivate people who are on temporary benefit. And eventually temporary entitlements are almost always made permanent.

What's more, in countries like Sweden and Norway, the focus on temporary payments in recent years has prompted a rise in new claims from young people – again mostly on the grounds of mental disorder. The reason is that temporary disability benefits have lowered the threshold for new claims (OECD, 2013b; OECD, 2013d).

It has proven to be very difficult to activate young people who are about to claim disability benefit and to strike the right balance between more rigorous requirements and better support. Recent reforms in Denmark (see Factsheet 5.3) and Austria (see Factsheet 5.4) have sought to strengthen activation by restricting entitlements to disability benefit and offering a more comprehensive and interdisciplinary rehabilitation and integration approach instead. Such changes apply particularly to young people, as initial outcomes in Denmark confirm. It remains to be seen, however, whether the new rehabilitation models are effective and if reforms can help young people enter or stay in employment.

A promising initiative for helping young people suffering from psychotic disorders into employment is Australia's *Orygen* Youth Health, a psychosocial recovery programme. It was adapted from Individual Placement and Support (IPS), a scheme originally developed for adults. As with IPS, an employment advisor works alongside the clinical team to support returns to school, training or employment (Factsheet 2.13). Although *Orygen* focuses chiefly on young people with psychotic illness and has not yet been as widely evaluated and implemented as adult IPS, it is a promising example of integrated health, education, and employment support. Developing similar programmes for registered young jobseekers who suffer from mild-to-moderate mental ill-health is an avenue worth exploring.

Today, support for young people with poor mental health seeking to make the school-to-work transition is substandard. It often comes too late – namely, after young people have left school – and only if they voluntarily register with the PES. And the longer they are out of work, the slimmer their chances of joining the labour market.

Key messages

Disability benefit claims usually spell the end of career prospects. Action to assist school-to-work transitions needs to start when students are still in education – be they in mainstream or special-needs establishments – and should be the work of job coaches with understanding of mental health. Given the high lifetime costs of being unable to enter the labour market, investing in strong support for the school-to-work transition is likely to pay off handsomely.

The following steps could help make support for the school-to-work transition effective:

- Improve early detection of mental ill-health in order to help those with mental health problems make the transition to higher education or work, e.g. with the support of specialised job coaches in secondary and vocational education.
- Involve the PES as early as possible, e.g. by requiring school leavers to register with the local employment office and guaranteeing training for young people who fail to find work.
- Use multidisciplinary rehabilitation to curb young people's disability benefit claims.

REFERENCES

Homlong, L., E. Rosvold and O. Haavet (2013), "Can Use of Healthcare Services Among 15-16 Year-olds Predict an Increased Level of High School Dropout? A Longitudinal Community Study", *BMJ Open*.

Kessler, R. and P. Wang (2008), "The Descriptive Epidemiology of Commonly Occurring Mental Disorders in the United States", *Annual Review of Public Health*, Vol. 29, pp. 115-129.

Kessler, R. et al. (2005), "Lifetime Prevalence and Age-of-Onset Distributions of DSM-IV Disorders in the National Comorbidity Survey Replication", *Archives of General Psychiatry*, No. 62, pp. 593-603.

Kim-Cohen, J. et al. (2003), "Prior Juvenile Diagnoses in Adults with Mental Disorder: Developmental Follow-Back of a Prospective-Longitudinal Cohort", *Archives of General Psychiatry*, Vol. 60, pp. 709-717.

Langeveld, J. et al. (2011), "Teachers' Awareness for Psychotic Symptoms in Secondary School: The Effects of an Early Detection Programme and Information Campaign", *Early Intervention in Psychiatry*, Vol. 5, pp. 115-121.

McLeod, J. and D. Fettes (2007), "Trajectories of Failure: The Educational Careers of Children with Mental Health Problems", *American Journal of Sociology*, Vol. 113, No. 3, pp. 653-701.

Merikangas, K. et al. (2010), "Lifetime Prevalence of Mental Disorders in US Adolescents: Results from the National Comorbidity Study-Adolescent Supplemente (NCS-A)", *Journal of American Academic Child and Adolescent Psychiatry*, Vol. 49, No. 10, pp. 980-989.

MindMatters (2014), "Background, Framework and Rationale: MindMatters Redevelopment", www.mindmatters.edu.au/docs/default-source/fact-sheets/mindmatters---background-framework-and-rationale.pdf?sfvrsn=12.

Mroz, T. and T. Savage (2006), "The Long-term Effects of Youth Unemployment", *Journal of Human Resources*, Vol. 41, No. 2, pp. 259-293.

OECD (forthcoming 2015), *Mental Health and Work: Austria*, OECD Publishing, Paris.

OECD (2014a), *Mental Health and Work: Switzerland*, OECD Publishing, Paris, http://dx.doi.org/10.1787/9789264204973-en.

OECD (2014b), *Mental Health and Work: Netherlands*, OECD Publishing, Paris, http://dx.doi.org/10.1787/9789264223301-en.

OECD (2014c), *Employment Outlook 2014*, OECD Publishing, Paris, www.oecd.org/employment/oecdemploymentoutlook.htm.

OECD (2013a), *Mental Health and Work: Belgium*, OECD Publishing, Paris. http://dx.doi.org/10.1787/9789264187566-en.

OECD (2013b), *Mental Health and Work: Norway*, OECD Publishing, Paris, http://dx/doi/org/10.1787/9789264178984-en.

OECD (2013c), *Mental Health and Work: Denmark*, OECD Publishing, Paris, http://dx/doi/org/10.1787/9789264188631-en.

OECD (2013d), *Mental Health and Work: Sweden,* OECD Publishing, Paris, http://dx.doi.org/10.1787/9789264188730-en.

OECD (2012), *Sick on the Job? Myths and Realities about Mental Health and Work*, OECD Publishing, Paris, http://dx.doi.org/10.1787/9789264124523-en.

OECD (2010), *Creating Effective Teaching and Learning Environments: First Results from TALIS*, OECD Publishing, Paris. http://dx/doi/org/10.1787/9789264068780-en.

Ormel, J. et al. (2014), "Mental Health in Dutch Adolescents: A TRAILS Report on Prevalence, Severity, Age of Onset, Continuity and Co-morbidity of DSM Disorders", *Psychological Medicine*, Epub ahead of print.

Philip, J. et al. (2014), "The Mental Health in Austrian Teenagers (MHAT) Study: Preliminary Results from a Pilot Study", *Neuropsychiatrie*, Epub ahead of print.

Royal College of Psychiatrists (2011), "Mental Health of Students in Higher Education", *College Report No. CR166*, Royal College of Psychiatrists, London.

Skre, I. et al. (2013), "A School Intervention for Mental Health Literacy in Adolescents: Effects of a Non-randomized Cluster Controlled Trial", *BMC Public Health*, Vol. 13, No. 873, pp. 1-15.

Slee, P. et al. (2009), *KidsMatter Primary Evaluation Final Report,* Centre for Analysis of Education Futures, Flinders University of South Australia, Bedford Park.

Strandh, M. et al. (2014), "Unemployment and Mental Health Scarring During the Life Course", *European Journal of Public Health*, Vol. 24, No. 3, pp. 440-445.

Veldman, K. et al. (2014), "Mental Health Problems and Educational Attainment in Adolescence: 9-year Follow-up of the TRAILS Study", *PLoS One*, Vol. 9, No. 7, pp. 1-7.

Weare, K. and M. Nind (2011), "Mental Health Promotion and Problem Prevention in Schools: What Does the Evidence Say?", *Health Promotion International*, Vol. 26, No. S1, pp. i29-169.

Wyn, J. et al. (2000), "MindMatters, A Whole-school Approach Promoting Mental Health and Wellbeing", *Australian and New Zealand Journal of Psychiatry*, Vol. 34, pp. 594-601.

FACTSHEETS 2.1 TO 2.13

Factsheet 2.1
Norway: Improving the mental health literacy of teachers and students

Context

Teachers play a crucial role in recognising mental ill-health among students and taking action accordingly. Breaking the stigma that attaches to students affected by mental ill-health can help secure them social support and inclusion. It is important to improve the mental health literacy of both students and teachers to prevent negative educational outcomes.

Programme

In Norway, the Mental Health in Schools co-operative project, which ran from 2004 to 2011, provided different mental health training programmes directed at teachers and students. The project, part of the government's strategic plan for mental health, aimed to raise awareness of mental health conditions, increase available support, and foster confidence in the effects of treatment.

Specifically, six different mental health programmes were run, all with the goal of fostering knowledge on how students can safeguard their own mental health, where they can get help, and how they can provide support for each other. One programme specifically focused on teachers to increase their i) understanding of mental health, ii) competency in dealing with students suffering from mental ill-health and iii) knowledge of models of co-operation between schools and health and social services. The ambition was to create a more open atmosphere conducive to discussing emotional problems in schools.

Outcomes

A non-randomised controlled study evaluated the effects of one of the mental health programmes – Mental Health for Everyone. The programme focused on teaching young people about mental health and helped students to express their feelings and become more aware of their own and others' mental health. It showed that mental health literacy improved significantly more among students who attended the programme than among those who did not. They recognised symptom profiles better and held less prejudices. A study evaluating information campaigns in Norway for increasing teachers' ability to spot the early signs of psychosis revealed that those who were reached by the campaign had more confidence in the effectiveness of psychosis treatment and were better able to identify psychosis. Such information campaigns could be a basis for closer collaboration between the education and the mental health care systems.

There has been no investigation of whether training for teachers in identifying a broad range of signs of poor mental health has been successful. It is crucial that its scope should not be confined to identifying students with more easily recognisable problems, such as defiant behaviour, hyperactivity, or conduct disorders. It should encompass less visible, less disruptive mental health problems such as anxiety and depression.

Further reading

Langeveld, J. et al. (2011), "Teachers' Awareness for Psychotic Symptoms in Secondary School: The Effects of an Early Detection Programme and Information Campaign", *Early Intervention in Psychiatry*, Vol. 5, pp. 115-121.

OECD (2013), *Mental Health and Work: Norway*, OECD Publishing, Paris, http://dx/doi/org/10.1787/9789264178984-en.

Skre, I. et al. (2013), "A School Intervention for Mental Health Literacy in Adolescents: Effects of a Non-randomized cluster Controlled Trial", *BMC Public Health*, Vol. 13, No. 873, pp. 1-15.

Factsheet 2.2
Australia: KidsMatter and MindMatters – Promoting mental health programmes in schools

Context

Young people who suffer from mental ill-health run a higher risk of attaining low levels of education and leaving school early than their healthy peers. Promoting mental health programmes in schools can improve mental health literacy among teachers and students and prevent early school leaving.

Programme

The Australian Government funds two mental health promotion programmes in schools: KidsMatter for primary schools and MindMatters for secondary schools.

KidsMatter aims to encourage partnerships between the education sector, early childhood professionals, the health system, and local communities in order to optimise children's mental health and well-being and to intervene early in children's lives where necessary. MindMatters builds on the mental health promotion, prevention, and early intervention frameworks developed for KidsMatter, but has been adapted to secondary schools contexts and adolescent development. Aligning MindMatters with KidsMatter through a consistent framework can support the large number of schools with both primary and secondary intakes.

Both programmes provide training in promoting mental health and help schools to identify their strengths and weaknesses in that regard. To that end, the programmes foster collaboration between teachers, parents, students, and the wider school community. They guide schools in choosing an available intervention programme in four major areas: i) positive school community; ii) student skills for resilience; iii) parents and families (*e.g.* information support and good communication); and iv) support for students experiencing mental ill-health.

Outcomes

A pilot phase of KidsMatter was trialled in 101 schools across Australia during 2007-8. A comprehensive evaluation (albeit without a comparison group) found a general improvement in students' mental health and well-being – greater optimism, coping skills and mental health difficulties – and in teachers' knowledge of mental health and ability to support their students. No robust measurement has yet been taken of how the MindMatters programme improves mental health literacy, implements interventions, or achieves mental health outcomes. Nor is it known how many secondary schools have integrated the programme into the curriculum. In 2011, the Commonwealth Department of Health and Ageing commenced work with the Principals Australia Institute on how to consistently and continuously measure the outcomes of KidsMatter and MindMatters.

Further reading

Graetz, B. et al. (2008), "KidsMatter: A Population Health Model to Support Student Mental Health and Well-being in Primary Schools", *International Journal of Mental Health Promotion*, Vol. 10, pp. 13-20.

OECD (forthcoming 2015), *Mental Health and Work: Australia*, OECD Publishing, Paris.

Slee, P. et al. (2009), *KidsMatter Primary Evaluation Final Report*, Centre for Analysis of Education Futures, Flinders University of South Australia, Bedford Park.

Factsheet 2.3
Belgium: Internal care structure in schools

Context

Childhood and adolescence are crucial times for promoting good mental health and preventing mental illness. Organising school-based mental health services with a central role for the teacher as primary actor is one promising way of addressing the issue.

Programme

Flanders has a scheme, *interne leerlingenbegeleiding* (internal care structure), that operates within schools. Each school receives funding that allows it to relieve teachers of part of their teaching duties or to hire specialised staff (a psychologist, pedagogue, medical professional, or social worker) so that they can provide extra care for pupils in need. These teachers are called "care teachers". All primary schools are obliged to conduct a three-level care policy with some teachers co-ordinating action at the school level, some coaching and supporting their co-workers, and others guiding students. However, should the need arise, care teachers are allowed to fill in at other levels than the one to which they are assigned. In some schools, the care teacher engages primarily in one-to-one interventions (e.g. encouraging pupils to talk about their problems at school or at home). In other schools, the care teacher focuses more on group-based approaches (e.g. bullying prevention programmes), or devising new policies (e.g. healthy school schemes).

Outcomes

A recent evaluation shows that the internal care policy with the teacher as primary actor has become widely accepted in primary education in Flanders thanks to a range of policy initiatives and increased spending from the Flemish Government. Primary schools have, on average, the full-time equivalent of 0.6 care teacher, with the 25% largest schools employing between 0.75 and 1 full-time care teacher. In addition, schools with at least 10% of their pupils (25% in secondary education) in a risk group (e.g. foreign language spoken at home, poorly educated mother, or household in receipt of a school subsidy) receive additional resources equivalent to one to two full-time teachers. The same study points out, however, that secondary schools typically have a much less well developed internal care structure as the issue has received much less attention and resources from the government.

Further reading

OECD (2013), *Mental Health and Work: Belgium*, OECD Publishing, Paris, http://dx.doi.org/10.1787/9789264187566-en.

Struyf, E. et al. (2012), "Zorgbeleid in het Gewoon Basisonderwijs en Secundair Onderwijs in Vlaanderen: Kenmerken, Predictoren en Samenhang met Taakopvatting, en Handelingsbekwaamheid van Leerkrachten" [Care policy in primary and secondary education in Flanders: Characteristics, predictors and congruence of tasks, and competency of teachers], Onderzoek in opdracht van de Vlaamse Minister van Onderwijs en Vorming in het kader van het onderwijskundig beleids- en praktijkgericht wetenschappelijk onderzoek (OBPWO 09.05), Brussels.

Factsheet 2.4
Sweden: Youth clinics help young people with multiple problems

Context

Many young people with mental health problems do not receive the right support, if any at all, because they have no dealings with the relevant public services. Those who are not in education or employment are a prime example as they have typically lost touch with either the education or the employment system. Making sure that they receive support is a daunting challenge.

Programme

Youth clinics are an easily accessible, free public service for young people up to 20 years of age. Young people can make contact voluntarily through the clinics' open house policy. The clinics play an important role in general health promotion because of their close contact with a large proportion of the teenage population. They are run jointly by municipalities and regions, providing services to young people with multiple problems, particularly mental health problems. Municipalities or regional councils fund the clinics, either separately or jointly. Although there are some differences in the way that municipalities organise their youth clinics, the general focus is the same.

All youth clinics have at least one midwife, a general practitioner, a social worker and a psychologist. Their main activities include prevention and treatment services for young people with i) psychological and social problems and ii) sexuality issues (*e.g.* unwanted pregnancies and sexually transmitted infections). Workers in youth clinics actively work to identify early signs of mental illness and deal with concerns related to adolescents' social development. Depending on the severity of the illness, psychological treatment measures can take the form of short or long therapies that focus on crisis care, support, and/or patients' lack of insight. The work of the various professionals involved consists of individual conversations, investigation, treatment, and group activities. Outreach activities are also essential part of the clinics' work. They include study visits to school classes and informing schools about the available health services.

Outcomes

Around 1.3 million young people have registered with youth clinics since their inception in 2002. There is no evidence available on the effectiveness of the programme. However, it has strengths that are recognised as important to designing services for young people. First, the service mix within a single youth-friendly setting addresses young people's low use of and engagement in traditional primary and specialist (mental) health care. Second, integrating mental health programmes and services into general youth and welfare programmes could be a way forward, notably in low-resource settings. The third distinct strength is that youth health programmes are less stigmatising when multiple youth-friendly services are provided under one roof and are thus better able to reach out to young people with common mental illnesses.

Further reading

OECD (2013), *Mental Health and Work: Sweden,* OECD Publishing, Paris, http://dx.doi.org/10.1787/9789264188730-en.

Patel, V. et al. (2007), "Mental Health of Young People: A Global Public-Health Challenge", *The Lancet*, No. 369, pp. 1302-1313.

Factsheet 2.5
Australia: Headspace – Providing services for young people with mental ill-health

Context

Mental health problems are extremely frequent during the transition from childhood to adulthood – they occur even more often than later in life. Yet young people are less likely than any other groups to seek professional help for mental ill-health. Reasons include lack of awareness and poor service accessibility.

Programme

Headspace addresses the mismatch between the need for and supply of mental health services among young people between 12 and 25 years old. As at December 2014, there were 70 headspace centres across Australia, a number that will be scaled up to 100 by 2016. They bring together a range of professionals from psychologists, social workers, alcohol and drug workers, to GPs, career counsellors, vocational workers and youth workers. Headspace centres are accessible, youth-friendly, integrated service hubs that provide evidence-based interventions and support to young people with mental health and well-being needs. Each centre offers medical and vocational services as part of the aim to provide holistic and integrated support.

Headspace's access threshold is very low: anyone can walk in. The centres are thus ideally placed to reach young people with non-diagnosed common mental illness. Services are provided largely free of charge with high confidentiality. Headspace works together with and refers to other services, such as government-funded employment schemes and the Department for Social Services (which assesses eligibility for income support and refers claimants to employment services). Headspace also has a support programme for secondary schools affected by suicide.

Outcomes

A recent study into the characteristics of headspace clients, between January and June 2013 (across all 55 centres open during this time), showed that the majority had problems with how they felt – most often sad, depressed and/or anxious. Over half presented very high levels of psychological distress. About 15% came with no mental disorder, 17% with a sub-threshold condition, about 40% with mild to moderate mental illness, close to 20% with a full-threshold diagnosis, and 6% with a serious, on-going mental disorder.

Almost 50% attended school and 20% were in higher education – figures that demonstrate headspace's potential as a programme for preventing early school leaving among young people with mental health issues. That one-third not engaged in education, training or employment indicates the vulnerability of youngsters with mental health problems. No details are known so far about the types of services used most frequently or the sustainability of interventions.

Further reading

OECD (forthcoming 2015), *Mental Health and Work: Australia*, OECD Publishing, Paris.

Rickwood, D., N. Van Dyke and N. Telford (2013), "Innovation in Youth Mental Health Services in Australia: Common Characteristics Across the First Headspace Centres", *Early Intervention in Psychiatry*, Epub ahead of print, http://dx.doi.org/10.1111/eip.12071.

Rickwood, D. et al. (2014), "Headspace – Australia's Innovation in Youth Mental Health: Who Are the Clients and Why Are They Presenting?", *Medical Journal of Australia*, Vol. 200, No. 2, pp. 108-111.

Factsheet 2.6
Belgium: Student guidance centres

Context

With the average age of onset of mental disorders being 14 years old, the education system has an important role to play in early identification of mental ill-health. Providing individual, multidisciplinary support for students with behavioural problems can contribute to the timely, co-ordinated treatment of young people with mental health problems.

Programme

In Flanders, student guidance centres (Centra voor Leerlingenbegeleiding – CLBs) assist schools in four core domains – learning strategies, educational career planning, psychosocial functioning, and preventive health care. The centres work with multidisciplinary teams consisting of psychologists (typically directors of centres), doctors, nurses, social workers, and educationalists. The CLBs also perform regular medical check-ups and are structurally linked to both the Flemish Department for Education and the Flemish Department for Welfare, Public Health and Family.

They operate on the principle of universal surveillance for all students on the one hand and, on the other, provide individual, multidisciplinary, and intensive counselling to students with greater needs. The work of the centres is mainly demand-driven and they intervene after a request from a student, parent or school. However, they also play a key role in the prevention of early school leaving and access to special and integrated education.

Besides giving information, support and guidance, the centres typically have a clear overview of the external services to which they can refer people if they cannot resolve issues themselves.

Outcomes

All schools are required to work with a student guidance centre, with each CLB caseworkers responsible for about 400 students on average. Yet practices vary greatly across centres and they do not always have enough staff to meet all their tasks. There is growing demand from schools, parents and students for support from the CLB centres, in particular with respect to psychosocial problems. Long waiting lists for external services, especially in the mental health sector, have increased the workload for CLB caseworkers as they support the students until they get specialised care. Due to lack of time, centres tend to undertake little prevention or early detection.

Further reading

OECD (2013), *Mental Health and Work: Belgium*, OECD Publishing, Paris, http://dx.doi.org/10.1787/9789264187566-en.

Vermaut, H. et al. (2009), "Het CLB-Decreet: Tussen Wens en Realisatie", Evaluatie Acht Jaar na de Invoering van het CLB-Decreet, Hoger Instituut voor de Arbeid, Katholieke Universiteit Leuven.

Factsheet 2.7
Netherlands: Regional care and advice teams for young people at school

Context

Early identification and co-ordinated treatment of students with mental ill-health is important for supporting those with psychosocial problems. The education system has a key role to play.

Programme

In the Netherlands, schools are part of regional care and advice teams (ZAT) that support students with psychosocial and/or behavioural problems. The teams include other youth care specialists such as paediatricians, social workers, psychologists, educationalists, education officers, and the police. There are separate teams for primary, secondary and vocational education.

The ZATs' main tasks are to i) conduct interdisciplinary problem analysis of the cases that come before them; ii) further explore the problems of students or families; iii) co-ordinate the support services necessary for a specific case; iv) advise school representatives; v) provide support to students and/or families; vi) refer to external support; vii) prevent early school leaving (mainly in vocational school care and advice teams).

Outcomes

Almost all secondary and vocational schools, but only 67% of primary establishments, take part in ZATs. Teams are confronted with high caseloads: 8 200 students in primary education and 721 and 3 200 in secondary and vocational education, respectively. Of the total primary school population, about 1% of all pupils are discussed in an academic year, while in secondary education the figure is 4%. (No statistics are available for vocational establishments.) The inference is that a large group of students with problems is being missed, as national data have shown that about 20% of Dutch young people experience mental health problems. Consequently, the ZAT teams support those who suffer from more severe psychosocial problems.

Each year, schools evaluate the ZAT teams. Overall, they rate them well for expertise, teamwork, clear administration and reporting of agreements, speed of response and effective problem management. In primary and secondary education, teams have been criticised for the lack of preventive programmes and the limited scale on which support programmes are provided. Teams in primary education do not work closely enough with local youth care providers. In secondary education, problems are encountered with feedback from the teams to students, parents and teachers. And in vocational education, timely referral of students to the ZAT teams and to other external parties has been found wanting.

Further reading

OECD (2014), *Mental Health and Work: Netherlands*, OECD Publishing, Paris, http://dx.doi.org/10.1787/9789264223301-en.

Steenhoven, P. van der and D. van Veen (2012), "Monitor deelnemerszorg en ZAT's in het middelbaar beroepsonderwijs 2011", Nederlands Jeugdinstituut, Utrecht.

Steenhoven, P. van der and D. van Veen (2011a), "Monitor ZAT's, zorgteams en leerlingenzorg in het primair onderwijs 2010", Nederlands Jeugdinstituut, Utrecht.

Steenhoven, P. van der and D. van Veen (2011b), "Monitor leerlingenzorg en ZAT's in het voortgezet onderwijs 2010", Nederlands Jeugdinstituut, Utrecht.

Factsheet 2.8
Netherlands: Preventing early school leaving

Context

Young people with mental health problems are a risk group that is particularly prone to early school leaving (ESL), which seriously reduces their levels of educational attainment and labour market prospects. Policies to prevent early school leaving and offer timely support to young people who have dropped out are essential, therefore.

Programme

Since 2007, the Netherlands has introduced several measures to curb ESL. All young people in education receive an "education number" to facilitate the tracking of ESL. In line with this move, a national digital School Absenteeism Desk has been put in place. Schools report to the desk absenteeism (defined as missing 16 hours within four consecutive school weeks) and ESL (defined as leaving school before having acquired a basic qualification). Since 2009, it has been compulsory for all schools to report absenteeism and ESL to the desk.

A nationwide programme to address ESL, called "Aanval op schooluitval", has also been initiated. Its chief goals are: i) scrutinise more closely the transition from pre-vocational secondary education to vocational education; ii) take more and better action at school (schools receive financial rewards for lowering ESL percentages to certain levels); iii) cater better to pupils who would rather "work with their hands"; iv) support career orientation and study choices more effectively; v) offer more attractive syllabi, that include sports and culture, to keep youth in school; vi) agree with employers basic qualification requirements for early school leavers aged 18 to 23.

The Netherlands has also set up 39 regional registration and co-ordination centres to further tackle ESL in collaboration with schools and municipalities. Students under the age of 23 who leave school without a basic qualification fall under the responsibility of the centres. They seek to guide students back into education, possibly in combination with work, in order to obtain a basic qualification. If education is no longer a feasible option, the centres help their wards find a sustainable job (often working with employment services).

Outcomes

A clear downward trend has been observed in the number of new early school leavers per school year since the measures to tackle ESL were implemented. The number almost halved from over 50 000 in school year 2005-06 to around 28 000 in 2012-13, which is 2.1% of the total school population (the statistics are preliminary). The bulk early leavers (79%) come from vocational education, 18% from secondary education, and the remaining 3% from adult education.

Further reading

OCW (2011), "Schooluitval voorkomen in Nederland: Speerpunten huidige aanpak en doorkijk naar vervolgbeleid; resultaat schooljaar 2009-2010 (voorlopige cijfers)" [Preventing school dropout in the Netherlands: Priorities of the current approach and perspective on follow-up policy; Result for school year 2009-10 preliminary numbers], Ministerie van Onderwijs, Cultuur en Wetenschap, Den Haag.

OCW (2013), "Aanpak voortijdig schoolverlaten" [Approach to early school leaving], Ministerie van Onderwijs, Cultuur en Wetenschap, Den Haag.

OECD (2014), *Mental Health and Work: Netherlands*, OECD Publishing, Paris, http://dx.doi.org/10.1787/9789264223301-en.

Factsheet 2.9
Australia: Youth connections – reconnecting disengaged young people with education, training and employment

Context

Young people who suffer from mental ill-health, diagnosed or not, are at a higher risk of disengaging from education and, consequently, facing poor labour market prospects. Special centres for case management can improve support for early school leavers and help them return to school or otherwise make the transition to work.

Programme

Youth Connections was a safety net scheme for young people who had disengaged from education, or were at risk of doing so. It provided individually-tailored case management to help them re-connect with education or training and build resilience, skills and attributes that promote positive life choices and well-being.

The programme had three components: i) individual support services; ii) outreach and re-engagement activities to track young people who have dropped out of education; and iii) activities targeted at strengthening services in the region to identify and respond more effectively to young people at risk of disengagement. Case management included mentoring, advocacy and referral to other service providers. The most common barriers addressed were low self-esteem, low literacy, and numeracy and behavioural problems.

Providers were funded by the federal government, complemented by state programmes. The amount of funding depended on the size and nature of each service region. Though the agreements between the federal and state governments ended in 2013, the Australian Government continued funding Youth Connections until the end of 2014.

Outcomes

The service was delivered in 113 service regions by 67 organisations and provided support services to more than 87 870 young people. 26 079 (29%) of these young people had suspected or diagnosed mental health issues. During the life of the programme, approximately 54 150 young people receiving support commenced education, re-engaged in education or strengthened their education engagement, approximately another 40 740 improved educational performance, attendance or behaviour and 4 490 engaged in employment (Youth Connections participants could achieve multiple outcomes).

A survey among case management providers suggests that Youth Connections is effective in establishing a long-term effect through lasting re-connection: six months after completing the programme, 93% of participants were in education, training, or employment. A significant proportion experienced improved psychological outcomes. The main reasons for not achieving outcomes are a failure to engage when initially contacted and withdrawals during the programme.

The main success factors included the very low caseload of 25-30 adolescents, the flexibility of the service, and links to others services. The majority of staff working with the young people had Youth Work or Social Work qualifications and were trained to recognise mental health problems and provide crisis intervention.

Further reading

Dandolopartners (2014), Final Evaluation of the National Partnership on Youth Attainment and Transitions, Dandelopartners, Melbourne.

OECD (forthcoming 2015), *Mental Health and Work: Australia*, OECD Publishing, Paris.

Factsheet 2.10
Austria: Youth coaching – Helping pupils stay in the education system

Context

Young people with multiple problems, which may include mental health issues, are at a high risk of leaving the education system without a qualification. Premature drop-out permanently affects their labour market prospects and calls for early intervention.

Programme

The aim of the Youth Coaching programme is to help young people stay in the education system as long as possible and to re-engage those who are neither employed nor in education or training (NEET). The three target groups are young people in their ninth school year (the last year of compulsory education) typically in the 15-16 age group; NEETs under the age of 19; and young people with a disability or special educational needs under 25 years old. Those eligible typically display a combination of individual conditions and social disadvantages and thus at a high risk of failing to complete school. Young people at risk access the programme chiefly through teachers who identify them (for those in their last school year) and through agencies like the employment service.

Youth Coaching is a graded three-step process. Step one is a three-hour initial consultation, including educational counselling and resulting in a mutually-agreed target. Step two comprises eight hours of counselling, during which students are required to take the initial agreement further and, if necessary, consult external experts such as social workers. Step three involves 30 hours of individual case management, in which youth coaches set out goals for implementing the target agreement and conclude with a clearance report. In this process, youth coaches refer their clients to services like debt or counselling and, if necessary, organise psychological therapy. The entire process may be spread out over no more than one year. An important element of the programme is the involvement of both parents and teachers and a strong focus on students' resources.

Outcomes

In its trial phase, Youth Coaching applied primarily to pupils in the ninth school year. They are easily reached through their class teachers although access procedures to the programme differ widely between regions and are in most cases highly non-transparent. For other target groups, better outreach methods will be needed, such as close collaboration with other actors (e.g. youth workers).

Of those who have gone through the whole programme so far (only 7% have dropped out), 85% achieved outcomes in line with target agreements. In total, 30% ended up in step-3 case management, though for the NEET group the proportion is expected to be much higher – raising significant issues of funding due to the large current caseload of some 100 students per caseworker.

Finally, there appears to be little conflict with other mental health care professionals (such as social workers, school psychologists and advisory teachers for children with mental and behavioural problems). Youth coaches actually seem to function like hubs for carers.

Further reading

OECD (forthcoming 2015), *Mental Health and Work: Austria*, OECD Publishing, Paris.

Steiner, M. et al. (2013), "Evaluierung Jugendcoaching-Endbericht", Studie im Auftrag des Bundesministeriums für Arbeit, Soziales und Konsumentenschutz, Vienna.

Factsheet 2.11
Denmark: Municipal youth guidance centres

Context

Young people who suffer from mental ill-health are greatly at risk of leaving school early, which dims their labour market prospects. Early action to ensure a smooth transition from lower- to upper-secondary education and from upper-secondary education to work is needed.

Programme

Municipal Youth Guidance Centres are responsible for i) counselling young people up to the age of 25 in their critical transition from lower- to upper-secondary education, and ii) following up on those who drop out of upper-secondary education.

Guidance counsellors are responsible for preparing education plans for all pupils for the time after they complete lower-secondary school. Planning involves counsellors meeting pupils and parents and building on pupils' school records, which provide information on their achievements, interests, expectations for the future, and how they wish to develop.

Planning starts several years before the end of compulsory schooling. Youth guidance counselors assess the pupil's academic, social and personal competences in the 8th grade. Children assessed as not having the competenes needed to be ready for further education must participate in an individually adapted, focused education and guidance programme in grade 8 and 9 in co-operation between the school and the guidance centre. The goal is that the pupil becomes ready to receive an upper secondary education by the end of grade 9 or 10.

The transition process between lower and upper secondary education is monitored and pupils 15 to 17 years old who fail to turn up for upper secondary education after compulsory school are monitored to prevent early school leaving. In the event of a pupil's non-attendance, the guidance counsellor has to get in touch with his or her parents within five days of being notified by the school and initiate action within 30 days. Counsellors are not allowed to provide any treatment or therapy but they can identify problems and refer pupils or parents to specialists – a social worker in case of severe social problems in the family, for example, or a psychologist in the event of mental illness.

The centres co-operate closely with the educational institutions and the municipal job centre, for which young people in general and 18-19 year-olds in particular are also a target group (all young people can get guidance from the job centre for labour market questions and employment options). The guidance centres have acces to a database with a full overview of the education and training of each person under age 25 within the municipality who has not finished upper secondary education. This enables a quicker identification of vulnerable youth.

Outcomes

There are 53 centres in Denmark with around 1 000 counsellors covering the 98 municipalities. The Ministry of Education has developed guidelines for a quality assurance system to be set up by each centre including figures regarding the scope, results and effects of the guidance provided, and a procedure for evaluating the services provided through user and employee surveys. Centres are also required to publish objectives, methods, planned activities and performance on the Internet.

Further reading

Euroguidance Denmark (2014), *Guidance in Education – The Educational Guidance System in Denmark*, Danish Agency for Higher Education, Copenhagen.

OECD (2013), *Mental Health and Work: Denmark,* OECD Publishing, Paris, http://dx/doi/org/10.1787/9789264188631-en.

Factsheet 2.12
Sweden: Navigator centres for young unemployed people

Context

High unemployment among young people who suffer from poor mental health is a problem in many OECD countries. Several have therefore invested in public employment service youth activation programmes. Ensuring co-ordinated and interdisciplinary support for young unemployed people is crucial to integrating them into the labour market.

Programme

During 2005-07, the Swedish National Board for Youth Affairs piloted eleven municipal navigator centres with a common "single-door" to provide support for young people. The navigator centres are a good model of co-ordinated employment, educational and health support for young people between 16 and 25 years of age facing high entry barriers to the labour market. The navigator centres focus their attention on individuals who are harder to motivate than those usually encountered by the employment service. They include young people who suffer, or have suffered, from social phobias, depression, or the effects of drug abuse. Many are on social assistance benefit and have never been integrated into the labour market.

The navigator centres provide services mainly through a one-stop shop formula that range from curriculum vitae writing skills, educational and vocational counselling, and motivational interviewing to preventive health care. Young people may also be referred to mental health professionals in the county where the centre is located. Or, centres themselves may deliver support depending on the nature of the young person's disorder and how the centre is organised. If referrals are made through municipal employment units, the public employment services, or the Social Insurance Agency, young people are required to take up the support provision that is offered to them.

Outcomes

Evaluations of the navigator centres across the country are not available. But evidence from the pilot phase suggests that out of the 2 000 young people who have so far been placed in a navigator centre, between 45% and 70% have moved on to education, employment, or work experience. Qualitative evidence suggests that navigator centres are a good way of filling the gap left by the employment service, social services and the local education committees between which young people are shuttled. Ensuring that all municipalities offer navigator-centre-type services would ease access to both employment and health support. Alternatively, navigator centres could be turned into a national initiative subject to a rigorous evaluation of the programme.

Further reading

OECD (2013), *Mental Health and Work: Sweden,* OECD Publishing, Paris, http://dx.doi.org/10.1787/9789264188730-en.

Factsheet 2.13
Australia: Orygen youth health – Embedding employment services in a clinical setting

Context

Health services tend to have little employment focus or expertise and are also generally poorly connected with employment agencies and job brokers. Yet the vocational services provided in parallel to health services have been shown not only to help people into employment but also to improve health and well-being outcomes.

Programme

Orygen Youth Health is a state-funded hospital-based youth mental health service. It runs an experimental psychosocial recovery programme, which is in fact Individual Placement and Support (IPS) adapted to young people. This means that employment counsellors are directly employed by the health service and provide support in attaining educational goals or finding and maintaining employment in line with the IPS model.

Orygen focuses on three disorder groups: first-episode psychoses, mood disorders, and personality disorders. However, Orygen does not wait until people have been assigned a disability tag and has a strong focus on indicated prevention when the first signs of mental illness arise. Referrals may thus also come from schools, families and the community.

Returning to school, training or employment are common goals for young people attending the Psychosocial Recovery Programme. Young people can work on their job interview skills, update their resume, explore their skills and identify training they might want to pursue. A Group Programme may be offered as a first step in vocational recovery providing structure and routine and opportunities to participate in meaningful activities with others. Qualified teachers are available on site to support young people in staying at, or returning to, school. Vocational group programmes such as catering and horticulture are offered and co-facilitated by clinicians and teachers. Those ready to enter work have access to employment consultants from outside agencies and the consultants employed at Orygen.

Outcomes

The effectiveness of the IPS service for young people with first-episode psychosis is currently being evaluated in a randomised controlled trial. First – unpublished – results are positive: the integrated service is more effective than health intervention alone (85% of subjects moved into education or employment compared to 29% in the control group which received the usual clinical case management care, some of which have a vocational orientation). Factors that contribute to the success of Orygen's employment counsellors include the low caseload of around 20 clients and the focus on prevention and early intervention (before clients are caught in inactivity).

Funding employment specialists remains an issue for integrated services of this type. It requires convincing people that the employment specialist is of more value than an additional clinician. A further worry is that capacity is insufficient for offering such service to everyone in the region, e.g. there are 2 500 referrals every year but resources only for 700-800 clients.

Further reading

Killackey, E. et al. (2013), "A Randomized Controlled Trial of Vocational Intervention for Young People with First-episode Psychosis: Method", *Perspectives in Early Intervention*, Vol. 7, No. 3, pp. 329-337.

OECD (forthcoming 2015), *Mental Health and Work: Australia*, OECD Publishing, Paris.

Chapter 3

Creating employment-oriented mental health care systems

People with mental ill-health need timely, adequate treatment in order to prevent a deterioration of their situation. Under-treatment is a persistent problem, since only about 50% of people with severe mental illness and about 30% of the people with moderate mental health conditions receive treatment. Moreover, targeting the right form and intensity of treatment at the right people remains a challenge in many OECD countries. Fostering the labour market participation of people who suffer from poor mental health requires policy action. Co-ordination between the health and employment sectors is crucial to that end.

Policy conclusions:

- *Assure timely access to recommended effective treatment.*
- *Provide training and support to general practitioners to enable them to treat mental illness.*
- *Give general practitioners incentives and tools for addressing work and sickness issues.*
- *Strengthen the employment focus of the mental health system.*

Health care systems can prevent impairment of the ability to work and improve the labour market participation of people who suffer from mental ill-health through timely, adequate treatment. It is essential that health care providers understand that work has a positive effect on the mental health recovery process and that they should seek to help people with mental health problems into the workplace. That being said, work-related problems can also cause mental illness or be caused by it. The inextricable links between mental health and work call for the delivery of integrated mental health and employment support services.

Under-treatment is pervasive across the OECD

Many countries struggle to treat mental illness. The report *Sick on the Job? Myths and realities about mental health and work* (OECD, 2012) has shown that in OECD countries only about 50% of people with severe mental ill-health and 30% of those with moderate complaints receive treatment. And most people who do receive treatment do so from non-specialists, mainly general practitioners. Very few are in the care of mental health professionals (Figure 3.1, Panel A).

Most people with mental health problems do not find their way into the health care system. Yet many experience an unmet need for treatment. Australian data for 2007 showed that about 20% of people with a mental illness that had lasted more than 12 months and who had not received treatment reported that they felt the need for it. Even among those who had received treatment, some 40% said that it only partially met their needs (Figure 3.1, Panel B). Similar results were found in a large-scale survey in six European countries: only about half of the people with mental health care needs received treatment (Alonso et al., 2007).

To ensure proper mental health treatment that fosters labour market participation, OECD countries should address four main policy issues:

1. timely access to adequate treatment,
2. training and support for general practitioners (GPs) in treating mental ill-health,
3. incentives and tools for GPs to help them address work and sickness issues,
4. a strong employment focus in the mental health system as a whole.

Timely access to adequate treatment

Many of the obstacles to timely treatment are common to all OECD countries. First, the stigma that still attaches to poor mental health makes people reluctant to seek treatment (Alonso et al., 2009). Second, GPs, who are in most cases the first to see patients and responsible for referring them to mental health care services, do not always recognise mental ill-health and the need for referral.

Another worrying impediment to timely treatment is that mental health care specialists are often overbooked and waiting times are long. In Belgium, Denmark, and the Netherlands, for example, waiting times of over a month have been reported to get an appointment, while in Austria it takes between two and eight months to receive a place in therapy (OECD, 2013a; OECD, 2013c; OECD, 2014b; OECD, 2015a). Having to bide their time for so long can put people off seeking treatment, with serious repercussions on work outcomes when delays in treatment prevent them from resuming their job. In

Sweden, for example, it was found that GPs prescribe unnecessarily long sick leave because waiting times for specialists were so long (OECD, 2013d). As the chances of returning to work dwindle rapidly over time it is alarming that obtaining timely treatment should be such a struggle (Koopmans et al., 2008).

Figure 3.1. **Needs for mental health care are often not met**

A. Share of people being treated by a specialist or non-specialist by severity of their mental ill-health, 2010

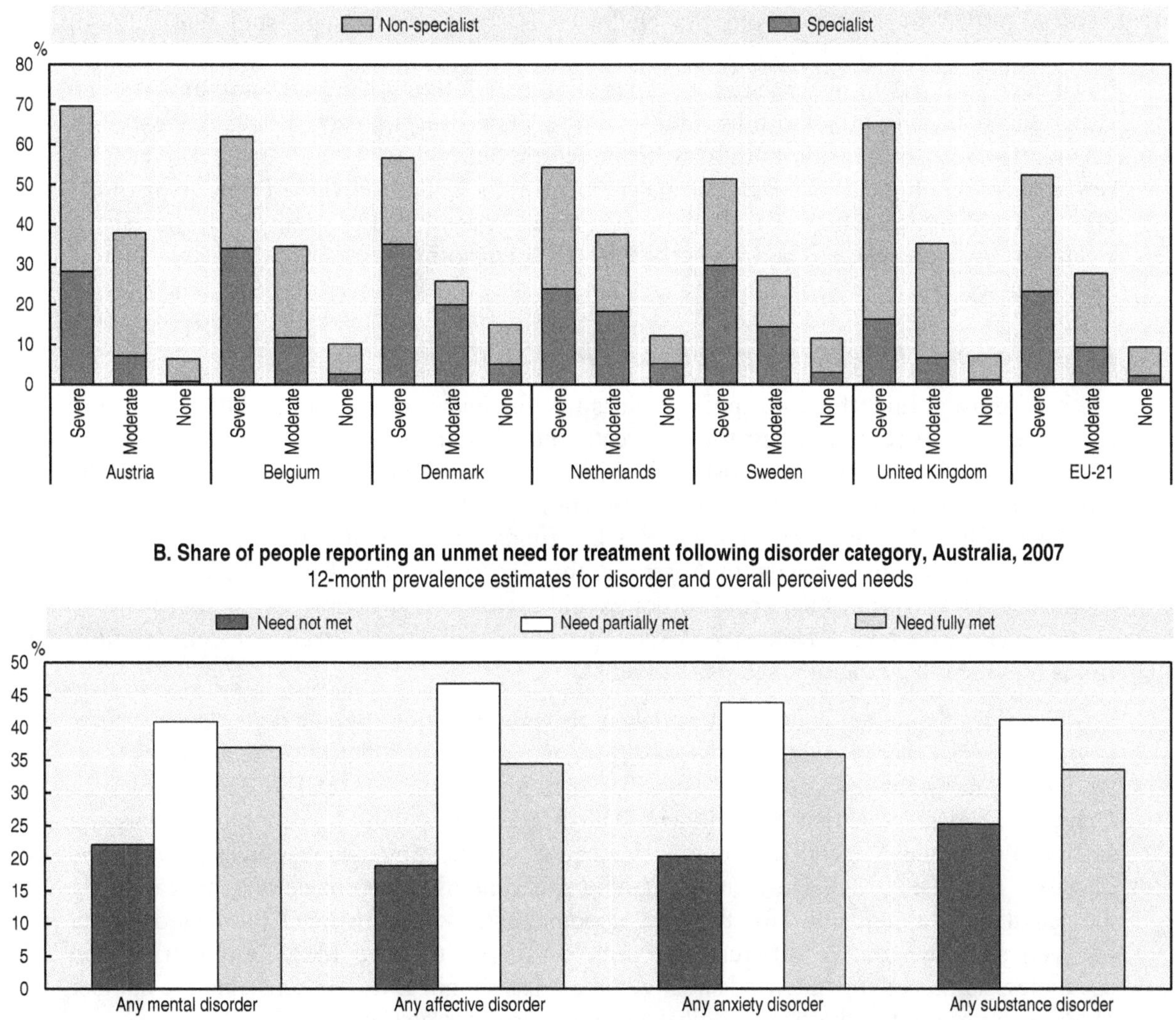

Note: EU-21 covers the 21 European countries in the Eurobarometer survey.

Source: Panel A: OECD calculations based on the Eurobarometer 2010 and Panel B: Meadows, G. and P. Burgess (2009), "Perceived Need for Mental Health Care: Findings from the 2007 Australian Survey of Mental Health and Wellbeing", *Australian and New Zealand Journal of Psychiatry*, Vol. 43, pp. 624-634.

StatLink http://dx.doi.org/10.1787/888933184112

Adequate mental health treatment remains challenging

Relatively few patients actually enter the mental health care system. When they do, the treatment they receive is not always adequate. Prescriptions for psychotropic drugs (e.g. antidepressants) have increased rapidly over the past two decades in many countries

(Figure 3.2, Panel A), and such medication remains the preferred treatment for people with mental ill-health (Figure 3.2, Panel B). It is a questionable trend, as it has been shown that for a number of mental illnesses a combination of medication and psychotherapy is the most effective treatment (Cuijpers et al., 2014; Huhn et al., 2014), and one that is now recommended in the guidelines of the United Kingdom's National Institute for Health and Care Excellence (NICE).

Targeting the right form and intensity of treatment at the right people is not a given, as exemplified by a study from the Netherlands. Its findings suggested that 20% of patients receiving mental health care from a specialist, a psychiatrist or psychotherapist, had never suffered from a mental disorder (Figure 3.2, Panel C), and another 20% had experienced trouble at some other point during their lives but not during the previous 12 months. The findings do not mean those people did not need care – in fact over 50% reported psychological or social impairments in their daily lives (Trimbos-instituut, 2012). They indicate that not all people seeking mental health care need specialised treatment and that some could be served by GPs and other primary carers, e.g. mental health nurses.

Policy action to better serve people with mental ill-health

The most straightforward policy measure for making mental health care more available is to increase funding for the treatment of the common disorders – depression and anxiety – that account for most mental ill-health. The United Kingdom and Australia have rolled out national programmes to that end. The British initiative, *Increased Access to Psychological Therapies* (Factsheet 3.1), funds teams that offer evidence-based psychological therapy services. In Australia, the *Access to Allied Psychological Services* initiative (ATAPS) funds the provision of psychological therapy services for six to twelve sessions (Factsheet 3.2). Denmark, which has emulated the Australian example, fully funds treatment by an authorised psychologist.

To cut waiting times, countries have taken different measures. Scotland guarantees access to psychological therapy within 18 weeks (England will soon follow) – still a long time to wait, particularly for young people, even if it is an improvement (OECD, 2014c). Although Denmark guarantees a first appointment with a therapist within two months, it has not sufficiently shortened overall waiting times because so much time and resources are spent on diagnosis (OECD, 2013c). The Danish example underlines the importance of cutting not only the length of waiting times for the first appointment, usually devoted to diagnosis, but between sessions, too. A different approach is simply to have more psychiatrists and psychologists, something the Swedish Government has sought to do by increasing the number of places for trainees in the psychological education programme (OECD, 2013d).

It may also be worthwhile to further investigate the potential of electronic psychological therapy services (OECD, 2014d). A number of studies have shown that eCBT, i.e. web-based cognitive behavioural therapy (CBT), is effective in easing mental health complaints, at least in the short term (Spek et al., 2007; So et al., 2014). Although eCBT is available in a wide range of countries, it is not used yet on a large scale. It would be of great practical value in Australia, for example, with its many wide, remote areas. Yet, although the government funds eCBT as part of its ATAPS initiative, it accounts for less than 0.5% of all ATAPS treatment (OECD, 2015b). Just like face-to-face treatment, however, eCBT requires compliance and follow-up. E-mail reminders might be the answer, as they can be embedded in the eCBT interface (Christensen et al., 2009).

Figure 3.2. **Providing the right treatment to the right people is challenging**

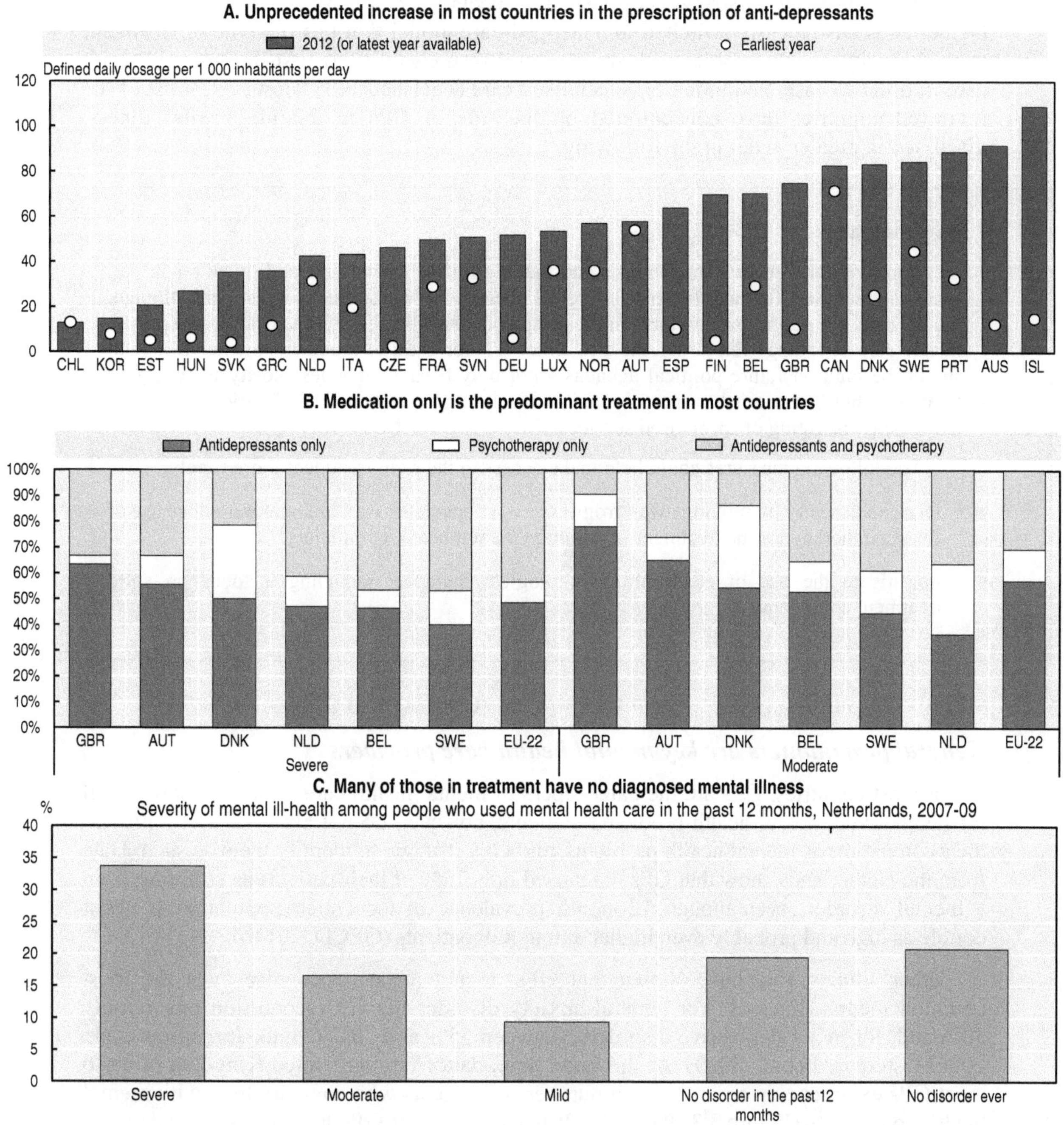

Note: EU-22 is an unweighted average of the 22 countries in the Eurobarometer survey.

a. Professional treatment for a psychological or emotional problem in the last 12 months.

Source: Panel A. *OECD Health Database*, Pharmaceutical Market dataset; Panel B: OECD calculations based on Eurobarometer, 2005; Panel C: ten Have, M., J. Nuyen, A. Beekman and R. de Graaf (2013), "Common Mental Disorder Severity and its Association with Treatment Contact and Treatment Intensity for Mental Health Problems", *Psychological Medicine*, No. 3, pp. 2203 2213, www.ncbi.nlm.nih.gov/pubmed/23388154.

StatLink http://dx.doi.org/10.1787/888933184124

In contrast to action to cut waiting times, policy development to ensure adequate care and a better targeting of scarce and expensive specialist treatment is moving slowly. The Netherlands has recently switched to a stepped-care model that ties the type of treatment to the severity of the disorder and gives greater responsibility to first-line mental health care in order to ease the burden on specialised care (Factsheet 3.3). However, most of the reviewed countries have concentrated on the role of GPs in treating mental illness, discussed in greater detail in the following.

Key messages

Improving treatment to meet needs and making it timelier requires additional resources, such as increased funding for psychological therapy services. Such investment, though, would help cut public expenditure on sickness and disability benefits and also on somatic health care spending. Exploring the use of eCBT for mild-to-moderate mental ill-health should be high on future political agendas – not only because it is less costly than regular treatment, but because it has the potential to reach to greater numbers of patients and may allow better targeting of specialised services.

The following measures could help make access to the right treatment more timely:

- Increase capacity by moving away from expensive specialist care and making wider use of first-line therapy for the treatment of common mental health complaints.
- Investigate the use of electronic psychological therapies including a focus on solid treatment compliance.

Training and supporting general practitioners to treat mental illness

General practitioners are key mental health care providers

In most countries, GPs are the gatekeepers of mental health care – the first port of call for people with mental health problems. Patients, however, do not always directly present their complaints as mental health problems, and GPs struggle to identify them as such. Data from the Netherlands show that GPs diagnosed only 12% of their patients as suffering from a mental disorder, even though 12-month prevalence in the Dutch population is about double as high and probably even higher among GP patients (OECD, 2014b).

Other studies, too, have shown that GPs do not always recognise even the most common mental illnesses. For general anxiety disorder the GP recognition rate is only 30% and, for major depressive disorders, between 55% and 75% (Munk-Jørgensen et al., 2006; Ostergaard et al., 2010). At the same time, data from the United Kingdom point to most GPs experiencing an increase in numbers of patients who come to them with mental health complaints (Figure 3.3, Panel A). It is essential that GPs have the knowledge and skills to identify and address mental ill-health. Yet only a few countries provide training to that effect in the general GP curriculum.

GPs are not only gatekeepers of mental health care, but also the main providers of treatment. Their role is growing increasingly important in many countries, a trend borne out by available data from Australia, for example (Figure 3.3, Panel B). And they refer relatively few patients to mental health specialists – just 15% in both Switzerland and the Netherlands, for example (OECD, 2014a; OECD, 2014b). It may thus be inferred that the only treatment the vast majority of mental health patients receive is from their GP.

Figure 3.3. **General practitioners are treating more and more mental illness**

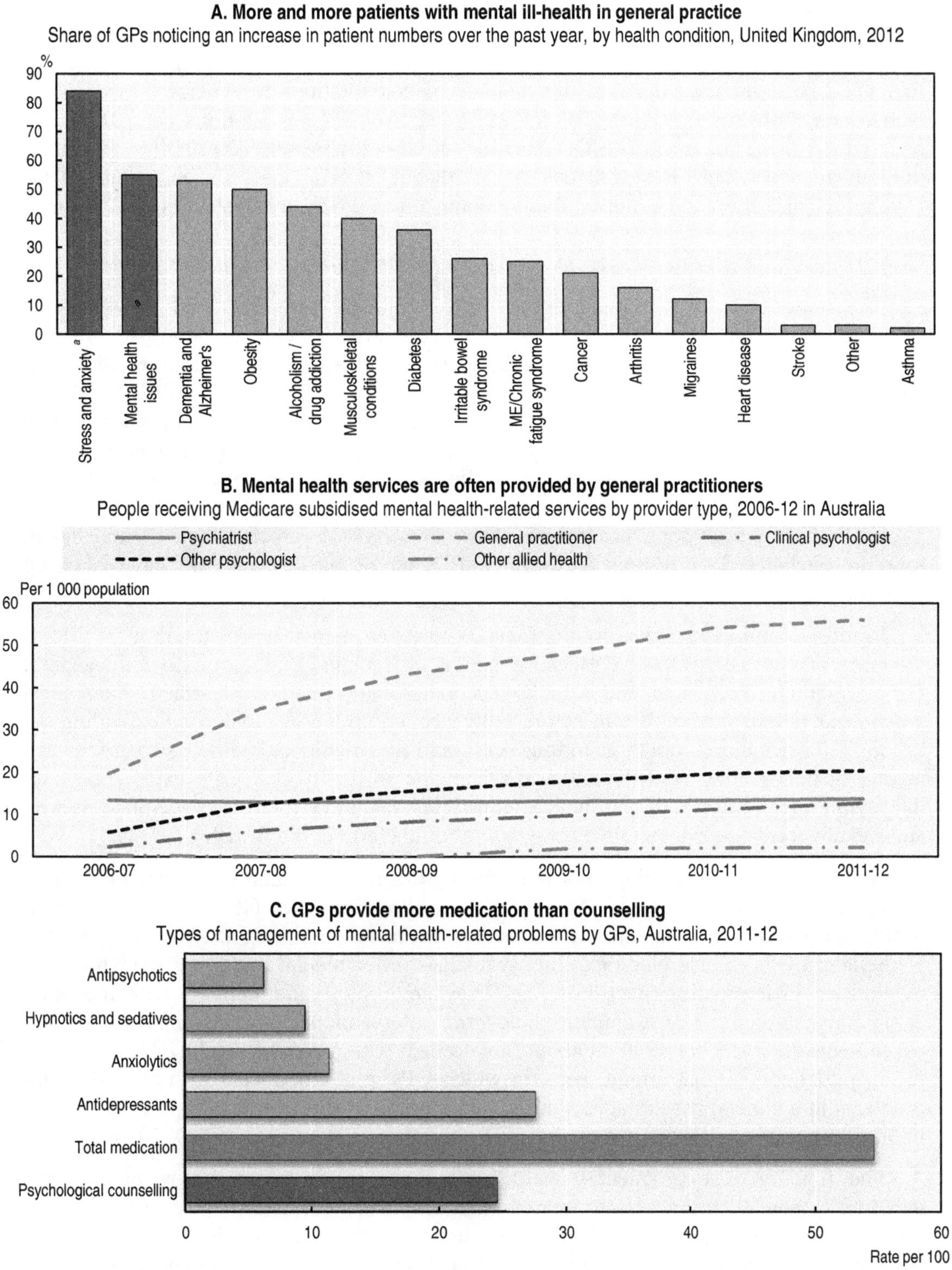

a. Excludes stress and anxiety.

Source: Panel A: *Aviva Health of the Nation Index Report*, 2013; Panel B: Medicare Benefits Schedule data (Department of Health and Ageing, Australia); and Panel C: OECD compilation based on data from the Australian Institute of Health and Welfare (http://mhsa.aihw.gov.au/home).

StatLink http://dx.doi.org/10.1787/888933184131

That most people with mental ill-health are cared for only by their GPs is a cause for concern, as many GPs have neither the time nor the training to treat mental health problems – a fact reflected, for example, in the clear preference of GPs in Australia (and other countries) for medication rather than psychological counselling (Figure 3.3, Panel C). To compound matters, the number of consultations is generally low. In the Netherlands, Austria and Australia, for example, two GP consultations per patient has been found to be the norm (OECD, 2014b; OECD, 2015a; OECD, 2015b) – which is unlikely to be enough. Research has shown that it takes at least six consultations for psychological therapy to be more effective than the usual GP care (Bower et al., 2011).

Countries are taking measures to give general practitioners greater support

The importance of GPs as mental health treatment providers and their lack of resources for playing that role have prompted countries to change policy in order to support them more effectively. Denmark, Austria and Australia have invested in GP mental health training, albeit to varying degrees (OECD, 2013c; OECD, 2015a; OECD, 2015b). Denmark provides on-line courses on stress, anxiety and depression, while Austria and Australia offer more extensive extra-curricular training on mental health treatment. Governments have increased funding for psychological therapy consultations as an incentive for GPs to take up training and deliver mental health treatment. Australia pays GPs higher rates for consultations when they have completed their mental health training (Factsheet 3.4). In both Australia and Denmark, most of the GPs have taken up such training.

In most countries reviewed by the OECD, however, mental health training for GPs is voluntary and not very extensive. Because there is little mental health training in the general GP curriculum throughout the OECD, adequate diagnosis and treatment cannot be guaranteed. The United Kingdom has recently opened up the discussion on extending the general GP curriculum from three to four years, and specifically including a strong focus on mental health training (OECD, 2014c). Given the difficulty that GPs experience with diagnosing mental ill-health and their responsibility for initial treatment, adequate referral and sickness certification, all OECD countries should consider the British example.

Another way of supporting GPs is to fund extra mental health personnel in primary care. Australia's *Mental Health Nurse Incentive Program* pays GPs to employ mental health nurses to treat patients with severe mental ill-health (Factsheet 3.5). In the Netherlands, GPs receive funding to hire specialists (often mental health nurses) who come to work in their practice (Factsheet 3.6). They care chiefly for patients with moderate complaints through, for example, short-term interventions, relapse prevention, and psycho-education (i.e. information about how to deal with mental ill-health). New Zealand recently trialled a similar arrangement, in which GPs referred patients with mental health problems to a clinical psychologist stationed in a primary care practice (Dath et al., 2014). In other countries such support is often lacking or rather inconsistent (OECD, 2014d).

The funding of extra mental health care personnel in primary care has several benefits: i) more timely access to treatment; ii) improved compliance because treatment takes place in the familiar, stigma-free setting of the GP practice; and iii) closer collaboration with and more effective referrals to specialists (Dozeman and van Straten, 2012; Dath et al., 2014). GPs have been very positive about the extra support they have enjoyed and, in the Netherlands and Australia, demand for mental health nurses quickly outstripped supply (OECD, 2014b; OECD, 2015b).

Key messages

A number of countries have taken steps to improve mental health treatment in GP practices. Such efforts are an acknowledgement of the importance of a strong safety net for people affected by mental ill-health. For many of them, the GP is their first and only point of call in the health care system.

Despite improvements, proper mental health training needs to take its place in the general GP curriculum and GPs must be properly remunerated for the extra time that they put into mental health care. Otherwise good quality treatment cannot be guaranteed. Funding mental health professionals as support staff in GP practices might be the most promising way to go, as they have the required expertise, can devote more time to patients with mental ill-health than GPs and, importantly, have strong backing from the GP community.

The following measures could help in enabling GPs to provide proper mental health treatment:

- Expand the GP curriculum to include mental health training.
- Properly remunerate GPs for talking therapy time with patients.
- Fund mental health nurses and psychologists to support GPs in their practices.

Incentives and tools for general practitioners to address work issues

GPs must be competent to address work and sickness issues

There is a vast body of evidence showing that people with mental ill-health are one of the highest risk groups when it comes to long-term sickness absence (OECD, 2012). Data from Norway add to this evidence by showing that, over the past decade, the share of long-term absentees with mental disorders has grown (Figure 3.4, Panel A). Moreover, irrespective of diagnosis, most absences due to mental ill-health are long term (Figure 3.4, Panel B).

GPs need to be knowledgeable about the impact of work on mental health, and vice versa, given that:

- Most people with mental ill-health who seek treatment will see only their GP.
- People with mental ill-health are between 30% and 50% more likely to take sick leave.
- GPs are in most OECD countries responsible for certifying sickness.

A common misconception among GPs, and health care providers in general, is that people with mental ill-health need to be cured before they can return to work. However, numerous studies have shown that a good job contributes to good mental health (Thomas et al., 2005; Paul and Moser, 2009). Conversely, long absences from work increase the risk of permanent work disability (Kivimäki et al., 2004). Clearly, timely return to work is paramount.

Figure 3.4. **Absences due to mental illness tend to be long term**

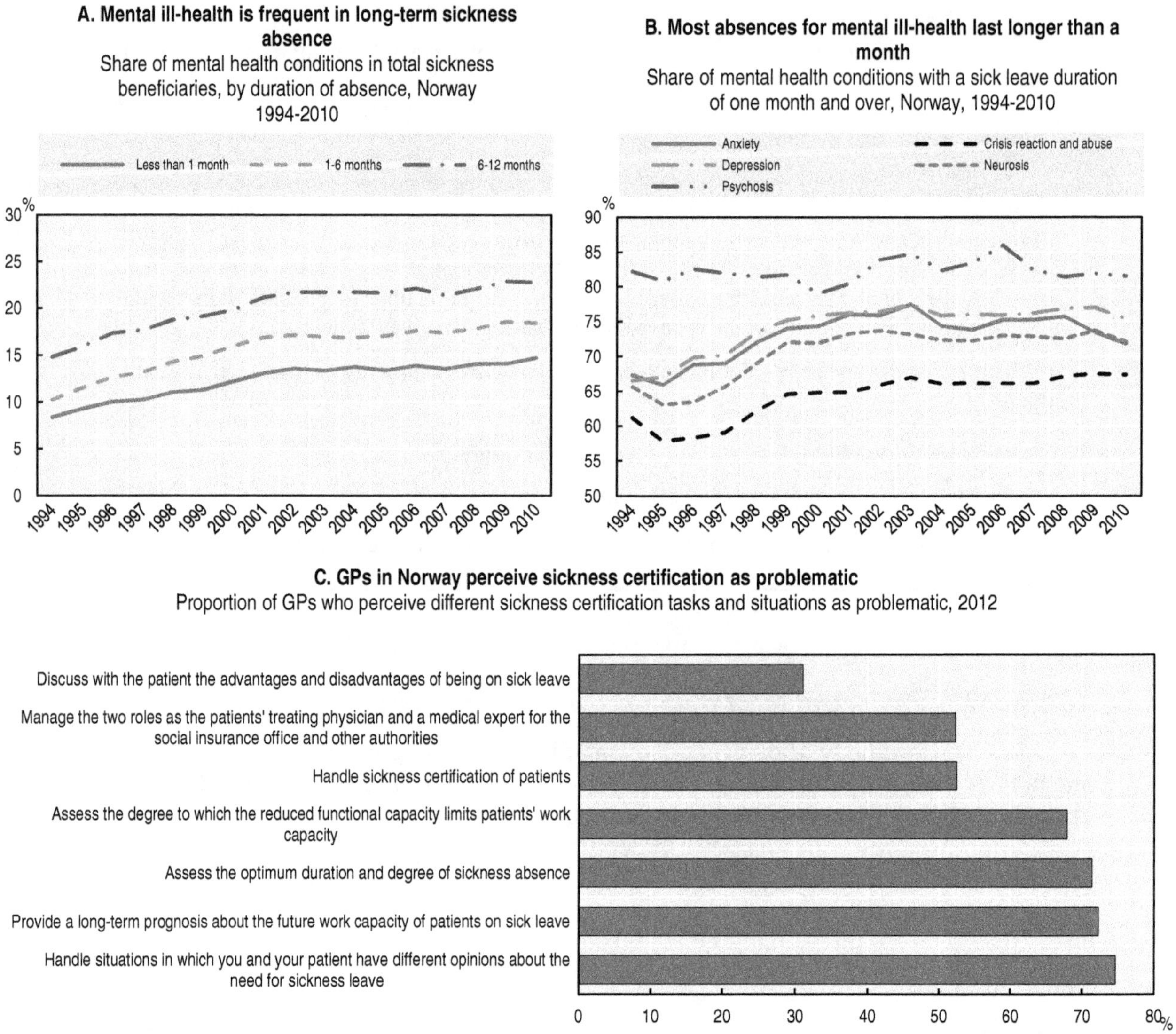

Source: Panel A: Norwegian Labour and Welfare Administration, NAV; Panel B: OECD questionnaire on mental health; and Panel C: Winde, L. et al. (2012), "General Practitioners' Experiences with Sickness Certification: A Comparison of Survey Data from Sweden and Norway", *BMC Family Practice*, Vol. 13:10.

StatLink http://dx.doi.org/10.1787/888933184146

GPs struggle to address work-related issues. Figure 3.4, Panel C, illustrates how Norwegian GPs evaluate the way in which they go about certifying sickness. About 70% have trouble assessing the capacity to work and gauging the length of sick leave. Similarly, in the state of Victoria, Australia, GPs have been found to be more likely to certify people with mental health complaints as "unfit for work" – 94% were given this certificate compared to 78% of patients with back pains and strains.

Help GPs understand the work and mental health interplay

The importance of the role of GPs in improving work outcomes for people with mental ill-health is now starting to be acknowledged. Accordingly, a few countries have invested in developing GPs' understanding of work-related mental health issues. In 2010, the United Kingdom switched from "sick notes" to "fit notes" (short for "statement of fitness to work"). The move focused GPs' minds on the role of work, as they are now required to provide recommendations and thereby advise patients and employers on how they could adapt work and what they could do to speed up return to work (Factsheet 3.7).

Sweden and the Netherlands have introduced GP guidelines on the interplay between mental health and work and GPs' responsibilities (Factsheet 3.8; Factsheet 3.9). To help doctors assess a patient before certifying sickness, the Swedish guidelines include advice on the expected lengths of sick leave for people with different mental illnesses. However, guidelines are a relatively passive tool and research has shown that health care providers' compliance with guidelines is often poor (Gagliardi et al., 2011). Guideline compliance would therefore have to be monitored.

A more proactive approach comes from Denmark, where mental health e-training for GPs offers additional courses on how patients with mental ill-health can remain at work and how doctors can help them do so. The Danish e-training programme also gives GPs guidance on filling in the obligatory work ability report on whether a patient is fit for work (OECD, 2013c). In Norway, an on-line tool is available for physicians to compare their sickness certification practice against all other physicians and which can support them when assessing future patients (OECD, 2013b).

There are no examples of bringing extra staff into GP practice to address employment issues in the same way as Australia and the Netherlands have done with mental health professionals. It may, however, be worth exploring whether mental health nurses could receive additional training in employment issues or whether employment specialists could work side-by-side with them and the GP.

GPs, patients, and their employers should communicate to share understanding of the work context and seek ways to enable patients to go on working at a level that matches the severity of their mental health problem. In this regard, it needs to be pointed out that partial work resumption is not possible in a number of countries, which puts GPs in the invidious position of making "all-or-nothing" decisions i.e. of having to choose between full-time work or no work at all while neither is often the optimum for people struggling with mental ill-health.

Arguments against communication between GPs and employers often refer to the issue of privacy and confidentiality. In this regard, the Dutch occupational health care model – with its close lines of communication between occupational physicians and employers – provides a helpful perspective. Doctors cannot, of course, divulge medical information. But there is no need for them to do so in discussions with an employer about what a worker can or cannot do and how to foster a supportive work environment, which is all employers need to know to fulfil their responsibility towards their employees (NVAB, 2011). As for GPs, Denmark is the only country reviewed by the OECD that remunerates GPs for talking to employers (OECD, 2013c). In Switzerland, written communication between employers and GPs is possible. It can be part of the "expanded medical sickness certification" which, if a patient agrees, allows a GP to receive information from the patient's employer about the workplace and the tasks that the job entails (Factsheet 3.10).

Key messages

Although most OECD countries assign GPs a central role that allows them to intervene in people's working lives through sickness certification, they are given little direction on how to fulfil their role properly. When it comes to mental health, determining the ability to work is heavily dependent on factors that are not only disease related, but workplace related, too.

GPs should be offered financial incentives for talking to patients' employers as they would be for a consultation. Governments should also give GPs incentives for building employment support into their practices and, by the same token, make them accountable for a patient's sick leave.

Strategies for helping GPs to address work-related issues include:

- Change the terms of reference of sickness certification to focus on what people can do rather than what they cannot.
- Develop illness-specific guidelines for GPs on sickness certification and return-to-work practices and monitor their use.
- Fund employment specialists to support GPs in their practice.

A strong employment focus for the mental health system as a whole

The link between treatment and employment is strong

Just as GPs need to address work issues, mental health care must recognise the importance of employment. Data from Switzerland and Denmark, for example, show that people with mental health problems who are in work have better outcomes with respect to treatment take-up, duration, and costs than those who are unemployed or inactive (Figure 3.5, Panels A and B).

Indeed, being in work greatly shortens the duration of treatment. Supporting people with mental ill-health in finding work should therefore be of concern to the whole mental health care system.

Although there is scant evidence as to whether treatment time shortens after unemployed patients find work, there are studies showing that the mental health of unemployed people improves after they resume or enter employment (Thomas et al., 2005; OECD, 2008).

There might be a number of explanations for the relationship between employment status and treatment duration, but its strength points to the importance of work. Resuming or starting a job not only boosts employment and well-being, it is also a good cost-containment strategy for the health care system itself.

Figure 3.5. **Employment reduces the cost and duration of treatment**

A. Lower treatment duration for those in employment

Treatment duration[a] of patients in private psychiatric practice, by illness-severity and employment status in Switzerland, 2009

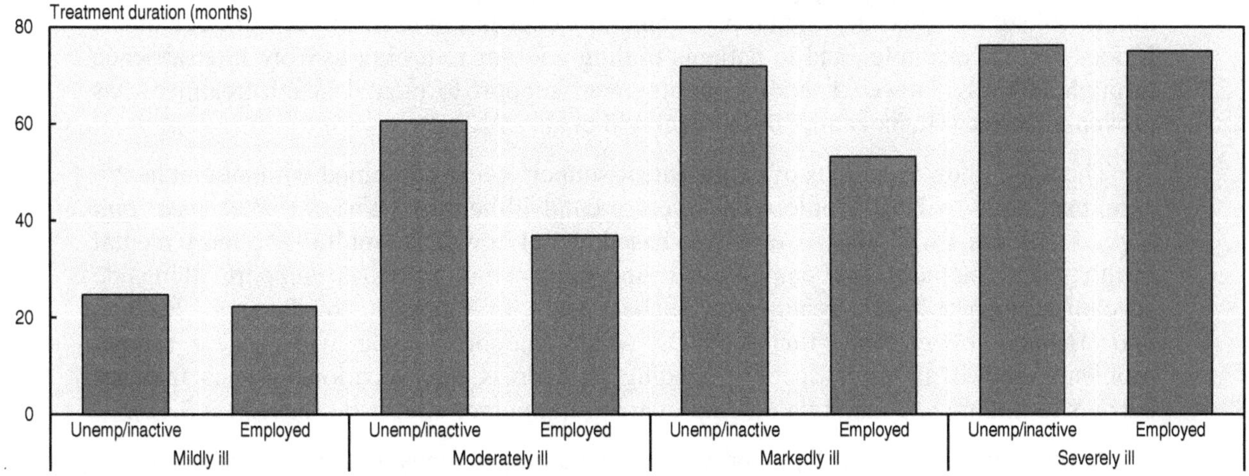

B. Lesser, shorter and cheaper treatment for those employed

Selected Danish outpatient treatment indicators by employment status[b] in 2011: incidence of treatment; average cost per patient and duration of outpatient visits

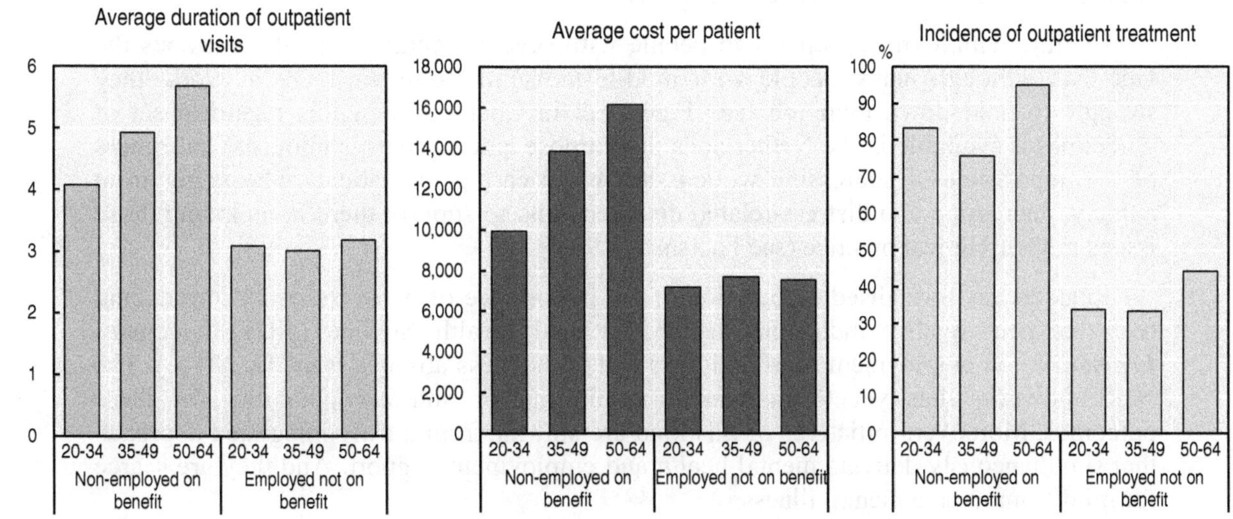

Note: "Inactive" refers to all persons who are not classified as employed or unemployed.

a. "Treatment duration" is the sum of the months already in treatment and the expected number of months patients will stay in treatment in the future; it may comprise several treatment episodes.

b. The group "non-employed" includes all patients receiving (public or private) social benefits, including unemployment benefit, social assistance, sickness benefit, (pre)rehabilitation benefit, disability benefit and early retirement.

Source: Panel A: Baer, N. et al. (2013), "Depressionen in der Schweizer Bevölkerung", Schweizerisches Gesundheitsobservatorium; calculations based on a survey of private psychiatrists in the canton of Berne (Amsler, F. et al., 2010, "Schlussbericht zur Evaluation der institutionellen ambulanten und teilstationären Psychiatrieversorgung des Kantons Bern unter besonderer Berücksichtigung der Pilotprojekte") and Panel B: e-Health clinical database (National Institute for Health Data and Disease Control).

StatLink http://dx.doi.org/10.1787/888933184153

Only treatment and employment support combined improve work outcomes

Treatment alone does not produce good work outcomes for people with mental ill-health. They do not simply recover from their symptoms and go back to work. A number of studies have shown that psychotherapy does not in itself affect work outcomes. It does not, for example, lead to patients finding a job or returning to work after absence through sickness. However, adding employment support to mental health treatment has proven effective (Blonk et al., 2006; Lagerveld et al., 2012).

There are a few examples of employment support being combined with mental health care, especially to help people with severe mental ill-health. *Individual Placement and Support* (IPS) is a well-known, evidence-based model in which a multidisciplinary mental health team includes an employment specialist who provides support alongside specialised mental health treatment (Factsheet 3.11). In Australia, the *Personal Helpers and Mentors Programme* funds NGOs which support people with severe mental problems, and it allocates specific funding to address non-vocational issues that are barriers to finding and maintaining employment, training or education (Factsheet 3.12).

Another promising development is to bring a stronger focus on employment into self-management programmes that are available in a few countries. Specifically, Denmark is trialling a self-management programme on return-to-work among people with anxiety and depression through gaining self-confidence, managing health problems and developing strategies for return-to-work (Factsheet 3.13).

Limiting employment support to people with severe mental ill-health overlooks the fact that, although many people with mild-to-moderate complaints are in work, they struggle to hold down their job (see Figure 1.2 in Chapter 1). In this regard, a set of guidelines is available in the Netherlands. Its purpose is to raise psychologists' awareness of the importance of addressing work issues when caring for patients who suffer from anxiety, depression and distress-related disorders, and to support them in including those issues in their clinical practice (see Factsheet 3.9).

England has formalised recognition of the importance of work issues by introducing two treatment quality indicators in the National Health Service (NHS) *Outcomes Framework* on employment rates and days lost to sickness absence (OECD, 2014c). The NHS, however, has yet to implement monitoring of and accountability for these outcomes. Moreover, initiatives of this kind are still far from a truly integrated approach that simultaneously delivers mental health and employment support. And they are scarce for mild-to-moderate mental illness.

To date, the United Kingdom and Norway are among the few countries to have piloted a nationwide programme of integrated mental health and employment support for people suffering from mild-to-moderate mental ill-health.

In 2009, two years after the United Kingdom introduced its *Increased Access to Psychological Therapies* (IAPT) programme to improve treatment rates among people with common mental illness, employment advisors were added to the programme (Factsheet 3.14). These advisors work alongside IAPT therapists, providing practical advice and making relevant interventions to help people remain in, or enter, the workplace. The extension of IAPT to include employment advisors has not yet been rigorously evaluated. However, a comparison of patients who received support from the employment advisors with those who did not revealed that the advisors had added value: return to work after sickness absence had improved and patients were remaining in work (Hogarth et al., 2013).

A similar structure can be found in Norway, where *Centres for Work Coping* offer both CBT and specialist employment services to people with common mental disorders who are either still in work, or on sick leave, or inactive (Factsheet 3.15). One important facet of the centres' activity is that employment counsellors communicate actively with patients' employers. No evaluation of the centres has yet been undertaken.

Back in the United Kingdom, the NHS recently made a start on piloting a combined mental health and employment service specifically for health care professionals – a high-risk group when it comes to mental ill-health and related sickness absence. Although evaluation still needs to take place, potential success factors are the collaboration of mental health, employment, and various other specialists in a multidisciplinary team, a low caseload, and a focus on gradual return to work (where possible). The service is freely available to doctors but, because it is a small-scale operation with a very low caseload, it can only serve 2% per year of all its potential customers (Factsheet 3.16). Such an initiative would also be relevant for teachers and line managers, following the argument that priority access to adequate mental health treatment for these front-line actors in mental health promotion of others would benefit the greater community.

Key messages

The importance of integrated mental health and employment support is widely accepted when it comes to severe mental ill-health. But the mental health sector is only just starting to realise that work issues also play an important role in the successful recovery of patients with mild-to-moderate mental ill-health. With the exception of the United Kingdom and Norway, programmes to incorporate work-related knowledge in general mental health care are still scarce and need to be piloted. To drive the implementation of such integrated approaches, it is essential that there should be funding for rigorous evaluation, which would include evaluating the business case for investing in employment support in mental health care.

A stronger employment focus of the mental health system can be developed and achieved in the following way:

- Add employment-related outcomes to the quality assurance and outcomes frameworks of the health system.
- Incorporate employment support into the treatment plan for people with common mental health complaints.
- Develop employment support programmes (building on the experiences with IPS) for people suffering from common mental ill-health.

REFERENCES

Alonso, J. et al. (2007), "Population Level of Unmet Need for Mental Healthcare in Europe", *British Journal of Psychiatry*, Vol. 190, pp. 299-306.

Alonso, J., A. Buron, S. Rojas-Farreras et al. (2009), "Perceived Stigma among Individuals with Common Mental Disorders", *Journal of Affective Disorders*, Vol. 118, pp. 180-186.

Amsler, F. et al. (2010),"Schlussbericht zur Evaluation der institutionellen ambulanten und teilstationären Psychiatrieversorgung des Kantons Bern unter besonderer Berücksichtigung der Pilotprojekte".

Baer, N., D. Schuler, S. Füglister-Dousse and F. Moreau-Gruet (2013), "Depressionen in der Schweizer Bevölkerung. Daten zur Epidemiologie, Behandlung und sozial-beruflichen Integration" [Depression in the Swiss Population. Data on the Epidemiology, Treatment and Social-Professional Integration], *Obsan Bericht No. 56*, Schweizerisches Gesundheitsobservatorium, Neuchâtel.

Blonk, R. et al. (2006), "Return to Work: A Comparison of Two Cognitive Behavioural Interventions in Cases of Work-related Psychological Complaints Among the Self-employed", *Work & Stress*, Vol. 20, No. 2, pp. 129-144.

Bower, P. et al. (2011), "Counselling for Mental Health and Psychosocial Problems in Primary Care", *Cochrane Database of Systematic Reviews*, Vol. 9, Art. No.: CD001025, http://dx.doi.org/10.1002/14651858.CD001025.pub3.

Christensen, H., K. Griffiths and L. Farrer (2009), "Adherence in Internet Interventions for Anxiety and Depression: Systematic Review", *Journal of Medical Internet Research*, Vol. 11, No. 2, pp. e13.

Cuijpers, P. et al. (2014), "Adding Psychotherapy to Antidepressant Medication in Depression and Anxiety Disorders: A Meta-analysis", *World Psychiatry*, Vol. 31, No. 1, pp. 56-67.

Dath, S. et al. (2014), "A Clinical Psychologist in GP-land: An Evaluation of Brief Psychological Interventions in Primary Care", *New Zealand Medical Journal*, Vol. 127, No. 1391, pp. 62-74.

Dozeman, E. and A. van Straten (2012), "De praktijkondersteuner GGZ in Amsterdam: Op weg naar een sterke basis GGZ" [The mental health specialist in GP practices in Amsterdam: Heading towards strong primary mental health care], Vrije Universiteit, Amsterdam.

Gagliardi, A. et al. (2011), "How Can We Improve Guideline Use? A Conceptual Framework of Implementability", *Implementation Science,* Vol. 6, No. 26, pp. 1-11.

Hogarth, T., C. Hasluck, L. Gambin, H. Behle, Y. Li and C. Lyonette (2013), "Evaluation of Employment Advisers in the Improving Access to Psychological Therapies programme", *DWP Research Report*, Vol. 826, London.

Huhn, M. et al. (2014), "Efficacy of Pharmacotherapy and Psychotherapy for Adult Psychiatric Disorders: A Systematic Overview of Meta-analyses", *JAMA Psychiatry*, Vol. 71, No. 6, pp. 706-715.

Kivimäki, M. et al. (2004), "Sickness Absence as a Risk Marker of Future Disability Pension: The 10-town study", *Journal of Epidemiology and Community Health*, Vol. 58, pp. 710-711.

Koopmans, P., C. Roelen and J. Groothoff (2008),"Frequent and Long-term Absence as a Risk Factor for Work Disability and Job Termination Among Employees in the Private Sector", *Occupational and Environmental Medicine*, Vol. 65, pp. 494-499.

Lagerveld, S. et al. (2012), "Work-focused Treatment of Common Mental Disorders and Return to Work: A Comparative Outcome Study", *Journal of Occupational Health Psychology*, Vol. 17, No. 2, pp. 220-234.

Meadows, G. and P. Burgess (2009), "Perceived Need for Mental Health Care: Findings from the 2007 Australian Survey of Mental Health and Wellbeing", *Australian and New Zealand Journal of Psychiatry*, Vol. 43, pp. 624-634.

Munk-Jørgensen, P. et al. (2006), "Prevalence of Generalised Anxiety Disorder in General Practice in Denmark, Finland, Norway, and Sweden", *Psychiatric Services*, Vol. 57, No. 12, http://dx.doi.org/10.1176/appi.ps.57.12.1738.

NVAB – Netherlands Society of Occupational Medicine (2011), "Leidraad bedrijfsarts en privacy: Hoe om te gaan met privacy-gevoelige informatie in de bedrijfsgezondheidszorg en in het bijzonder met medische gegvens bij ziekteverzuim" [Guideline occupational physician and privacy: How to deal with private information in occupational health care and specifically with medical information in sickness management], Nederlandse Vereninging voor Arbeids- en Bedrijfsgeneeskunde, Utrecht.

OECD (forthcoming 2015a), *Mental Health and Work: Austria*, OECD Publishing, Paris.

OECD (forthcoming 2015b), *Mental Health and Work: Australia*, OECD Publishing, Paris.

OECD (2014a), *Mental Health and Work: Switzerland*, OECD Publishing, Paris, http://dx.doi.org/10.1787/9789264204973-en.

OECD (2014b), *Mental Health and Work: Netherlands*, OECD Publishing, Paris, http://dx.doi.org/10.1787/9789264223301-en.

OECD (2014c), *Mental Health and Work: United Kingdom*, OECD Publishing, Paris, http://dx.doi.org/10.1787/9789264204997-en.

OECD (2014d), *Making Mental Health Count: The Social and Economic Costs of Neglecting Mental Health Care*, OECD Publishing, Paris, http://dx/doi/org/10.1787/9789264208445-en.

OECD (2013a), *Mental Health and Work: Belgium*, OECD Publishing, Paris. http://dx.doi.org/10.1787/9789264187566-en.

OECD (2013b), *Mental Health and Work: Norway*, OECD Publishing, Paris, http://dx/doi/org/10.1787/9789264178984-en.

OECD (2013c), *Mental Health and Work: Denmark*, OECD Publishing, Paris, http://dx/doi/org/10.1787/9789264188631-en.

OECD (2013d), *Mental Health and Work: Sweden,* OECD Publishing, Paris, http://dx.doi.org/10.1787/9789264188730-en.

OECD (2012), *Sick on the Job? Myths and Realities about Mental Health and Work*, OECD Publishing, Paris, http://dx.doi.org/10.1787/9789264124523-en.

OECD (2008), *OECD Employment Outlook 2008*, Chapter 4 "Are All Jobs Good for Your Health? The Impact of Work Status and Working Conditions on Mental Health", OECD Publishing, Paris, http://dx.doi.org/10.1787/empl_outlook-2008-en.

Ostergaard, S. et al. (2010), "Psychiatric Caseness Is a Marker of Major Depressive Episode in General Practice", *Scandinavian Journal of Primary Health Care*, Vol. 28, No. 4, pp. 211-215.

Paul, K. and K. Moser (2009), "Unemployment Impairs Mental Health: Meta-analyses", *Journal of Vocational Behavior,* Vol. 74, No. 3, pp. 264-282.

So, M. et al. (2014), "Is Computerized CBT Really Helpful for Adult Depression? A Meta-analytic Re-evaluation of CCBT for Adult Depression in Terms of Clinical Implementation and Methodological Validity", *BMC Psychiatry*, Vol. 13, No. 113, pp. 1-14.

Spek, V. et al. (2007), "Internet-based Cognitive Behaviour Therapy for Symptoms of Depression and Anxiety: A Meta-analysis", *Psychological Medicine*, Vol. 37, pp. 319-328.

ten Have, M., J. Nuyen, A. Beekman and R. de Graaf (2013), "Common Mental Disorder Severity and its Association with Treatment Contact and Treatment Intensity for Mental Health Problems", *Psychological Medicine*, No. 3, pp. 2203 2213, http://www.ncbi.nlm.nih.gov/pubmed/23388154.

Thomas, C., M. Benzeval and S. Stansfeld (2005), "Employment Transitions and Mental Health: An Analysis from the British Household Panel Survey", *Journal of Epidemiology and Community Health,* Vol. 59, pp. 243-249.

Trimbos-instituut (2012), "Trendrapportage GGZ 2012 Deel 2B: Ernst van de psychische aandoening als voorspeller van de aard en intensiteit van zorggebruik, Resultaten van de "Netherlands Mental Health Survey and Incidence Study-2" (NEMESIS-2)" [Trend analysis on mental health care 2012 Part 2B: Severity of the mental disorder as predictor of the type and intensity of health care use, Results of the "Netherlands Mental Health Survey and Incidence Study-2" (NEMESIS-2)], Trimbos-instituut, Utrecht.

Winde, L. et al. (2012), "General Practitioners' Experiences with Sickness Certification: A Comparison of Survey Data from Sweden and Norway", *BMC Family Practice*, Vol. 13:10.

FACTSHEETS 3.1 to 3.16

Factsheet 3.1. United Kingdom: Providing faster access to psychological therapies

Factsheet 3.2. Australia: Access to allied psychological services (ATAPS)

Factsheet 3.3. Netherlands: Stepped care model for primary mental health care

Factsheet 3.4. Australia: Extensive training courses for general practitioners

Factsheet 3.5. Australia: Engaging mental health nurses in the treatment process

Factsheet 3.6. Netherlands: Mental health specialists supporting general practitioners

Factsheet 3.7. United Kingdom: Fit note to increase work-related knowledge among general practitioners

Factsheet 3.8. Sweden: Guidelines for general practitioners to focus on work

Factsheet 3.9. Netherlands: Guidelines for health care professionals

Factsheet 3.10. Switzerland: Expanded medical certificates to improve co-operation

Factsheet 3.11. United States: Individual placement and support by the health sector

Factsheet 3.12. Australia: Personal helpers and mentors service – Community mental health care

Factsheet 3.13. Denmark: Self-management programme for return-to-work

Factsheet 3.14. United Kingdom: Employment advisors working alongside psychological therapists

Factsheet 3.15. Norway: Centres for at work and coping offer therapy and employment services

Factsheet 3.16. United Kingdom: Doctors for doctors – Supporting the health of health professionals

Factsheet 3.1
United Kingdom: Providing faster access to psychological therapies

Context

Research demonstrates that effective psychological treatment can improve symptoms of mild-to-moderate mental health problems. Nevertheless, in many OECD countries, a wide gap exists between the need of mental health treatment and the actual treatment received. Improving the availability of treatment could play an important role in addressing the gap.

Programme

The "Improving Access to Psychological Therapies" (IAPT) initiative aims to provide faster access to evidence-based psychological therapies, especially through cognitive behavioural therapy. IAPT services were initially targeted at people of working age, but in 2010, the programme was opened to adults of all ages. Access to IAPT services is by self-referral or referral from the general practitioner. Therapies are short-term (with a maximum of 20 sessions) and are delivered by service teams typically made up of psychologists, psychotherapists, therapists, graduate primary care workers, and administrative staff. They target people with mild-to-moderate mental health problems. The IAPT programme will be fully rolled out in England by the end of 2015.

Outcomes

An evaluation of the first three years of the IAPT programme shows that around 1.1 million people accessed the first phase of the programme and that numbers have increased steadily. Recovery rates have now reached 45% and are on track for the target rate of at least 50%.

Further reading

Department of Health (2012), "IAPT Three-year Report: The First Million Patients", London.

Hogarth, T. et al. (2013), "Evaluation of Employment Advisers in the Improving Access to Psychological Therapies Programme", *DWP Research Report*, No. 826, London.

OECD (2013), *Mental Health and Work: United Kingdom*, OECD Publishing, Paris, http://dx.doi.org/10.1787/9789264204997-en.

Factsheet 3.2
Australia: Access to allied psychological services (ATAPS)

Context

Providing psychotherapy is often an effective way to reduce mental ill-health. However, few people receive adequate treatment due to long waiting times and lack of funding. Increased funding for psychotherapy could improve timely treatment and serve people with poor mental health more effectively.

Programme

In response to the low treatment rates for people with mild-to-moderate mental illness, the Australian Government introduced the Access to Allied Psychological Services (ATAPS) initiative. Commencing in 2003, the initiative has funded the provision of short-term psychological services through fund-holding arrangements. It enables general practitioners (GPs) to refer patients with high-prevalence mental disorders for six sessions of evidence-based mental health care with allied health professionals (i.e. psychologists, social workers, mental health nurses, occupational therapists and Aboriginal and Torres Strait Islander health workers with specific mental health qualifications). After the six sessions, the GP may decide to refer a patient for an additional six sessions if the report of the allied health professional deems it necessary. In exceptional circumstances (e.g. a significant change in a patient's clinical condition or care circumstances) up to 18 individual sessions per calendar year can be provided.

Outcomes

The on-going evaluation of the ATAPS programme, since 2003, by the University of Melbourne has shown it has delivered effective, evidence-based services which have improved mental health outcomes for people in hard to reach populations, including people from low socioeconomic areas; individuals at risk of suicide and self-harm; individuals who are homeless or at risk of homelessness; and people in rural and remote areas. Overall, also due to other policy initiatives aimed at improving access to psychological services, the treatment rate in Australia has increased in the past decade; roughly from 37% to 46%, according to some estimates.

Further reading

Department of Health and Ageing (2010), "Outcomes and Proposed Next Steps: Review of the Access to Allied Psychological Services Component of the Better Outcomes in Mental Health Care Program", Commonwealth of Australia, Canberra.

OECD (forthcoming 2015), *Mental Health and Work: Australia*, OECD Publishing, Paris.

Factsheet 3.3
Netherlands: Stepped care model for primary mental health care

Context

To improve mental health care and make it more timely and appropriate, it is important that its type and intensity should match the severity of the condition. To that end, a stepped care model that delineates milder treatment for less severe problems and provides clear guidelines on when and how to increase treatment could be helpful.

Programme

In 2014, a stepped care model for primary mental health care was introduced in the Netherlands. It specifies four care trajectories (short, medium, intensive, chronic) that can be offered in primary mental health care (chiefly by first-line psychologists), with treatment intensity increasing from trajectory to trajectory. Patients are assigned to trajectories on the basis of five criteria: i) type of disorder, ii) symptom severity, iii) risk level, iv) complexity and v) chronicity of the problem or disorder.

Outcomes

The government has provided an indication of which treatment components can be part of each trajectory with an estimation of total treatment times. In coming years, however, the trajectories need to be further developed on the basis of practical experience. As the model has only recently been implemented, no results are available yet. Nevertheless, the government will monitor aspects of the model such as referrals to different trajectories and patient's treatment process (e.g. whether patients often switch trajectories).

Further reading

OECD (2014), "Mental Health Analysis Profiles (MHaP): Netherlands", *OECD Health Working Paper*, OECD Publishing, Paris, http://dx.doi.org/10.1787/5jz158z60dzn-en.

OECD (2014), *Mental Health and Work: Netherlands*, OECD Publishing, Paris, http://dx.doi.org/10.1787/9789264223301-en.

VWS (2013), "Voorhangbrief POH-GGZ en Generalistische Basis GGZ" [Prelimary letter on POH-GGZ and Generalist Basic mental health care], Ministerie van Volksgezondheid, Welzijn en Sport, Den Haag.

Factsheet 3.4
Australia: Extensive training courses for general practitioners

Context

General practitioners (GPs) are often the gatekeepers of mental health care and main treatment providers. However, they struggle to identify mental ill-health. While GPs' knowledge and skills are very important, few countries include specific training on mental health issues in the GP curriculum.

Programme

Australia offers GPs extensive extra-curricular training courses on mental health treatment. The Australian Department of Health funds the General Practice Mental Health Standards Collaboration (GPMHSC), which is responsible for GP education and training in mental health. The GPMHSC offers different types of accredited activities through which GPs can acquire different competencies and continue their professional development.

For example, Mental Health Skills Training provides training in mental health assessment, treatment planning, and a review of mental illnesses that commonly present in general practice. GPs have a financial incentive to obtain accreditation for Mental Health Skills Training as they can then claim higher fees for GP mental health services that are rebated by the Medicare Benefit Schedule. The Focussed Psychological Strategies Skills Training enables GPs to register as a focused provider of psychological strategies, which is a prerequisite for providing care that is rebated by the Medicare Benefit Schedule.

Outcomes

Currently, about 90% of GPs (almost 24 000 of an estimated 26 000) have completed the Mental Health Skills Training and are registered with Medicare Australia to access the higher rebate. Yet, according to survey data, still only 12% of all GP encounters are mental health-related (i.e. encounters in which at least one mental-health-related problem is managed). This is significantly lower than the actual mental health prevalence.

Further reading

AIHW (2014), "Mental Health Services in Australia", Australian Institute of Health and Welfare, http://mhsa.aihw.gov.au/home/, accessed 2 September 2014.

General Practice Mental Health Standards Collaboration (2013), "Mental Health Education Standards 2014-2016: A Handbook for GPs", The Royal Australian College of General Practitioners, Melbourne.

OECD (forthcoming 2015), *Mental Health and Work: Australia*, OECD Publishing, Paris.

Factsheet 3.5
Australia: Engaging mental health nurses in the treatment process

Context

General practitioners (GPs) are one of the main mental health treatment providers. However, they often lack the resources to fulfil that role. Different OECD countries are therefore taking measures to better support GPs. One measure is funding for extra mental health care personnel in primary care.

Programme

The Australian Mental Health Nurse Incentive Programme funds GPs to enable them to hire mental health nurses in the treatment of patients with more severe mental health problems. The nurses provide services such as monitoring patients' mental state, managing medication, and improving links to other health professionals and clinical service providers. These services are provided in a range of settings, such as clinics or patients' home, and are provided at little or no cost to the patient.

Outcomes

An evaluation of the programme showed that it resulted in greater continuity of care, better follow-up, timely access to support, and increased compliance with treatment plans. Patients also showed higher levels of employment. Of the 72 surveyed clients, 19% obtained full-time or part-time work, 13% entered voluntary work, and 7% started or resumed their studies. Cost savings were realized through reduced hospital admissions, which were equivalent to the average direct subsidy levels of providing the programme. However, the evaluation also showed that demand was higher than the demand offered by the number of available nurses. Of 47 medical practitioners surveyed about how to cope with patient demand, the most frequent responses were using waiting lists (47%) and triage (28%).

Further reading

Department of Health and Ageing (2012), *Evaluation of the Mental Health Nurse Incentive Program: Final Report*, Commonwealth of Australia, Canberra.

OECD (forthcoming 2015), *Mental Health and Work: Australia*, OECD Publishing, Paris.

Factsheet 3.6
Netherlands: Mental health specialists supporting general practitioners

Context

The first port of call made by people with mental health problems is often their general practitioner (GP) who plays an important role in recognising and treating mental illness. Although GPs are therefore ideally placed as the first to flag and act upon mental ill-health, they are not trained and could benefit from mental health support services in their practice.

Programme

Since 2008, the Dutch Government has funded the use of a mental health specialist in GP practices to better enable GPs to support patients with mental health problems. The POH-GGZ (Dutch abbreviation for Practice Support Professional for Mental Health Care) supports the GP in diagnosing, treating, and referring patients with mental health problems. More specifically, the POH-GGZ's responsibilities are: problem analysis and screening, developing and discussing the treatment plan, providing psycho-education, guiding and supporting self-management, conducting interventions aimed at behavioural change, indicated prevention, and relapse prevention. The POH-GGZ is not authorised to prescribe medication. The professional background of POH-GGZs is usually psychiatric nursing (63%), psychologist (10%), social worker (7%), or general nurse (6%).

Outcomes

Over the past years, the use of POH-GGZs by GPs increased from 11% in 2009 to 34% in 2011 and 62% in 2013. An evaluation of GPs' experiences with POH-GGZs showed that 90% assessed co-operation with the POH-GGZ as good or excellent. GPs valued the POH-GGZ because of easy communication, low thresholds for patients and expertise on mental disorders, counselling and referrals to specialised mental health care. Patients valued the way they were treated by the POH-GGZ and the quick, client-centred actions. Necessary improvements mentioned were: more transparency for patients (e.g. what is the POH-GGZ's role and what does the POH-GGZ communicate to the GP), greater familiarity with POH-GGZs, and incorporating the POH-GGZ in the neighbourhood's care team.

Further reading

Dozeman, E. and A. van Straten (2012), "De praktijkondersteuner GGZ in Amsterdam: Op weg naar een sterke basis GGZ" [The mental health specialist in GP practices in Amsterdam: Heading towards strong primary mental health care], Vrije Universiteit, Amsterdam.

OECD (2014), *Mental Health and Work: Netherlands*, OECD Publishing, Paris, http://dx.doi.org/10.1787/9789264223301-en.

ter Horst, L. and S. Haverkamp (2012), Ervaringen van patiënten met de praktijkondersteuner huisartsenzorg GGZ [Experiences of patients with the mental health specialist in GP practices], Zorgbelang Noord-Holland, Haarlem.

Verbeek, M., A. Knispel and J. Nuijen (2011), "GGZ in tabellen" [Mental health care shown in tables], Trimbos-instituut, Utrecht.

Factsheet 3.7
United Kingdom: Fit note to increase work-related knowledge among general practitioners

Context

General practitioners (GPs) play an important role in improving work outcomes for people with mental ill-health. They prevent labour market exclusion by acting as gate-keepers to sickness and disability benefits, and they are critical in motivating patients to make a quick return to work. Work-related knowledge among GPs is therefore crucial.

Programme

Since 2010, GPs have had to provide the Statement of Fitness for Work (known as "fit note" in place of the previous "sick note") across England, Wales and Scotland. GPs are now not only required to assess whether their patients (the sick employees) are able to work but to suggest basic changes to the work environment or job role, or other steps to help employees return to work earlier. For instance, if a patient is classified in the "maybe fit for work" category, the doctor is required to specify at least one of four options outlining common return-to-work approaches – a phased return to work; amended duties; altered hours; and workplace adaptations. GPs are now also required to assess a patient's fitness for (any) work (rather than fitness for a specific job). The changes also mean a move towards an electronic fit note which, in theory at least, should generate new, standardised data (including causes of absence) and bring transparency to a hitherto rather undisclosed process.

Outcomes

Qualitative evaluations suggest that the fit note is being used by GPs to initiate discussions about work with their patients and that it has also improved the information flow between employers and employees. Although fit notes have facilitated dialogue between GPs, employees and employers, there is a long way to go to make the most from the new approach. One particular challenge for better use of the fit note is the lack of workplace knowledge among GPs generally. GPs are not equally confident in using all the return-to-work options on the fit note and differentiating between the return-to-work options. Challenges also remain in issuing fit notes for those with mental health problems. There is some evidence that because they have little knowledge of mental health problems and interact little with workplaces, GPs may have a greater tendency to write patients with poor mental health off sick for longer periods.

Further reading

Chenery, V. (2013), "An Evaluation of the Statement of Fitness for Work (Fit note): A Survey of Employees", *DWP Research Report*, No. 840, London.

OECD (2013), *Mental Health and Work: United Kingdom*, OECD Publishing, Paris, http://dx.doi.org/10.1787/9789264204997-en.

Shiels, C. et al. (2013), "An Evaluation of the Statement of Fitness for Work (fit note): Quantitative Survey of Fit Notes", *DWP Research Report*, No. 841, London.

Factsheet 3.8
Sweden: Guidelines for general practitioners to focus on work

Context

General practitioners (GPs) are in a key position as gatekeepers of sickness and disability benefits in most OECD countries. Yet, many do not have the right skills or knowledge for prescribing sick leave, especially when it comes to patients suffering from mild-to-moderate mental health problems. The result can be unnecessarily long sickness absences.

Programme

In 2005 the Swedish National Board of Health and Welfare developed new ways to improve the quality of sickness certification in an effort to reduce high levels of sickness absence. To date, the board has published 120 illness-specific guidelines on anxiety, depression, and schizophrenic conditions. They include criteria for judging individual cases – e.g. expected prognosis, effective treatment, and the length of sickness absence. The guidelines are based on a combination of available scientific evidence and consensus among different specialists. For example, the guidelines on depression recommend that people with uncomplicated first-time depression can achieve improved functionality within three months of adequate treatment.

Outcomes

The newly developed diagnosis-specific medical guidelines for GPs have had a significant impact on their attitudes towards prescribing sick leave. Evidence suggests that sickness absence guidelines for the most frequent illnesses have contributed to a much reduced incidence and shorter spells of sickness absence and a much narrower distribution of diagnoses. In a recent national survey of all general practitioners, around 76% reported the use of national sickness guidelines. Nearly two-thirds reported that the guidelines had facilitated their contacts with patients and one-third spoke of improved communication with social insurance officers, other health care staff, and employers.

Further reading

OECD (2013), *Mental Health and Work: Sweden*, OECD Publishing, Paris, http://dx.doi.org/10.1787/9789264188730-en.

Skaner, Y. et al. (2011), "Use and Usefulness of Guidelines for Sickness Certification: Results from a National Survey of All General Practitioners in Sweden", *BMJ Open*, Vol. 1, No. 1, http://bmjopen.bmj.com/content/1/2/e000303.full.

Factsheet 3.9
Netherlands: Guidelines for health care professionals

Context

People who suffer from mental ill-health frequently struggle with work-related problems, which health care providers often fail to address. The combination of medical, social and work-related problems results in treatment by general practitioners (GPs), occupational physicians (OPs) and psychologists. They need to co-ordinate their interventions and act upon work issues.

Programme

To manage the work-related problems of people with mental disorders and to better co-ordinate treatment provided by GPs, OPs and psychologists, the Netherlands has developed sets of treatment guidelines.

The guidelines set forth a three-phase process for helping health care professionals support people with mild-to-moderate mental health problems in their return to work: 1) discuss why the sickness absence occurred, educate the worker about his or her future employment prospects and advise on organising a daily routine during the sickness absence; 2) address the problems that caused the sickness absence and coax the worker into proposing solutions for returning to work; and 3) implement the solutions while returning to work gradually. The guidelines also offer additional information on the roles of the different health care providers and when contact or referral is deemed necessary.

In addition to the three profession-specific sets of guidelines, a multidisciplinary guideline is available on co-operation between GPs, OPs and psychologists in treating work-related distress and burn-out.

Outcomes

Specifically, the OP guideline has been evaluated in a cluster-randomised controlled trial and proved to be effective in improving return-to-work. On average, people treated in accordance with the guideline returned to work 17 days earlier than those treated by OPs who did not use the guideline.

Evaluations of OPs' adherence to their guideline have shown limited compliance, with some studies finding that OPs only follow 50% of the guideline recommendations. Nevertheless, greater compliance is related to reductions in sickness absence. With regards to the guideline for psychologists, one study showed that about 58% of the psychologists used their guideline, but no data are available on compliance rates.

Further reading

LVE/NHG/NVAB (2011), Richtlijn: Eén lijn in de eerste lijn bij overspanning en burnout: Multidisciplinaire richtlijn bij overspanning en burnout voor eerstelijns professionals, LVE (Amsterdam), NHG (Utrecht) and NVAB (Utrecht).

Nieuwenhuijsen, K. et al. (2003), "Quality of Rehabilitation Among Workers with Adjustment Disorders According to Practice Guidelines: A Retrospective Cohort Study", *Occupational and Environmental Medicine*, Vol. 60, Suppl. 1, pp. i21-i25.

NVAB (2007), *Richtlijn: Handelen van de Bedrijfsarts bij Werkenden met Psychische Problemen*, Nederlandse Verenining voor Arbeids- en Bedrijfsgeneeskunde, Utrecht.

OECD (2014), *Mental Health and Work: Netherlands*, OECD Publishing, Paris, http://dx.doi.org/10.1787/9789264223301-en.

Rebergen, D. et al. (2006), "Adherence to Mental Health Guideline by Dutch Occupational Physicians", *Occupational Medicine (London)*, Vol. 56, No. 7, pp. 461-468.

Factsheet 3.10
Switzerland: Expanded medical certificates to improve co-operation

Context

Co-operation between general practitioners (GPs) and patients' employers is important for gaining a common understanding of the work context and finding opportunities for enabling patients to continue working. Due to confidentiality issues, however, physicians are not allowed to make contact with employers. There is consequently a lack of communication between GPs and employers, which makes it very difficult for GPs to judge a patient's ability to work.

Programme

To supply employers with more work-related information about employees on sick leave, strengthen the chances of earlier (often part-time) return-to-work, and improve co-operation between employers and physicians, some regional associations of employers and physicians have drawn up an "expanded medical sickness certificate".

Employers can ask treating physicians for an expanded medical certificate. It provides more information than the ordinary one which indicates only the cause of absence (accident, illness, or pregnancy) and the grade and duration of the incapacity to work. The employer has to send a description of the workplace and patient's tasks to the GP. The description must be signed by the employee, who, thereby, consents to the request for an expanded medical certificate. The employer may also specify whether he or she wishes to communicate with the physician. Based on the workplace description, the GP describes what work tasks the employee can or cannot conduct while he or she is on (part-time) sick leave.

The forms for workplace descriptions and medical certificates are downloadable on the home pages of employers' organisations, physicians' associations, and private daily allowances insurers. The employer has to pay CHF 60 for a certificate.

Outcomes

Since 2005, the expanded sickness certificate has been implemented in different regions and is now available across Switzerland. While there has been no formal evaluation, anecdotal evidence suggests that joint work between employers' and physicians' associations may be effective in improving dialogue and mutual trust between employers and physicians. An important factor seems to be the agreement between employers and physicians, which served as the base for the new certificate. However, use of the certificate does not so far seem widespread, partly due to a lack of information among employers and because employees need to give their consent before employers may request the certificate.

Further reading

Ebnöther, E. (2014), "Das Arztzeugnis im Brennpunkt unterschiedlicher Interessen" [The sickness certificate viewed from different perspectives], *Schweizerische Ärztezeitung*, Vol. 95, No. 4, pp. 108-111.

OECD (2014), *Mental Health and Work: Switzerland*, OECD Publishing, Paris, p://dx.doi.org/10.1787/9789264204973-en.

Links to the expanded sickness certificate ("Erweitertes Arbeitsunfähigkeitszeugnis") and the workplace description ("Arbeitsplatzbeschreibung") on the webpage of the Swiss Insurance Medicine: www.swiss-insurance-medicine.ch/de/arbeitsunfaehigkeitszeugnisse.html.

Factsheet 3.11
United States: Individual placement and support by the health sector

Context

Mental health treatment alone does not improve work outcomes for people suffering from mental ill-health. To remain in or return to work, they also need employment support. Adding such support to mental health treatment has shown to be effective in improving work outcomes.

Programme

The Individual Placement and Support (IPS) model is an approach to helping people with severe mental illness get back into employment. IPS directly tackles the lack of integration of mental health care and employment services and the disconnection between different specialists. The key principles of the model include: i) competitive employment; ii) eligibility based on individual choice – no exclusions; iii) customised job search; iv) job search within four weeks; v) employment specialists and clinical teams work together and are closely located to each other; vi) continuous in-work support; vii) employers are approached with the individual's needs in mind; and viii) support throughout the transition from benefits to work. IPS is currently widely offered in secondary mental health care settings rather than in the employment system – partly because the model's target group comprises individuals with severe mental health conditions.

Outcomes

There is strong evidence that IPS produces better outcomes than alternative vocational services at a lower cost overall to the health and social care systems. Research has shown that 55% of the individuals assigned to IPS worked for at least one day during the 18-month follow-up period, compared with 28% of those assigned to vocational services. People assigned to vocational services were significantly more likely to drop out of the service (45%) and to be readmitted to the hospital (31%) than people in the IPS arm of the trial –13% of drop-outs and 20% of readmission. Randomised controlled trials in the Unites States have also shown that IPS participants have much better employment outcomes than groups supported by more traditional approaches of "train and place" – *i.e.* providing vocational training and job preparation before undertaking the search for competitive employment.

Yet there are some limitations: programmes predominantly result in entry-level jobs in the service industry, around half of the clients leave their jobs within six months, and they do not normally work full-time in order not to jeopardise their social security benefits. In sum, successful job placement does not have much of an effect on the benefit system. Finally, supported employment programmes are not as widespread as might be expected, due to implementation barriers like fragmented funding which, in turn, leads to fragmented service provision. Since the IPS model is a resource- and staff-intensive service, the number of people it serves is small. Currently, it predominantly targets people with severe health problems and has not yet been adapted to the large and growing number of people whose mental health problems are more moderate.

Further reading

Drake, R. and G. Bond (2008), "Supported Employment: 1998-2008", Guest Editorial in the Special Issue on the 10th Anniversary on Supported Employment, *Psychiatric Rehabilitation Journal*, Vol. 31, No. 4, pp. 274-276.

Knapp, M. et al. (2013), "Supported Employment: Cost-effectiveness Across six European Sites", *World Psychiatry*, Vol. 12, No. 1, pp. 60-68.

Factsheet 3.12
Australia: Personal helpers and mentors service – Community mental health

Context

In most OECD countries employment support and mental health support are dealt with separately even though research has shown that being in work shortens treatment duration. Adding employment support to mental health treatment is essential to improving labour market outcomes for people with mental ill-health.

Programme

In 2007 the Australian Government introduced the Personal Helpers and Mentors Programme (PHaMs). PHaMs funds NGOs to provide increased opportunities for people aged 16 years and over whose lives are severely affected by mental illness by helping them to overcome social isolation and increase their connections to the community. PHaMs provides individual one-to-one support to help participants in their recovery journey and provides a co-ordinated and integrated approach to accessing support services. Services take into account not just mental health issues, but any additional physical and emotional well-being issues that impact mental health recovery. PHaMs commenced in 2007, and there are now 220 PHaMs services operating across Australia. Commencing in April 2013, some PHaMs services were specifically funded to assist people with mental illness to address barriers to achieving their employment and training goals.

Outcomes

Of the 13 219 people that took part in 2011-12, 65% had mood disorders and 36% anxiety complaints. Of the 4 024 participants who exited in 2011-12, 34% did so because they had reached their treatment goals. In 2013-14, performance data reported that 97% of the participants were maintaining progress against their relevant goals and 99% reported they were satisfied and that the service they received was appropriate to their needs. Also, a total of 1 737 participants on, or claiming, income support payments engaged with PHaMs employment services across 42 sites. These employment services work with participants to address non-vocational issues that are barriers to finding and maintaining employment, training or education, such as personal presentation, housing stability and family support for employment goals. No specific data are available on the number of people that were successful in obtaining work.

Further reading

Australian Government, Department of Social Services (2015), "Personal Helpers and Mentors website", www.dss.gov.au/our-responsibilities/mental-health/programs-services/personal-helpers-and-mentors-phams (accessed 12 January 2015).

Department of Families, Housing, Community Services and Indigenous Affairs (2011), Working with Australians to Promote Mental Health, Prevent Mental Illness and Support Recovery: Evaluation of the FaHCSIA Targeted Community Care Mental Health Initiatives, Final report, Commonwealth of Australia, Canberra.

Department of Social Services (2013), Part C1: Personal Helpers and Mentors Guidelines under the Targeted Community Care (Mental Health) Program, Commonwealth of Australia, Canberra.

OECD (forthcoming 2015), *Mental Health and Work: Australia*, OECD Publishing, Paris.

Factsheet 3.13
Denmark: Self-management programme for return-to-work

Context

To prevent that people with mental health problems exit the labour market, the provision of mental health treatment and employment support is equally important. Self-management programmes for people with mental ill-health to deal with health-related problems are common and provide a good setting to incorporate self-management techniques to maintain in or acquire work.

Programme

"Learn to manage" is the Danish version of the US self-management programme developed at Stanford University, California. The overall vision of "Learn to manage" is to create better health and self-management among people with long-term diseases such as depression, anxiety, arthritis, diabetes, and long-term pain conditions. The programme in Denmark contains four different interventions with different aims and target groups:

- Learn to manage anxiety and depression
- Learn to manage job and long-term disease
- Learn to manage long-term pain conditions
- Learn to manage chronic diseases

"Learn to manage job and long-term disease" is offered because people with long-term diseases are at great risk of exclusion from the labour market. It mainly focuses on helping people on sick leave gain self-confidence in their ability to control their symptoms, better manage their health problems and develop strategies to return to work. The main target group is people with anxiety, depression, stress and long-term pain conditions.

The partners are the Danish Health and Medicines Authority, the Danish Agency for Labour Market and Recruitment and the foundation TRYG. The programme is carried out by the Danish Committee for Health Education and financed by the municipalities.

Outcomes

The programme is evidence-based and has proven significant, positive effects on self-rated health, health distress, pain, fatigue, functional disability, physical activity, use of cognitive techniques and self-efficacy.

The module "Learn to manage job and long-term disease" is still in an implementation phase and trialled in 42 out of 98 municipalities. Two research institutions are evaluating the programme in the period 2014-17. The focus is on evaluating health status, health behaviour, self-efficacy, and return-to-work.

Further reading

The Danish National Board of Health (2009), Patient Education – A Health Technology Assessment.

www.patientuddannelse.info

http://patienteducation.stanford.edu/

www.patient.co.uk/doctor/expert-patient

Factsheet 3.14
United Kingdom: Employment advisors working alongside psychological therapists

Context

People with mental disorders often suffer from a combination of medical, social and work-related problems requiring services and support from a range of different actors. Yet health policies and services tend to operate in isolation from other systems and often focus on people with severe disorders.

Programme

To provide integrated employment and health services, the United Kingdom's National Health Service has introduced Employment Advisors (EAs) in the Improving Access to Psychological Therapies (IAPT) programme that it has rolled out across England. IAPT offers fast access to evidence-based psychological treatment for people with a common mental disorder. The EAs work alongside IAPT therapists, providing practical advice and relevant intervention to help people remain in work or enter the workplace. Access to IAPT services is by self-referral or referral from GPs.

Outcomes

EAs give added value to IAPT services both by facilitating quicker return-to-work from sick leave and increasing the likelihood of remaining in employment. Of those who were on sick leave when they entered the IAPT service and started seeing an employment advisor, 63% returned to work, 9% were still in employment but remained off sick, and the remaining 29% left employment after the service was completed. Of those who were working when they first saw an EA, 84% were still at work when they stopped seeing their EA.

People with employment and health problems highly value co-ordinated support from employment and health services. A key issue, however, is the extent to which such co-ordination would have occurred in any case, i.e. as a result of IAPT treatment alone. Analysis of the employment outcomes of those in IAPT who saw an employment advisor with those who did not has proved inconclusive.

While the programme demonstrates the considerable, innovative efforts made to integrate employment and health support, there are some shortcomings that can be improved. For instance, evidence suggests that employment support was not fully "integrated" with health support. Clients are not referred to employment advisors until their therapy session has ended. As a result support is delivered consecutively rather than in parallel.

Further reading

Hillage, J. et al. (2012), "Evaluation of the Fit for Work Service Pilots: First Year Report", *DWP Research Report*, No. 792, London.

Hogarth, T. et al. (2013), "Evaluation of Employment Advisers in the Improving Access to Psychological Therapies Programme", *DWP Research Report*, No. 826, London.

OECD (2014), *Mental Health and Work: United Kingdom*, OECD Publishing, Paris, http://dx.doi.org/10.1787/9789264204997-en.

Factsheet 3.15
Norway: Centres for at work and coping offer therapy and employment services

Context

People with mental ill-health often face work-related problems such as reduced ability to function in the workplace, sickness absence or unemployment. As work contributes to good mental health and can improve the effectiveness of mental health treatment, it is important to simultaneously provide therapy for mental ill-health and employment services for work-related problems.

Programme

In Norway the "centres for at work and coping" offer work-focused cognitive behavioural therapy and vocational rehabilitation services to people with mild-to-moderate mental health problems who are still at work, on sick leave, or inactive. How to cope with work problems is the main issue in both therapy and rehabilitation.

The services can include up to 15 sessions and are currently established in seven of Norway's 19 counties. The employment specialist is supposed not only to offer counselling but to actively seek contact with employers. There is close collaboration between therapists (employed by the Norwegian Labour and Welfare Department) and employment specialists.

Outcomes

A randomised controlled multicenter trial evaluated the effects of six centers and conducted a cost-benefit analysis – the "At Work and Coping" – study by Uni Research. The intervention group received "At Work and Coping", and the control group received treatment as usual, support from their general practitioner (GP) or vocational rehabilitation measures from the employment services.

For the clients that were mainly recruited from temporary disability benefits the results for the intervention group showed superior statistically significant results (more detailed results are not available at this moment). The concept of these centres is promising because they fully integrate an employment focus in treatment with a mental health focus in employment supports.

Further reading

Clinical trials, https://clinicaltrials.gov/ct2/show/NCT01146730?term=Centre+for+work+coping&rank=1.

Løvvik, C., W. Shaw, S. Øverland and S.E. Reme (2014), "Expectations and Illness Perceptions as Predictors of Benefit Recipiency Among Workers with Common Mental Disorders: Secondary Analysis from a Randomized Controlled Trial", BMJ Open, Vol. 4(e004321), http://dx.doi.org/10.1136/bmjopen-2013-004321.

Løvvik, C., S. Øverland, M. Hysing, E. Broadbent and S.E. Reme (2014), "Association Between Illness Perceptions and Return-to-Work Expectations in Workers with Common Mental Health Symptoms", Journal of Occupational Rehabilitation, Vol. 24, No. 1, pp. 160-170, http://dx.doi.org/10.1007/s10926-013-9439-8.

OECD (2013), Mental Health and Work: Norway, OECD Publishing, Paris, http://dx/doi/org/10.1787/9789264178984-en.

Olsen, I. B., Øverland, S., Reme, S. E., & Løvvik, C. (2014). Exploring work-related causal attributions of common mental disorders. Journal of Occupational Rehabilitation, http://dx.doi.org/10.1007/10926-014-9556-z.

Reme, S.E., A.L. Grasdal, C. Løvvik, S.A. Lie and S. Øverland (2015), "Work-focused Cognitive Behavioural Therapy and Individual Job Support to Increase Work Participation in Common Mental Disorders. A Randomized Controlled Multicenter Trial", Occupational and Environmental Medicine (under review).

Factsheet 3.16
United Kingdom: Doctors for doctors – Supporting the health of health professionals

Context

Although the prevalence of mental ill-health is high in the population at large, it is even higher in certain occupations due to a combination of occupational and individual risk factors. Doctors are particularly at risk. At the same time, they are least likely to disclose their problems, which leads to high incidences of absence.

Programme

The Practitioner Health Programme (PHP), put in place by the UK National Health Service (NHS) for Greater London in 2008, aims to address the widespread mental health problems of doctors while also reflecting the new employment responsibility of the health system. PHP, fully funded by the NHS, is a job-oriented stepped-care mental health service for health professionals. The service is free of charge, confidential (even anonymous if preferred), very easy to access (it is a walk-in service), and provides very fast intervention (therapy within only a week). Key characteristics include the involvement of a multidisciplinary team (such as general practitioners, psychiatrists, specialist nurses, psychologists and therapists); a very low caseload for the team; and a focus on graded return-to-work where possible (with the involvement of the employer). Every patient has a lead clinician who co-ordinates treatment and other supports, undertakes regular reviews, and discusses the patient's case at weekly team meetings.

PHP is not an occupational health service but can liaise with it. PHP provides assessments with respect to work and the workplace and supports return to work planning and implementation.

Outcomes

Over the first five years, from 2008 to 2013, more than 1 000 practitioners used the PHP. There were more women than men and the modal age was 30 years old. They were practitioners for whom the mainstream NHS care available was not accessible or did not meet the specific needs. Around 80% of the users presented with mental health problems (depression in 55% of such cases) and the remaining 20% with addiction problems (mostly alcohol dependence).

The service was effective in getting the practitioner patients well and back to work. On average over the five years, 76% remained in or returned to work whilst a practitioner patient and 79% of those treated for addition problems remained abstinent. Validated health questionnaires demonstrate improvements on all measures including mental health, social, and functioning at work. Such outcomes were made possible through the provision of a clear process and a focus on the goal of facilitating recovery and return-to-work or continuation with work. PHP has met an unmet need and has demonstrated that investment in such specialist services is both economically and clinically effective.

Further reading

NHS (2014), "The First Five Years of the NHS Practitioner Health Programme, 2008-2013, Supporting the Health of Health Professionals", www.php.nhs.net.

OECD (2014), *Mental Health and Work: United Kingdom*, OECD Publishing, Paris, http://dx.doi.org/10.1787/9789264204997-en.

Chapter 4

From workplace stress prevention to employer incentives and support for workers with mental health problems

Employers are ideally placed to help their employees deal with mental health problems and retain their jobs. Workers who suffer from mental ill-health take sick leave more frequently and are absent for longer than those who are mentally healthy. At the same time they also report reduced productivity at work more often. Stress prevention in the workplace is both a necessary and effective means of tackling existing mental health issues. However, the pervasiveness of mental health stigma complicates the solution of work problems that are related to mental health problems. If managers are to be able to identify mental health problems, they need adequate training and support.

Policy conclusions:

- *Enforce legislation for psychosocial risk prevention.*
- *Improve (line) managers' responses to workers' mental health issues.*
- *Design effective return-to-work management processes.*
- *Strengthen incentives and obligations for employers to prevent and address sick leave.*

Most people with a mental health problem have a job and go to work. Often, though, they are not fully productive. The workplace is thus a key area from which to develop policy that addresses the issue of mental health-related exclusion. Moreover, although work is a generally protective environment and fosters good mental health, it can also distress employees and worsen poor mental health. Stigmatising attitudes, evasive, counter-effective managerial interventions, and ignorance of psychosocial workplace risks are all factors that contribute to excluding workers with mental health problems from the labour market.

Although there is growing awareness of such risks and of the need for stress prevention in many OECD countries, there are few procedures or support mechanisms for translating that awareness into concrete action. The challenge is to provide effective early intervention and support for employers to address workplace risks and work problems. Mental health problems are related to performance deficits and interpersonal problems in the workplace. Not all mental ill-health can be prevented and employers must manage sickness absences, return-to-work, and workplace conflicts. Small and medium-sized enterprises (SMEs) in particular have little scope to adjust and are often left to their own devices.

Stigma and disclosure, a vicious circle

Awareness of mental health problems in the workplace and psychiatric treatment capacity have both grown in recent decades (Henderson et al., 2013). Yet the stigma that attaches to mental illness has not abated to the same degree. Prejudice is still very prevalent and is in sharp contrast to attitudes towards physical ill-health (Figure 4.1, Panel A). In 2005 as many as 65% of Danish employees, for example, were reluctant to work with someone who suffered from mood swings. Five years later more than one in two (55%) felt the same way. Yet only one in six would not wish to work with a blind colleague and only one-tenth with a co-worker in a wheelchair (OECD, 2013c).

Stigma complicates the management of mental-health-related work issues and makes it difficult for workers who suffer from mental ill-health to find, resume, and hold on to jobs (Stuart, 2006; Brohan et al., 2012). Many employers would not hire even highly-qualified applicants if they knew they had suffered from mental illness (Baer, 2007). Stigma makes it hard to fit back into the workplace, so making spells of unemployment even longer and increasing the number of disability benefit claimants (Rosholm and Andersen, 2010). Finally, many employees who suffer from poor mental health choose not to mention it because they fear discrimination and dismissal. As a result, co-workers and managers have trouble determining the reasons for their poor performance or interpersonal problems and do not offer support or understanding.

The pervasiveness of mental health stigma is surprising in view of the prevalence of mental ill-health in the working population, which is currently between 15% and 18% (OECD, 2012). Prejudice towards people with mental illness in general and the ability to collaborate closely with them in the workplace are common, not necessarily contradictory stances (Thornicroft et al., 2007).

Figure 4.1. **The stigma attached to workers with mild-to-moderate mental ill-health in Denmark persists despite improvements**

Percentage of workers who would be reluctant to work with a colleague who has mood swings

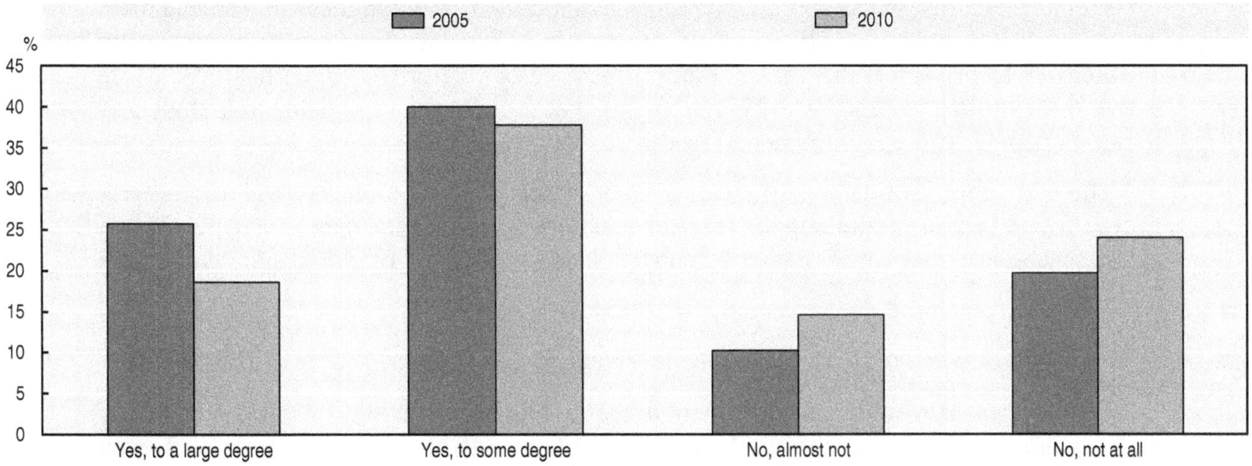

Source: Thomsen, L.B. and J. Høgelund (2011), "Handicap og beskaeftigelse. Udviklingen mellem 2002 og 2010", Report No. 11:08, Danish National Institute for Social Research, Copenhagen.

StatLink http://dx.doi.org/10.1787/888933184166

Fighting stigma is a challenging task. In the past decade, there have been workplace campaigns to that effect in a number of countries:

- The United Kingdom – the Shaw Trust in 2010; Munday in 2010; Time to Change in 2009; the "see me" anti-stigma campaign; the Mentally Healthy Workplace Programme.
- The United States, where most action has been to support military personnel suffering from posttraumatic stress disorder.
- Australia – the National Workplace Program from *beyondblue*; Business in Mind; Mental Health First Aid.
- Canada – the Copernicus Project: Risk Management for Workplace Mental Health; Mind Matters: Opening Minds.
- Continental European countries, like Denmark's "One of us" (OECD, 2013c) and Switzerland's "How are you?" (see also Malachowski and Kirsh, 2013; Szeto and Dobson, 2010).

Few of the campaigns have been evaluated extensively or for long periods, having got under way only in the last few years. Yet there are doubts as to whether they will yield sustainable results, as their awareness-raising approaches do not effectively change long-term behaviour when distressed employees are a burden on supervisors and co-workers (Clement et al., 2013; Corrigan et al., 2014; Baer et al., 2011; Corrigan and Shapiro, 2010).

Policies to curb stigma should seek not only to raise awareness but to build good relationships between workers with mental health problems and their colleagues. Supervisors, for example, should be fully instructed in how to behave in problematic situations. Similarly, policies should not only prevent discrimination but also encourage workers with mental ill-health to talk about their resulting work problems and supervisors to take early action in order to address workplace issues related to poor mental health. In other words, anti-stigma policies should give supervisors the backing they need.

Prejudice against workers with mental illness and their unwillingness to disclose them are frequent, interrelated problems. Self-stigma often prevents people from speaking up for themselves or tempts them to give up in the face of real or perceived hostility. More active policies than awareness-raising are needed to compel the workplace to include and maintain people with common mental health problems.

There are four particular key areas for workplace policy action: i) psychosocial risk prevention; ii) training and support for line managers; iii) the effective management of sickness absence and return-to-work; and iv) incentives and obligations for employers and employees.

Enforced legislation for psychosocial risk prevention

Employment is usually good for mental health. But poor-quality jobs, bad leadership, and psychosocial stress in the workplace can put mental health under strain and even trigger problems (Stansfeld and Candy, 2006). The cause-and-effect relationships between the work environment and mental health are multi-directional, as described in OECD (2012):

- Job-related strain and a poor psychosocial work environment can cause mental ill-health.
- Workers with mental health problems tend to work in lower-quality jobs and poorer work environments.
- Workers with mental health problems perceive their work situation more negatively because of their condition.

The relationship between the workplace and mental ill-health

Figure 4.2 (Panel A) shows how closely linked working conditions and mental ill-health are. There is evidence that more and more workers in most European countries are experiencing the joint effects of high job demands and low decision latitude – a combination that leads to job strain (OECD, 2012). Depending on the country, between 20% and 40% of employees report feeling job strain, a state that is associated with more frequent and longer sickness absences.

Many workers with a mental health problem in the United Kingdom report that they feel overwhelmed by the pressures of time at work, fear undesirable changes in their jobs, and do not feel secure in them (OECD, 2014b). Surveys in other countries yield comparable results. In Denmark, for example, workers with mental health problems report that they do not have enough time to complete all their tasks and receive little support from their supervisors. They also speak of limited co-operation with their colleagues and low appreciation of their work by management (OECD, 2013c).

However, it is important not to overstate the job strain paradigm. Depression is more closely related to high levels of stress in private life than to work strain (OECD, 2013a). And it is not even certain that work-induced psychological stress has increased. Data from Austria, for example, suggest that self-reported work strain has steadily declined in the past 15 years (OECD, 2015).

Figure 4.2. **Significant barriers and lack of incentives hinder better prevention policies**

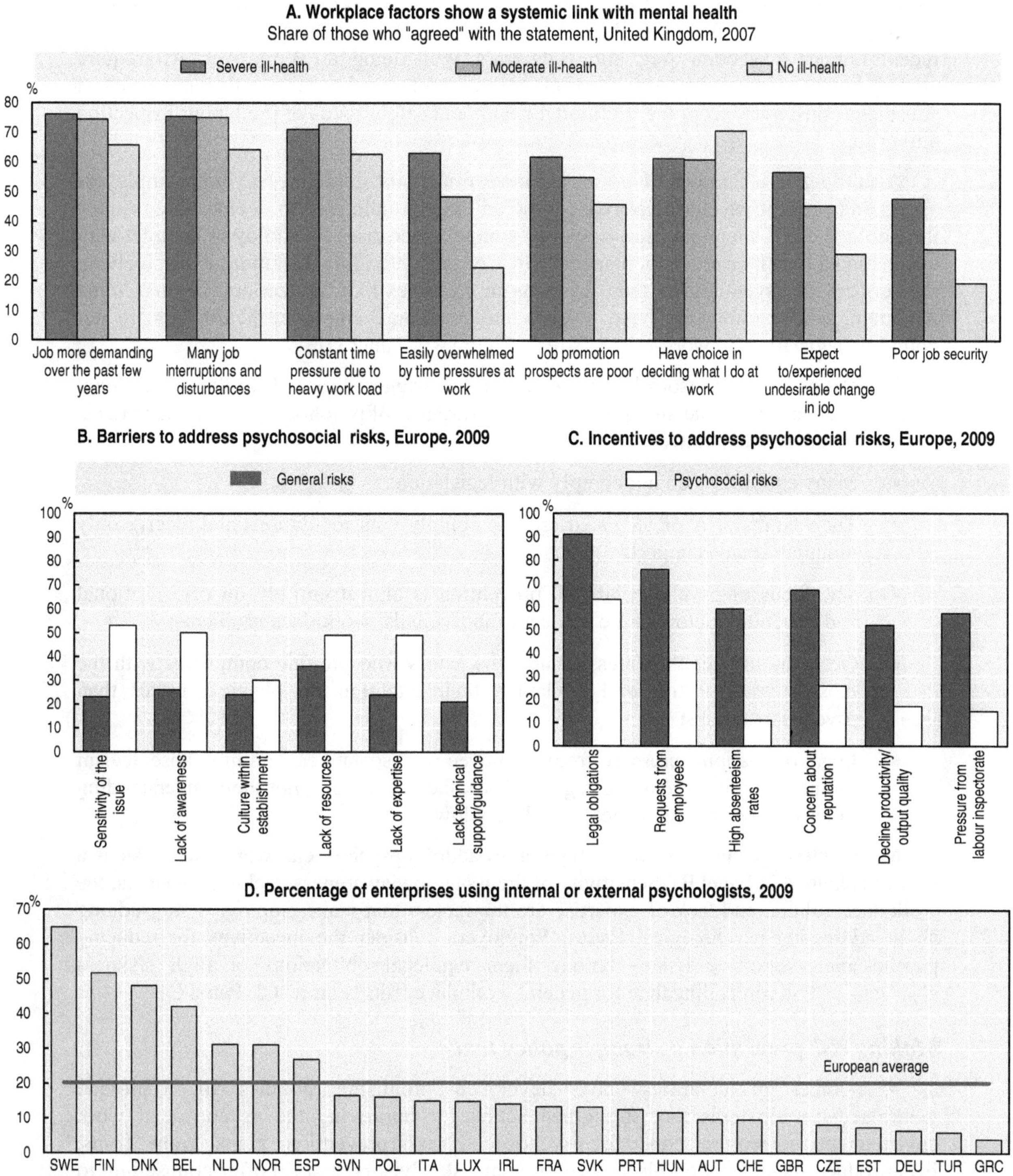

Note: EU-24 comprises the average of the 24 countries covered in the European survey of enterprises on new and emerging risks (ESENER).

Source: Panel A: OECD calculations based on Adult Psychiatric Morbidity Survey, 2007; and Panels B-D: OECD compilation based on the 2009 European survey of enterprises on new and emerging risks (ESENER) of the European Agency for Safety and Health at Work; https://osha.europa.eu/sub/esener/en.

StatLink http://dx.doi.org/10.1787/888933184174

The vast majority of countries have tackled psychosocial workplace risks and job strain through labour legislation. Examples are the Working Environment Acts of Norway, Sweden and Denmark, the Labour Conditions Law in the Netherlands, Austria's recent Labour Protection Act, and Belgium's Well-Being at Work Act. All require employers to routinely assess, prevent and control psychosocial risks at work – a substantial shift away from the traditional health and safety focus of the labour inspection authorities.

Accordingly, a number of countries have drawn up guidelines to help employers assess and prevent psychosocial risks, although they remain free to decide how to meet their obligations. Other countries, however, compel enterprises to employ or contract with occupational health or prevention specialists. Consequently, they call more extensively on the services of psychologists than do firms in countries like Switzerland or the United Kingdom, where employers have a legal duty to secure employee health but are not bound by legislation on work-related stress (Figure 4.2, Panel D).

Legislation on psychosocial risk prevention has triggered growth in the professional support and tools available and greater public awareness of psychosocial workplace risks. But the picture remains flawed:

- Many enterprises do not comply with legislation;
- The vast majority of SMEs struggle to comply with regulations and receive only minimal, if any, support;
- The focus of psychosocial risk prevention is almost entirely on organisational and structural factors to the neglect of individuals' workplace problems;
- Occupational health professionals – the actors who provide companies with the most support – still tend to lavish their attention on physical rather than psychosocial risks;
- Legal obligations, pressure from employee representatives, and high absenteeism prompt employers to address general risk factors at work, not their understanding of psychosocial risks, which is still very low.

Many enterprises perceive the obligation to address psychosocial workplace risks as a burden (Figure 4.2, Panel B). Sensitivity of the issue, low awareness, lacking resources, the workplace culture, and lack of expertise are the factors that make employers so grudging about addressing psychological issues. Employers consider the incentives for reducing psychosocial workplace risks – among them e.g. legal obligations or high sickness absence – as less compelling than for general workplace risks (Figure 4.2, Panel C).

Making risk prevention a stronger policy tool

A number of countries have developed promising policies to: i) provide workplace-specific tools that strengthen action for improving the psychosocial work environment, ii) require concrete psychosocial risk prevention plans from firms, iii) introduce specialist workplace psychosocial risk advisors, and iv) offer counselling to employers seeking help.

- Denmark has put in place sector- and job-specific guidance tools that describe in concrete terms risks and the resources a company may use to prevent problems (Factsheet 4.1). Inspectors from the Working Environment Authority (WEA) have been trained to use the tools and support employers. Preliminary results suggest employers find the guidance tools very useful.

- In Belgium, employers are required to draw up five-year prevention plans that meet the problems identified by their psychosocial risk assessments. They must establish annual action plans to prevent psychosocial distress at work and limit its consequences (Factsheet 4.2). Evaluations have shown that implementation has so far been weak. But the obligation to draw up concrete actions plans goes in the right direction.
- In Norway, employer support centres offer courses and support from specialised workplace counsellors (Factsheet 4.3). Tens of thousands of enterprises have received courses and counselling in managing problematic workplace situations.
- In Switzerland, cantonal disability benefit offices may advise employers on how to deal with employees who are perceived as difficult – long before they submit any disability benefit claim (see Factsheet 5.1). A guidebook is available to help labour inspectors identify mental health risks in a company.
- Austria's Labour Protection Act requires employers to evaluate psychological strain in the workplace, implement measures in the event of problems, and evaluate their effectiveness. Occupational psychologists can be mandated to evaluate workplace risks and develop measures accordingly (Factsheet 4.4).

Key messages

Over the past decade, many OECD countries have put in place more and more highly developed psychosocial risk prevention regulations. Although they yield new opportunities for preventing mental-health-related problems in the workplace, they need to be balanced with more specific, better targeted measures. Awareness raising and enforced psychosocial risk prevention may be successful when support is sufficiently specific, compulsory, and conducive to collaboration between employers and specialised services. Legislation is often poorly implemented and few policies support small and medium-sized enterprises. SMEs need highly practical tools to help them prevent and manage the psychosocial risks encountered in their particular work environments.

Ways to implement and enforce legislation to prevent psychosocial risk include:

- Specifying employer obligations in regard to psychosocial risk assessment and risk prevention.
- Providing targeted tools and support mechanisms that enable employers to make adjustments to the work environment.
- Directing labour inspectorate and occupational health service resources to psychosocial health issues.

Mental health training and support structures for line managers

Around two-thirds of all mental illness start before people enter the labour market. Measures to prevent mental health problems at work must be complemented by effective action to tackle existing mental health issues when they lead to reduced performance or workplace conflict.

Ignorance of the critical role of good management

Workers with a mental health problem are involved in workplace conflicts with superiors and co-workers twice as often as other workers (Figure 4.3, Panel A). Accordingly, difficulties in managing relationships with management and supervisors are the most frequent reason for employees to seek psychological help from employment advisors in the United Kingdom (Figure 4.3, Panel B).

Effective management of workplace conflicts is essential as they weigh heavily on the work environment and significantly heighten the risk of recurrent sickness absence (Arends et al., 2014). They can also weaken employee solidarity, which isolates the worker involved in the conflict and makes him or her more prone to dismissal (Baer et al., 2011). Although workplace conflicts are often related to mental health problems, employers usually fail to perceive a change in behaviour and conflicts as warning signs. Consequently, they may fail to manage situations adequately. Supervisory staff tends to feel too inhibited to deal with behavioural problems in a clear and timely manner. They shy away from asking or ordering an employee to seek professional help – something that many (larger) enterprises would do, however, to address drinking problems.

Large companies usually have in-house departments or contract outside consultants to prevent and manage mental-health-related work problems. The lack of such provision in SMEs is related to their ignorance (Figure 4.3, Panel C). Half of all very small firms consider that professional knowledge of burn-out and psychological strain is not relevant to them, even though managers – particularly in small firms – are often emotionally involved and do not have the resources to compensate for a worker's chronic performance problems. Not surprisingly, SMEs almost never offer their workers employee assistance, while big firms usually do (OECD, 2014b). The main challenge to policy in this respect is SMEs' low take-up of support services.

Figure 4.3. **Work conflicts correlate with mental health and are a main reason for seeking help**

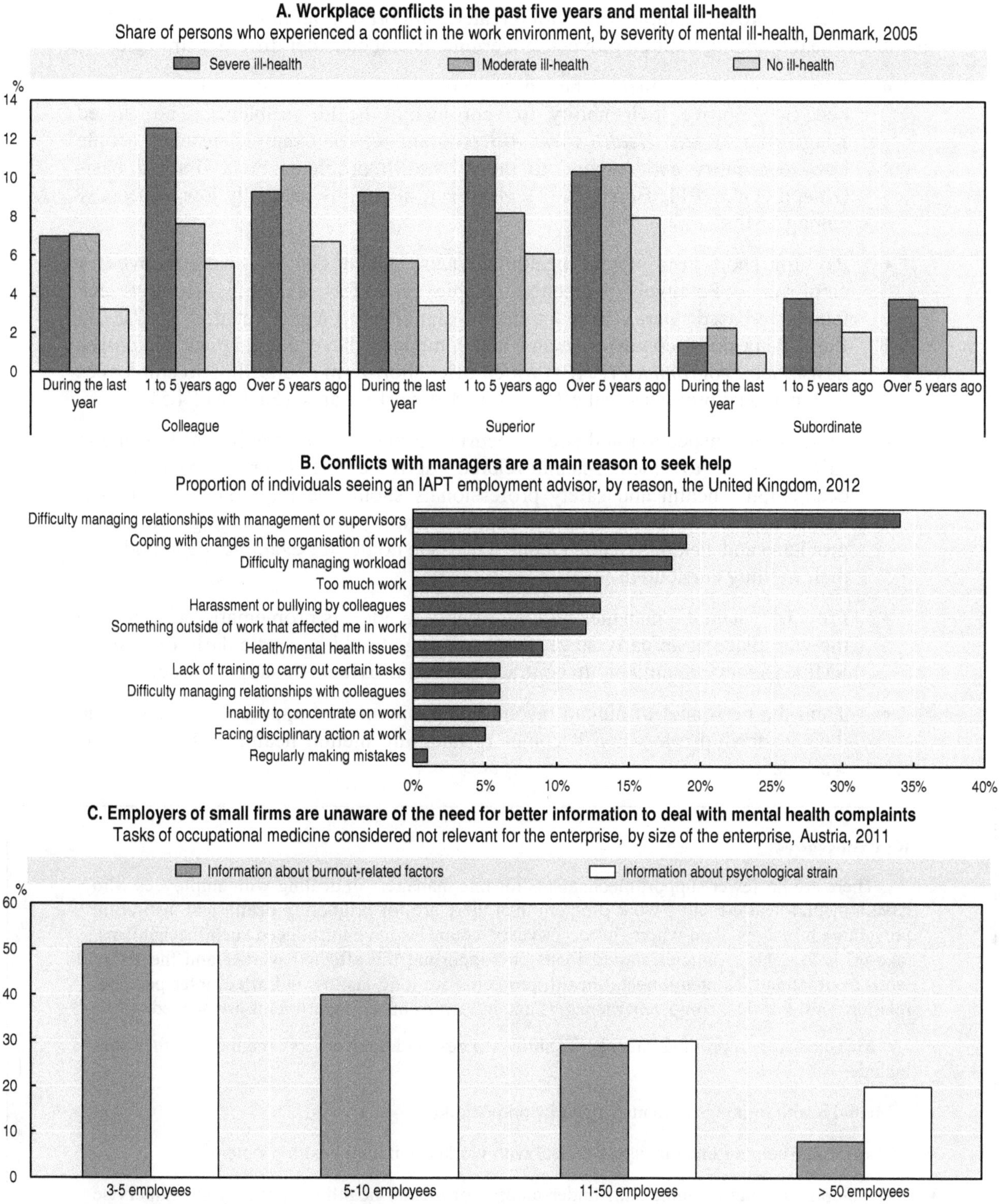

Source: Panel A: National Health Interview Survey 2005; Panel B: Hogarth, T. et al. (2013), "Evaluation of Employment Advisers in the Improving Access to Psychological Therapies Programme", *DWP Research Report No. 826*, London; and Panel C: OECD compilation based on data of: Spectra (2011), "The Position of Occupational Medicine in Enterprises. A Survey Commissioned by the Austrian Academy for Occupational Medicine".

StatLink http://dx.doi.org/10.1787/888933184182

Enabling management to deal with mental health problems

In order to provide employers with greater support for addressing and handling mental ill-health among their employees, governments can consider different strategies.

- Promote employee mental health screening and give managers the tools they need to improve their ability to spot mental health problems. The United Kingdom's *Mental Health First Aid* programme, for example, teaches people how to identify and respond to mental health problems on a first-aid basis (Knapp et al., 2011; Borril, 2011). However, take-up is generally low, especially among SMEs.
- Pay for short-term mental health services, which can be cost-effective for employers. Positively screened employees, for example, could seek telephone-based care from trained clinicians (Wang et al., 2007). In English-speaking countries, many big companies have put in place *Employee Assistance Programmes* (EAPs) which offer short-term counselling to employees with personal problems that affect their work performance (Factsheet 4.5).
- Shift labour inspection and social security resources from traditional health and safety tasks to mental-health-related activities. Labour inspectors and occupational health and safety professionals should be required to build their knowledge of how to actively support employers in managing workplace problems and sickness management. The issue could, for example, be included in their training curriculum.
- Provide systematic manager training in how to address problematic behaviour in the workplace at an early stage. Such training should be particularly directed at SMEs, as they are unlikely to contract external providers to supply the service.
- Train the personnel of human resource departments to support line managers in their leadership role when it comes to handling mental health problems in the workplace.

Key messages

There are far fewer support mechanisms for line managers in dealing with employees who have a mental-health-related work problem than there are for promoting health and instituting preventive measures. And where, in recent years, countries have introduced such mechanisms, take-up is low. New policies should focus on supporting the affected worker and the entire work environment, as many mental health problems are long-lasting and affect inter-personal relationships. For this, competent managers and human resource departments are needed.

Measures for improving managers' ability to respond to workers' mental health issues include:

- Mental health training for managers and workers alike.
- Toolkits for helping line managers to deal with workers' mental health problems.
- Developing human resource staff understanding of mental health so that they can supervise line managers in their dealings with workers who suffer from mental ill-health.
- Promoting employee mental health screening and employer-funded mental health first aid.

Actively managing return-to-work

Although some sickness absence is inevitable, it is a crucial issue from a medium and long-term policy perspective. Workers on long-term sick leave run a much higher risk of exiting the labour market and being granted permanent disability benefits. Active return-to-work management in the event of sick leave should be a strategic priority. And it should target workers who suffer from mental ill-health, as they are highly prevalent among long-term absentees.

Long absences make return-to-work difficult

Data for Sweden show that after 90 days of sickness absence, around 75% of workers with a physical problem are back to work. After 180 days, almost 90% are back. The corresponding percentages in mental health-related sick leave are just 50% and less than 70% (Figure 4.4, Panel B). These low figures are worrying in themselves. They are even more so because it is generally after around 90 days of sick leave that return-to-work becomes particularly difficult, as data for Belgium confirm (Figure 4.4, Panel A).

Factors intrinsic to their illness may mean that certain workers with mental health problems take long sick leaves – it takes time to recover from disturbed cognitive functions or exhaustion, for example. However, co-workers, employers, and treating physicians also contribute to absences that are longer than necessary in some of the following ways:

- Employers' and co-workers' behaviour is driven by fear avoidance, in the case of workplace conflicts, for example.
- General practitioners are uncertain and ineffective when certifying sickness and may prescribe unproductively long sickness spells because they feel pressured by the desire to "protect" patients from job strain and workplace conflict.
- Enterprises do not monitor sickness absence or have effective return-to-work measures in place. In European countries, only one in two takes systematic measures to support an employee's return to work after a long-term sickness absence (Figure 4.4, Panel C).

Countries are developing return-to-work strategies

Most countries are now developing strategies to support return-to-work. Most use – and sometimes combine – practices from five sets of measures.

Gradual early return-to-work

- Some countries seek to promote gradual return-to-work as early as possible instead of allowing workers to stay away sick until they are fully able to resume work. Norway recently made partial sick leave the default option for certifying physicians, so compelling them to justify why they may have prescribed full sick leave. At the same time, it introduced tools to support physicians, e.g. by online feedback about their certification behaviour (OECD, 2013c). Denmark's Flexjob system is another good example. The state subsidises the wage bill for employees who return to work on a full-time basis, but work fewer or less productive hours. Although *Flexjobs* are so far only seldom used for people who suffer from mental ill-health, they could help prevent recurrent sick leave and enable quicker return-to-work (Factsheet 4.6).

Figure 4.4. **Return to work becomes difficult after three month's sick leave**

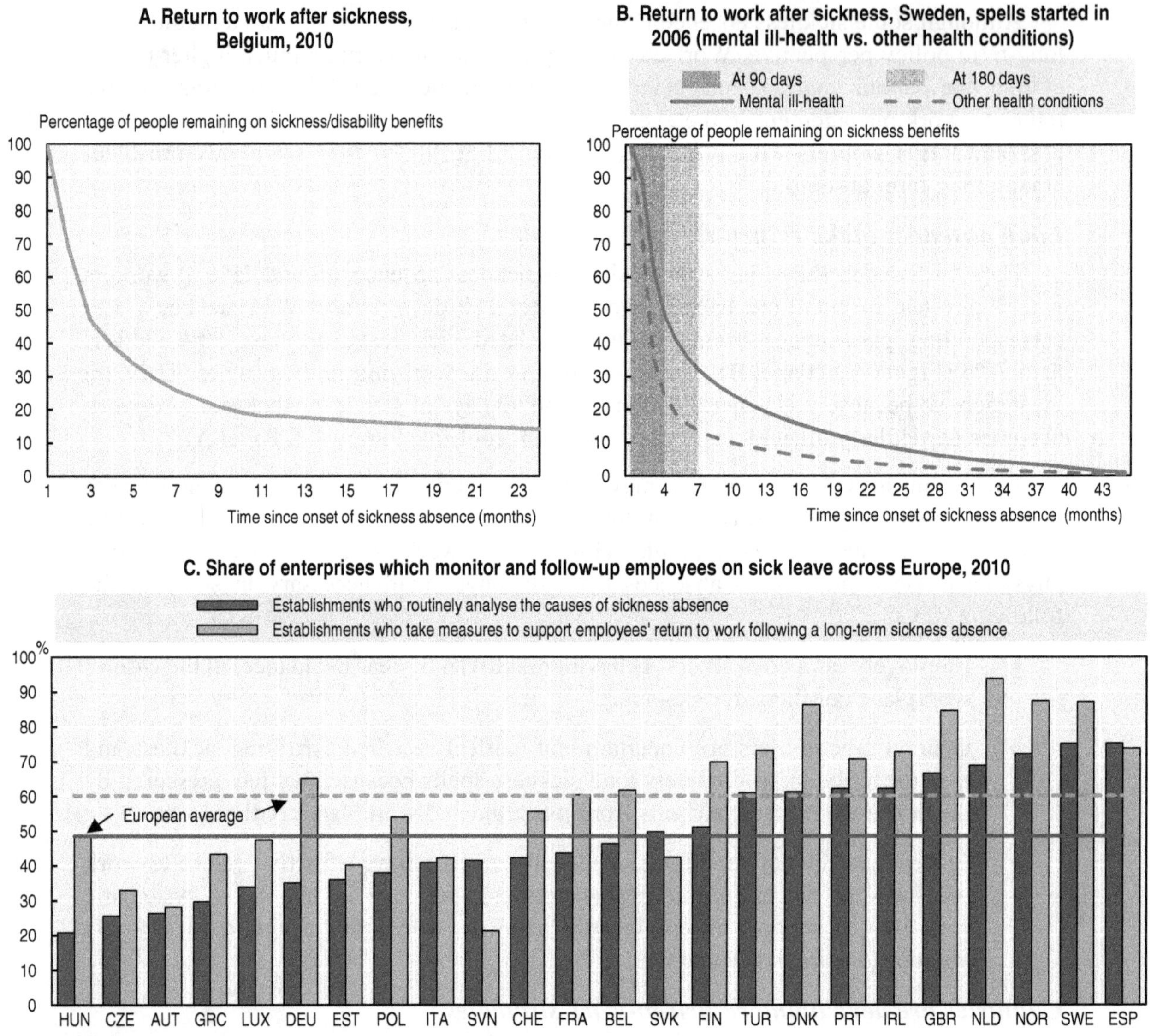

Note: Panel A: The National Institute for Sickness and Invalidity Insurance has only information on the sickness absences for which the mutualities pay sickness benefits, i.e. after the guaranteed wage period. To provide a consistent picture across blue-collar and white-collar people, the vertical axis shows the number of people receiving sickness or disability benefits as a percentage of the number of people receiving sickness benefits for at least one month. However, the time since onset of sickness absence (horizontal axis) includes the guaranteed wage period. The outflow curve is constructed on the basis of the duration of sickness benefits (first twelve months) and disability benefit outflows (from the thirteenth month onwards) for 2010.

Source: OECD calculations based on: Panel A: Data from the National Institute for Sickness and Invalidity Insurance; Panel B: Data provided by the Swedish Social Insurance Agency; and Panel C: The European survey of enterprises on new and emerging risks (ESENER) of the European Agency for Safety and Health at Work; https://osha.europa.eu/sub/esener/en.

StatLink http://dx.doi.org/10.1787/888933184192

Employer and employee seek joint workplace solution

The second broad strategy is to leverage the all-important employer-employee relationship and compel employers to address an employee's work problems at an early stage. To facilitate return-to-work an employer could, for example, work out a return-to-work plan jointly with the employee, and introduce concrete adjustments and a communications strategy in the workplace. Treating physicians and/or occupational doctors should be involved in this procedure as necessary.

The Netherlands, Norway, and Sweden have implemented a procedure which requires employer and employee to agree, within around eight weeks of sickness absence, to an action plan with different responsibilities incumbent on both sides (Factsheet 4.7; Factsheet 4.8; Factsheet 4.9). Such initiatives may be accompanied by guides and advice for employers, as in Denmark which recently published guidelines for managers on how to deal with workers on sick leave with a mental health problem.

A further example are the *Access to Work* grants in the United Kingdom for practical support to help people go back to, or stay in, work. People with mental health conditions may request the grant for work-related support (Factsheet 4.10). In Switzerland, employers often outsource casework to private insurance companies which work with the treating physician, employee and employer to draw up a back-to-work plan (Factsheet 4.11).

Fit notes versus sick notes

Changing sickness certification by requiring informative, capacity-oriented doctors' certificates is a third avenue. It is one that the United Kingdom has explored with the so-called "fit note" which it introduced in 2010. Physicians must focus on the work a patient can still do and describe in some detail what tasks he or she can reasonably perform and what workplace adjustments may be necessary (see Factsheet 3.7).

A similar trial in Switzerland tested so-called "expanded medical work incapacity certificates". Under this scheme, an employer sends the sick-listed employee's job description to the doctor and asks for an expanded certificate that describes in detail what he or she is capable of doing (see Factsheet 3.10). Denmark has done something similar with its new "fitness for work" assessment. It requires GPs to think about what patients can do and to describe the tasks and functions they can perform without worsening their condition. The Swedish Government, finally, has worked with medical associations to draw up diagnosis-specific sickness absence guidelines which, among other things, lay down the typical duration for a sick leave for a particular illness. They have been effective and welcomed by medical practitioners who feel to receive guidance (see Factsheet 3.8).

Early intervention for off-sick workers

A number of countries have developed early-intervention services to provide counselling and treatment referrals to sick-listed workers, usually with a case management approach. The Austrian Government, for example, came together with the social partners in 2013 to introduce *fit2work*, a programme of counselling services for supporting employees who have been sick for more than 40 days (Factsheet 4.12). The United Kingdom has trialled a similar programme in England, Wales, and Scotland. *Fit for Work* provides occupational assessments of employees and case-managed, multidisciplinary telephone advice to them in the first 4-12 weeks of sickness absence (Factsheet 4.13). However, neither in the Austrian nor in the British example the services have reached the target group of employees at an early stage of their sick leave – in most cases, only people on long-term absence or those already unemployed use the service.

Occupational doctors, professional certification

A fifth strategic course is to use the specialist knowledge of occupational physicians. The most prominent example is that of occupational doctors in the Netherlands, who are by law responsible for analysing workplace problems and producing return-to-work plans. Certifying sickness absence is exclusively their duty, not that of treating physicians. Certification is thus not complicated by the role conflict vis-à-vis patients that may affect a GP, though occupational physicians who work for and are answerable to an employer may experience a role conflict of a different nature.

Mental health competence of occupational doctors is generally limited, just like for GPs, and addressing mental-health-related work problems is a relatively new field. There are evidence-based guidelines in the Netherlands for occupational physicians on how to coach workers with mental health problems back to work, though doctors do not always adhere to them. A further point is that when occupational physicians also get involved in return-to-work, there has to be better collaboration, also with the treating doctor – something that is not always easy to achieve (Factsheet 4.14).

SMEs seldom have the resources to contract occupational health services. To address this issue, the United Kingdom introduced an occupational health advice service for small businesses which gives them "instant" access over the telephone to professional advice on all health conditions, particularly mental ill-health. The SMEs that have used the telephone service appear to have particularly appreciated it (Factsheet 4.15).

Key messages

Countries now widely acknowledge the importance of taking active measures to prevent unnecessary long-term sickness absence and stop workers with mental health problems from exiting the labour market. A number of governments have introduced promising policies to assertively promote early return-to-work. The stumbling block is the very low take-up and low compliance among the various actors – physicians, employers and employees.

Action to support an effective return-to-work management process should include:

- Putting in place fit-for-work counselling services to help sick-listed workers quickly.
- Promoting gradual return-to-work which can also help restore full work capacity.
- Strengthening the role of occupational physicians and occupational psychologists.

Incentives and obligations for employers to prevent and address sick leave

Several factors contribute to successfully preventing longer-term sick leave and managing return-to-work. Financial incentives and legal obligations for employers to actively follow up and support sick-listed employees play a crucial role.

Employer incentives are poorly developed

Incentives and obligations for employers are one factor that accounts for wide disparities between countries' sickness absence rates (Figure 4.5, Panel A). Absence rates are high in most Nordic countries where financial incentives for employers to actively manage long-term absences are limited. Companies have to provide sick pay only during the first two weeks of sickness absence – a minimal amount when it comes to sick-listed workers with mental illness who have an average absence rate that is around twice as high as that of workers with good mental health (Figure 4.5, Panel B).

There are further examples in other countries. In Switzerland, for example, although firms are required to provide sick pay for longer, the duration is related to the length of the employment contract (the same holds for the period in which dismissal is regarded as unfair in case of an illness). Employees with a mental health problem usually have shorter job tenures; this reduces an employer's obligation and incentive to actively do something about the absenteeism of workers with mental health conditions (Figure 4.5, Panel C).

Because employers and managers play a key role in the run-up to long-lasting sickness absences, during absences, and when employees return to work, they should be held accountable for the consequences. In other words, they have particular duties:

- It is their responsibility to settle workplace conflicts as they trigger many sickness absences.
- They should keep in regular contact with sick employees to shorten absences.
- They should adapt the workplace as possible to enable the sick employee to work, and co-operate in proper return-to-work procedures to increase the chances of job retention.
- They should co-operate and actively seek to communicate with sick employees' treating physicians and other relevant actors and authoritative parties.

Figure 4.5. **Employers have limited obligations for addressing the high rate of sickness absence among workers with mental ill-health**

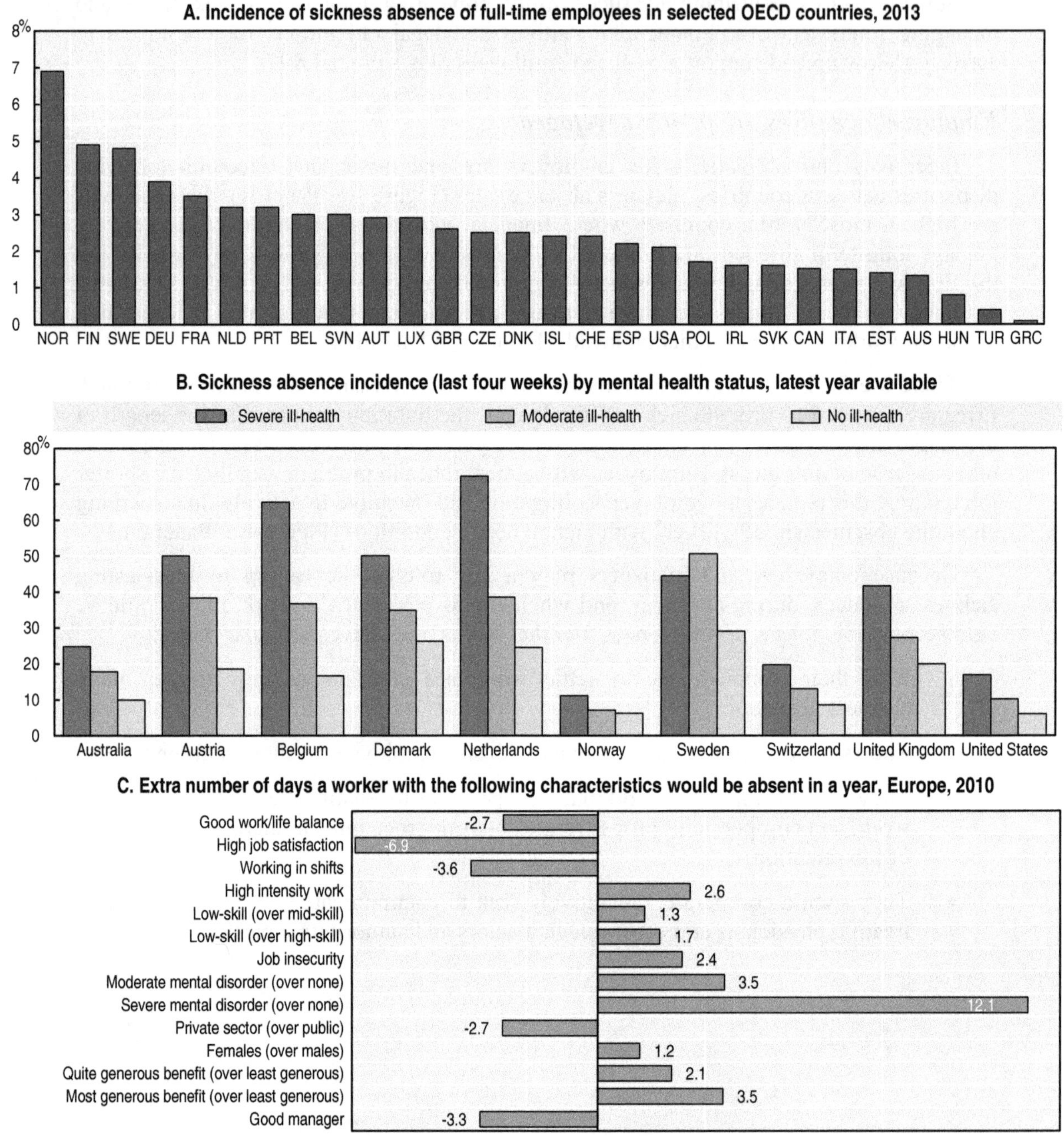

a. Absence is defined as follows: absence in the last four weeks for EU OECD countries, absence in the last two weeks in Australia (2004 instead of 2013) absence in the last week in Norway and absent for ten days or more in the last year in the United States (2012 instead of 2013).

Source: Panel A: European Labour Force Survey and national labour force surveys for Australia, Canada and the United States; Panel B: OECD calculations based on the Eurobarometer 2010 for Austria, Belgium, Denmark, the Netherlands, Sweden and the United Kingdom; National Health Survey 2011/12 for Australia, Swiss Health Survey 2010 for Switzerland and National Health Interview Survey 2008 for the United States; Panel C: OECD calculations based on European Working Conditions Survey 2010.

StatLink http://dx.doi.org/10.1787/888933184204

Better incentives for swift return-to-work management

There are indications that stiff employer obligations may help lower the incidence of sickness absence and foster job retention. The Netherlands has effectively reduced its rate of sickness absence with the stepwise introduction of the companies' obligation to provide sick pay for two years, actively draw up an action plan for ensuring a quick return-to-work, monitor sickness absences, record all actions taken, and adapt employees' tasks to their abilities (Factsheet 4.14).

There are also duties in the Netherlands incumbent on the sick-listed employee. He or she must see an occupational physician within the first six weeks of sickness absence, for example. Should employers and employees fail to agree on an action plan, they are liable to stiff sanctions. Employers who do not co-operate have to pay the worker's salary for a full third year. If it is employees, they may have their salary docked or stopped, be laid off, or have their disability benefits reduced later on.

Norway, Denmark, and Sweden have also ushered in duties for employers and employees to address actively and early workplace problems and return-to-work, hold meetings with caseworkers, develop action plans, and contact the treating physician (OECD, 2013b; OECD, 2013c; OECD, 2013d). Some countries, such as Sweden, also have strong statutory protection in place to prevent the dismissal of sick employees. However, in the Nordic countries these stronger obligations are not matched by corresponding financial incentives for either the employer or the worker.

Evidence across the countries reviewed by the OECD shows that regulations are fully effective only in combination with financial incentives and effective penalties for non-compliance; however, many of the reviewed countries do not enforce provisions for sanctions, particularly against sick employees (OECD, 2014a; OECD, 2013b), and their financial incentives are not deterrent enough. In Belgium, for example, administrative sanctions for employers who fail to conduct workplace risk analysis are lower than the cost of the analyses themselves (OECD, 2013d). Moreover, employers' sick-pay obligations are often short-lived and public sickness benefit for the employee is high relative to wages, so tempting employers and employees not to actively seek return-to-work solutions. This setup represents a moral hazard. Such shortcomings may explain in part why promising policies to beef up employer obligations have not yet achieved their full potential.

Key messages

Financial incentives for employers and employees to prevent long-term sickness absence are limited in many OECD countries. Only a few countries, especially the Netherlands, have gone further by giving employers a long-term responsibility for paying for sick leave and sanctioning them as well as employees when insufficient efforts have been undertaken to ensure return-to-work. In most countries, active return-to-work management is advocated for but not backed up with incentives or deterrents. Policies for return-to-work management therefore remain piecemeal and implementation often weak.

Strengthening employer incentives and obliging them to address the reasons for sick leave and foster return-to-work should include:

- Making employers responsible for developing and following up return-to-work plans for sick employees and monitoring the fulfilment of these plans.
- Compelling employers to be in contact with sick employees and where necessary also treating doctors to be able to adjust work.
- Extending employers' sick-pay obligations to spur them to action to prevent sickness absence and support returns to work.

REFERENCES

Arends, I., J. van der Klink, W. van Rhenen, M. de Boer, and U. Bültmann (2014), "Predictors of Recurrent Sickness Absence Among Workers Having Returned to Work After Sickness Absence Due to Common Mental Disorders", *Scandinavian Journal of Work, Environment and Health*, 40(2), pp.195-202

Baer, N. (2007), "Würden Sie einen psychisch behinderten Menschen anstellen?" [Would you hire a person with a psychiatric disability?], *Zeitschrift für Sozialhilfe*, Vol. 1/2007, pp. 32-33.

Baer, N., U. Frick, T. Fasel and W. Wiedermann (2011), "'Schwierige' Mitarbeiter: Wahrnehmung und Bewältigung Psychisch Bedingter Problemsituationen durch Vorgesetzte und Personalverantwortliche – eine Pilotstudie in Basel-Stadt und Basel-Landschaft" ["Difficult" Employees: Perception And Management of Psychological Related Problem Situations by Managers and HR Managers – A Pilot Study in Basel-Stadt and Basel-Landschaft], *FoP-IV Forschungsbericht*, No. 1/11, Bundesamt für Sozialversicherungen, Bern.

Borill, J. (2011), "Mental Health First Aid England and North East Mental Health Development Unit partnership project", Evaluation March 2011, NHS.

Brohan, E., C. Henderson, K. Wheat, E. Malcolm, S. Clement, E. Barley, M. Slade and G. Thornicroft (2012), "Systematic Review of Beliefs, Behaviours and Influencing Factors Associated with Disclosure of a Mental Health Problem in the Workplace", *BMC Psychiatry*, Vol. 12, No. 11, http://dx.doi.org/10.1186/1471-244X-12-11.

Clement, S., F. Lassmann, E. Barley, S. Evans-Lacko, P. Williams, S. Yamaguchi, M. Slade, N. Rüsch and G. Thornicroft (2013), "Mass Media Interventions for Reducing Mental Health-related Stigma, The Cochrane Collaboration", The Cochrane Library, http://onlinelibrary.wiley.com/doi/10.1002/14651858.CD009453.pub2/pdf.

Corrigan, P. and J. Shapiro (2010), "Measuring the Impact of Programs that Challenge the Public Stigma of Mental Illness", *Clinical Psychology Review*, Vol. 30, No. 8, pp. 907-922.

Corrigan, P. et al. (2014), "Listen to These Lessons", *Canadian Journal of Psychiatry*, Vol. 59, No. 10 (Suppl. 1), pp. S6-7.

Henderson, C., P. Williams, K. Little and G. Thornicroft (2013), "Mental Health Problems in the Workplace: Changes in Employers' Knowledge, Attitudes and Practices in England 2006-2010", *British Journal of Psychiatry*, Vol. 202 (Suppl. 55), pp. S70-S76.

Hogarth, T., C. Hasluck, L. Gambin, H. Behle, Y. Li and C. Lyonette (2013), "Evaluation of Employment Advisers in the Improving Access to Psychological Therapies programme", *DWP Research Report*, Vol. 826, London.

Knapp, M., D. McDaid and M. Parsonage(eds) (2011), "Mental Health Promotion and Mental Illness Prevention: The Economics Case", Department of Health, London.

Malachowski, C. and B. Kirsh (2013), "Workplace Anti-stigma Initiatives: A Scoping Study", *Psychiatric Services*, Vol. 64, pp. 694-702.

OECD (forthcoming 2015), *Mental Health and Work: Austria*, OECD Publishing, Paris.

OECD (2014a), *Mental Health and Work: Switzerland*, OECD Publishing, Paris, http://dx.doi.org/10.1787/9789264204973-en.

OECD (2014b), *Mental Health and Work: United Kingdom*, OECD Publishing, Paris, http://dx.doi.org/10.1787/9789264204997-en.

OECD (2013a), *Mental Health and Work: Belgium*, OECD Publishing, Paris. http://dx.doi.org/10.1787/9789264187566-en.

OECD (2013b), *Mental Health and Work: Norway*, OECD Publishing, Paris, http://dx/doi/org/10.1787/9789264178984-en.

OECD (2013c), *Mental Health and Work: Denmark*, OECD Publishing, Paris, http://dx/doi/org/10.1787/9789264188631-en.

OECD (2013d), *Mental Health and Work: Sweden*, OECD Publishing, Paris, http://dx.doi.org/10.1787/9789264188730-en.

OECD (2012), *Sick on the Job? Myths and Realities about Mental Health and Work*, OECD Publishing, Paris, http://dx.doi.org/10.1787/9789264124523-en.

Rosholm, M. and A.L. Andersen (2010), "The Effect of Changing Mental Health on Unemployment Duration and Destination States after Unemployment", Social Science Research Network, available at http://ssrn.com/abstract=1672026.

Spectra (2011), "The Position of Occupational Medicine in Enterprises. A Survey Commissioned by the Austrian Academy for Occupational Medicine", www.aam.at/downloads/image_arbeitsmedizin-report_unternehmen.pdf.

Stansfeld, S. and B. Candy (2006), "Psychoscial Work Environment and Mental Health – A Meta-analytic Review", *Scandinavian Journal of Work and Health*, Vol. 32, Special Issue No. 6, pp. 443-462.

Stuart, H. (2006), "Fighting Stigma and Discrimination is Fighting for Mental Health", *Canadian Public Policy*, Vol.31, pp. 21-28.

Szeto, A. and K. Dobson (2010), "Reducing the Stigma of Mental Disorders at Work: A Review of Current Workplace Anti-stigma Intervention Programs", *Applied and Preventive Psychology*, Vol. 14, pp. 41-56.

Thomsen, L.B. and J. Høgelund (2011), "Handicap og beskaeftigelse. Udviklingen mellem 2002 og 2010", *Report No. 11:08*, Danish National Institute for Social Research, Copenhagen.

Thornicroft , G., D. Rose, A. Kassam and N. Sartorius (2007), "Stigma: Ignorance, Prejudice or Discrimination?", *British Journal of Psychiatry*, Vol. 190, pp. 192-193.

Wang, P., G. Simon, J. Avorn et al. (2007), "Telephone Screening, Outreach and Care Management for Depressed Workers and Impact on Clinical and Work Productivity Outcomes: A Randomised Controlled Trial", *Journal of the American Medical Association*, Vol. 298, No. 12, pp. 1401-1411.

FACTSHEETS 4.1 to 4.15

Factsheet 4.1
Denmark: Assessing and monitoring the psychosocial work environment

Context

While psychosocial demands in the workplace have increased in recent decades, workplace risk assessment has not always kept pace. There is a need for stronger legislation on psychosocial risk assessment and better monitoring and support when problems have been identified. Workplace-specific tools can help to improve the psychosocial work environment.

Programme

Workplace health and safety in Denmark is regulated in the Working Environment Act, addressed through agreements between the social partners but overlooked by the Working Environment Authority (WEA). Legal provisions require employers to manage psychosocial work environment (PWE) risks in the workplace. Since 2007, the WEA has been responsible for inspecting the PWE in all enterprises. It is a big shift from the more traditional health and safety focus of the WEA and has prompted it to develop an inspection strategy.

Based on Danish research findings, the WEA has developed 24 sector- and job-specific guidance tools. Each guidance tool describes the prevalence of risk factors and the potential resources of a company to prevent problems – the aim being for each company to seek a balance between risks and prevention resources. The tool also describes the possible organisational consequences of an imbalance between risks and resources, such as bad reputation, loss of commitment, long delays, complaints from customers, high turnover rates, or long-term sickness absence rates.

WEA inspectors have been trained in how to use the guidance tools and how to assess and evaluate the PWE health and safety risks. The job of inspecting PWE risks has been facilitated through method descriptions and instructions, by templates on how to prepare improvement notices (in case improvements are needed), and through the sharing of best-practice examples. In each of the four regional WEA inspection centres, a task force has been established. The task forces comprise between six and eight highly skilled PWE inspectors who assist other inspectors in assessing PWE problems, preparing improvement notices, and giving guidance to enterprises that have received an improvement notice.

Outcomes

A full impact assessment of the WEA strategy and the guidance tools has not yet been carried out. However, preliminary results from focus group interviews with inspectors suggest that the guidance tools are used widely before, during, and after inspections and that employers consider them very useful. Although the number of improvement notices in relation to PWE problems has increased, they still comprise only 5% of all notices issued by the WEA in relation to health and safety aspects.

Further reading

OECD (2013), *Mental Health and Work: Denmark*, OECD Publishing, Paris, http://dx/doi/org/10.1787/9789264188631-en.

Senior Labour Inspectors Committee (2008), Report on the Evaluation of the Danish Working Environment Authority in 2008, Copenhagen.

Factsheet 4.2
Belgium: Services for prevention and protection at work

Context

Policies to prevent work-related stress are critical. At the same time, employees with mental disorders need adequate support to prevent long-term sickness absence. Similarly, employers need support to create a psychologically healthy work climate and help workers with mental ill-health to retain their job or resume work as quickly as possible.

Programme

In Belgium, employers are legally obliged to take all necessary preventive measures to preserve the well-being of their employees. Belgian legislation gives explicit instructions on how to deal with the mental health requirements mandated by law. All employers must carry out risk assessments to identify situations and risk factors at the workplace that can generate psychosocial distress. On the basis of such an assessment, the employer must draw up a five-year global prevention plan and an annual action plan to avoid psychosocial distress at work and limit its consequences. The risk analyses and prevention and action plans are conducted in collaboration with a team of prevention advisors and employee representatives.

Employers have to appoint a psychosocial prevention advisor to assist them in implementing the risk prevention policy. For companies with up to 50 employees, the prevention advisor must be from an external provider to avoid conflicts of interest. These external services employ both occupational doctors and prevention advisors who are specialised in one or more of the following five fields: safety at work, occupational medicine, ergonomics, occupational hygiene, and psychosocial aspects of work.

It is strongly recommended but not obligatory for an employer to appoint an internal confidential counsellor who is thoroughly familiar with the company's in-house workings.

Outcomes

An evaluation has revealed that the practical implementation of the legislation on well-being at work remains deficient. First, employers seldom carry out psychosocial risk analyses, chiefly because of the high cost involved and the resistance of employers who fear a negative analysis and the implications it may have on the organisation of work. Second, many employers are not aware of their legal obligations and the importance and advantages of prevention policies. Third, on the side of the employees, there is a lack of awareness of the role and existence of the psychosocial prevention advisors and confidential counsellors. Finally, prevention advisors have little to no time for the prevention of psychosocial risks in the workplace as they are fully occupied with individual complaints of harassment at work. They are not always trained to execute the wide range of possible risk assessments and prevention programmes, and are seldom familiar with the workplace. Because of the lack of financial incentives for employers to adapt the work and workplace, some are unwilling to co-operate, which discourages occupational health specialists from specialising in the field psychosocial risk prevention – less than 5% of prevention advisors are specialised in this field.

Further reading

OECD (2013), *Mental Health and Work: Belgium*, OECD Publishing, Paris, http://dx.doi.org/10.1787/9789264187566-en.

Service public fédéral Emploi, Travail et Concertation sociale (2011), Évaluation de la législation relative à la prévention de la charge psychosociale occasionnée par le travail, dont la violence et le harcèlement moral ou sexuel au travail, Brussels.

Factsheet 4.3
Norway: Supporting employers through specialised work advisors

Context

Many OECD countries have developed psychosocial risk prevention regulations in order to prevent mental health-related problems in the workplace. Specialised work advisors who can support employers is one way of dealing with psychosocial risks at work.

Programme

In order to support employers at an early stage in dealing with health-related problems in the workplace, the Norwegian Labour and Welfare Administration has implemented inclusive workplace support centres for employers in each of its 19 counties. The centres are based on the Working Environment Act, which promotes a healthy working environment, and the tripartite Inclusive Workplace Agreement, which seeks to reduce sickness absence and increase reintegration. The centres provide not only support for health promotion and sick-leave prevention, but also support for employers who have signed an IW-agreement.

One of the policy objectives is to motivate human resource staff in enterprises to engage more in health promotion. The centres have a strong information- and awareness-related approach, seeking to educate employers about the stigma that attaches to mental ill-health and to inform them about the professional support systems available for people with poor mental health. Recently, the centres have started a very promising trial scheme for providing advisors on work and mental health issues. It has now been extended to seven counties. Employers may also contact advisors directly in concrete problem situations for advice on possible work adjustments, for example.

Outcomes

Employer support centres provide a good structure for systematically offering early, highly competent interventions in the workplace. They have already built numerous contacts with employers which could be expanded, deepened, and made more systematic. Most of the services provided by the employer support centres have so far been in education and raising awareness. Although thousands of enterprises have been given courses and information about mental ill-health in the workplace, support for work-related problems does not yet seem to have received sufficient attention. If the centres are to deliver their full potential, they should i) be accessible to all employers; ii) be multidisciplinary and include mental health professionals; iii) collaborate with mental health specialists (e.g. psychiatrists) or care institutions and; iv) focus on employer counselling instead of awareness campaigns.

Further reading

OECD (2013), *Mental Health and Work: Norway*, OECD Publishing, Paris, http://dx/doi/org/10.1787/9789264178984-en.

Factsheet 4.4
Austria: Employer obligations to evaluate psychological work strain

Context

Preventing mental-health-related problems in the workplace is crucial to preventing long spells of sick and labour market drop-out. Obliging employers to evaluate work strain and involve occupational psychology is one promising way to address the issue.

Programme

The new Austrian Labour Protection Act came into force in January 2013. The act obliges employers to evaluate psychological strain in the workplace, implement specific measures in the event of problems, and evaluate the effectiveness of such measures. The new act's predecessor already compelled employers to comprehensively protect the health of their employees, which implicitly included mental health problems. The new act ushers in some important changes.

First, it identifies psychological strain (*e.g.* lack of social support or feedback from line managers, unclear or conflicting work targets, job monotony) as a risk factor. Second, it defines health as physical and mental. Third, it requires employers not only to secure a healthy work environment, but to actively evaluate whether there is psychological strain in their enterprise. Such evaluations should be carried out systematically, with a steering committee involving employee representatives and using standardised screening instruments or questionnaires. Fourth, the workplace evaluation must have a preventive focus – in other words, evaluate work tasks and how they are organised, the working environment, and operational procedures. Fifth, the act requires a workplace evaluation in the event of incidents with significantly elevated psychological strain. Sixth, occupational psychologists are explicitly included as qualified professionals (in addition to chemists, toxicologists, or ergonomists) who may be mandated to conduct evaluations as well as providing acknowledged preventive services.

Outcomes

The explicit recognition of psychosocial risks and the inclusion of occupational psychologists as professionals who can be mandated to evaluate workplace risks and develop suitable measures is promising. Although no evaluation is yet available, the role of occupational psychologists is still not wide-reaching enough. They are not acknowledged as preventive professionals and can be mandated only for up to 25% of the total time enterprises are obliged to engage occupational health and safety specialists every year. Moreover, the increased involvement of occupational psychologists intended by the new Labour Protection Act may not materialise because it is only voluntary for employers to work with them.

Further reading

OECD (forthcoming 2015), *Mental Health and Work: Austria*, OECD Publishing, Paris.

Factsheet 4.5
United States: Employee Assistance Programs to address productivity

Context

Although most people who suffer from mental ill-health have a job, they frequently show reduced productivity and greater sickness absence. Employers play a key role in securing good working conditions, addressing mental ill-health issues among their employees, and minimising productivity losses.

Programme

Employee Assistance Programs (EAPs) offer confidential, short-term counselling services for employees with personal problems that affect their work performance, whether or not those problems originate in the workplace. EAP services to individuals and their family include services and referrals related to mental health, drugs, alcohol and personal issues, such as divorce and parenting problems; wellness and health promotion; and work-related supports such as career counselling. EAPs also provide support to line managers, which may take the form of education on handling mental health, stress and addictions in the workplace, for example, or managing absence.

Outcomes

EAPs are free of charge for employees and their family members as they are pre-paid by the employers, and are typically available 24 hours a day. In the United States, EAPs are mandatory for federal agencies, while coverage in the private sector is around 65% among companies with more than 100 employees. EAPs are often offered by external providers.

EAPs have been shown to contribute to decreased absenteeism, greater employee retention, and significantly reduced medical costs through early identification and treatment of mental health issues. The programme has been criticized for its lack of impartiality in cases where an employee seeks assistance in work-related issues.

Further reading

Hargrave, G. et al. (2008), "EAP Treatment Impact on Presenteeism and Absenteeism: Implications for Return on Investment", *Journal of Workplace Behavioral Health*, Vol. 23, No. 3, pp. 283-293.

Lam, R. et al. (2012), "The Prevalence and Impact of Depression in Self-Referred Clients Attending an Employee Assistance Program", *Journal of Occupational and Environmental Medicine*, Vol. 54, No. 11, pp. 1395-1399.

ODEP (2009), *Employee Assistance Programs for a New Generation of Employees*, Office of Disability Employment Policy, U.S. Department of Labor, Washington, DC.

Factsheet 4.6
Denmark: Flexible wage subsidies for people with partial work capacity

Context

OECD countries have developed different strategies for supporting the return-to-work of workers with reduced work capacity. One example is to allow workers to work fewer hours at lower productivity levels, but to receive full wages through subsidies for employers.

Programme

The Danish "flexjob" scheme is a wage subsidy scheme targeted at people with reduced work capacity who are unable to work in the regular labour market but not incapacitated enough to be entitled to a disability benefit. The scheme was not originally created for people with mental health conditions and formally only some 15% of all flexjob users are registered as mental ill. The flexjob scheme has potential for people with poor mental health because it allows employees to be paid in full for working fewer hours with lower productivity and the employer to pay only for effective output.

A reform in 2013 addressed several weaknesses in the system: i) the gradual shift towards a higher subsidy; ii) the high share (around 50%) of flexjobs that employers assigned to employees in the company because they are allowed to convert existing positions into flexjobs; iii) the dominance of public municipal flexjobs; and iv) the frequent move to a flexjob on expiry of a sickness benefit entitlement. Moreover, the dead-end character of flexjobs has turned into a substantial financial problem, because the system has spread fast to include many people who used to work in unsubsidised jobs. The reform aims to eliminate these major flaws.

Outcomes

Very little is known about the use of flexjobs by people with mental health complaints. Many of the changes to the flexjob scheme will probably be especially helpful for clients with poor mental health who are among the most disadvantaged. The new system is temporary in principle, far more flexible in terms of hours and changes over time, and has a stronger focus on activating and reintegrating those eligible for a flexjob.

Since reform, the number of flexjob subsidies has continued to increase. The preliminary assessment of the reform says that it has been successful in several ways. There is a significantly higher percentage of flexjob users with mental health problems in the scheme, and the share of flexjobs in private companies is also considerably higher. At the same time, the number of people waiting to be placed in a flexjob and receiving a so-called "waiting allowance" has been noticeably reduced.

Further reading

OECD (2013), *Mental Health and Work: Denmark,* OECD Publishing, Paris, http://dx/doi/org/10.1787/9789264188631-en.

Factsheet 4.7
Netherlands: Strong financial incentives for employers and workers

Context

Sickness absence rates are high among workers who suffer from mental ill-health. For such workers, early sickness management and return-to-work policies are crucial in preventing long-term absence, disability, and labour market exits. Employer incentives to invest in sickness management can improve the labour market inclusion of those with poor mental health.

Programme

In the Netherlands, several policy changes have been introduced to compel employers (and workers) to face up to their responsibility in sickness matters. In particular, the Reduced Absenteeism Act (1994), the 2004 extension of the 1996 Wage Payment during Sickness Act, and the Gatekeeper Improvement Act (2002), have all contributed to significant improvements in sickness management.

When a worker becomes sick, the employer is obliged to continue paying 70%-100% of his or her salary for two years during which the worker is protected by law against lay-off. Moreover, employers are required to hire a case manager to oversee the return-to-work process. Within six weeks of going off sick, employees must visit an occupational physician who is paid by the employer. Within eight weeks, employer and employee are obliged to agree on an action plan, which spells out the responsibilities of both sides in ensuring a quick return to work. The employer is responsible for monitoring the return-to-work process every six weeks and for recording all actions undertaken – something often done by the return-to-work case manager. Both employer and employee may be penalised for not collaborating in the return-to-work process, which is assessed by the Employee Insurance Agency after two years of sickness absence.

If an employer cannot adjust a job to enable a sick worker to return to work, both are obliged to look for suitable work for the worker in another company. Occupational health services, reintegration offices, and employer branch organisations can facilitate the new job search. Some companies have a social worker, in addition to the return-to-work case manager, who provides support – such as work conflict mediation – in dealing with psychosocial problems that impact on work.

Outcomes

The sickness absence rate in the Netherlands has fallen sharply in the past 15 years and is now close to the OECD average. Yet it remains high among people suffering from mental ill-health. Moreover, not all employers live up to their responsibilities in return-to-work management. For example, every second employer has no guideline on when to contact an occupational physician in case of sickness absence. Employer sanctions are frequent: in one in five sickness absences longer than two years employers fail to meet their obligations.

Further reading

Jong, P. de, T. Everhardt and C. Schrijvershof (2011), *Toepassing van de wet Verbetering Poortwachter* [Application of the Gatekeeper Improvement Act], APE, Den Haag.

Koopmans, P., C. Roelen, and J. Groothoff (2008),"Frequent and Long-term Absence as a Risk Factor for Work Disability and Job Termination Among Employees in the Private Sector", *Occupational and Environmental Medicine*, Vol. 65, pp. 494-499.

OECD (2014), *Mental Health and Work: Netherlands*, OECD Publishing, Paris, http://dx.doi.org/10.1787/9789264223301-en.

Factsheet 4.8
Norway: A tripartite agreement to improve sick-leave outcomes

Context

Both employers and employees are responsible for active return-to-work management. Employers can contribute to the process by addressing work problems at an early stage and facilitating working conditions for employees with special needs.

Programme

In 2001, the Norwegian Government and the social partners signed an inclusive tripartite workplace agreement (IWA). It has been renewed several times so far, with the latest agreement being valid until 2018. The IWA seeks to: i) reduce sickness absence by at least 20% compared to 2001; ii) increase work participation among people with disabilities; and iii) raise the effective retirement age. In 2013, the agreement covered around 25% of all Norwegian enterprises and around 60% of all employees.

Signing up to the IWA requires enterprises to support its goals. In return, they benefit from the services of a liaison officer at the Norwegian Labour and Welfare Administration and special (possibly financial) support in preventing sickness absence and making workplace adjustments. IWA firms also have additional obligations: i) ensure a good working environment; ii) facilitate working conditions for special needs employees; iii) systematically prepare sick-leave statistics; and iv) seek and facilitate dialogue with sick-listed employees.

Outcomes

The tripartite structure provides a sustainable basis for initiating and implementing new policies and measures, and gives the social partners new responsibilities. It is particularly important, as the financial incentives for employers to increase job retention and avoid long-term absences are weak in Norway. The overall achievements from 2001 to 2014 concerning the three sub goals are:

i) Sickness absence was reduced by 12%;

ii) The employment rate of disabled persons remained almost constant (43%), but the incidence and prevalence of disability pensioners stagnated;

iii) The employment of persons 50 years and older increased by 18% (1½ years).

There are small differences between IW-enterprises and non-IW-enterprises when it comes to achievements and outcomes. Evaluations so far hardly seem to find direct causal effects from specific "IW-measures" on the outcomes. Nevertheless, more use of graded sick-leave seems to have a positive effect.

Further reading

Foss, L. et al. (2013), "Inclusive Working Life in Norway: A Registry-based Five-year Follow-up Study", *Journal of Occupational Medicine and Toxicology*, Vol. 8, No. 19, www.occup-med.com/content/8/1/19.

OECD (2013), *Mental Health and Work: Norway*, OECD Publishing, Paris, http://dx/doi/org/10.1787/9789264178984-en.

Factsheet 4.9
Sweden: Stricter sick-leave policy to prevent long-term absence

Context

Sickness absence rates are relatively high among workers with mental health problems. Early intervention and support for those on sickness benefits due to mental illness is crucial in preventing long-term sickness absence, disability, and early labour market exit.

Programme

Since 2003, Sweden has undertaken a series of reforms to address the long-term structural problems in its sickness and disability policies. The new sick-leave process provides incentives for a more active procedure and aims to prevent long periods of sick leave and ensuing permanent exclusion from the workplace. The main feature is a much stricter timeline for work-capacity assessment at different stages. It is first assessed in relation to the sick employee's own job, then – within no more than three months – in relation to other positions with the same employer and, last, after six months in relation to the regular labour market as a whole in order to facilitate early return-to-work.

Moreover, sickness benefit periods have been reduced to a maximum of 364 days within a time frame of 450, although payment can be extended to 914 days under certain conditions. This is in contrast to previous practice in which there was no limit on the number of days over which employees were entitled to sickness benefit. Sweden has also introduced an earned income tax credit (EITC) to strengthen the incentive to stay in work.

Outcomes

The extensive structural reforms to the sickness and disability system have been successful in tackling the large numbers of sickness and disability recipients. Long-term sick leave of more than one year initially fell by 80% from its peak in 2003, although it has increased again recently. The number of new disability benefit claims also fell by 80% during the decade after 2003.

It is argued that the EITC may have had a substantial impact on lengths of sickness absences. As employees on sick leave are not entitled to the credit, it entails an increase in income from work relative to compensation for sick leave. It is estimated that the EITC may have shortened average sick leave by around three days, or 7%.

The paradigm shift in sickness and disability policy towards early activation over this period is an example to be emulated by other OECD countries. However, whether reforms have been equally effective for people who suffer from mental ill-health merits further attention.

Further reading

Hartman, L. (2011), Swedish Policies for the Disabled. What Do We Know About the Effects?, Department of Economics, Uppsala University.

OECD (2013), *Mental Health and Work: Sweden*, OECD Publishing, Paris, http://dx.doi.org/10.1787/9789264188730-en.

Factsheet 4.10
United Kingdom: Access to work scheme offers practical work support

Context

Early intervention and support for workers on sickness benefits due to health problems is crucial in preventing long-term sickness absence, disability and early labour market exit. Although work-related changes may be essential in enabling return to work, employers do not always have the resources to make those changes.

Programme

Access to Work is a government-run scheme that targets workers and the self-employed with a disability or a health condition that will last for at least 12 months. The scheme provides flexible grants to workers and their employers for practical work support, typically for specialist equipment or transport to the workplace.

In 2011, Access to Work was also redesigned to include support for people experiencing depression, anxiety, stress, and other mental health issues affecting their work. The support offered may include: i) assessment of individual needs to identify coping strategies; ii) work-focused mental health support for six months, tailored to identified needs; iii) a personalised support plan, detailing the steps needed to remain in, or return to, work; iv) suggestions for adjustments in the workplace, or in work practices, that could help individuals fulfil their role; and v) advice and guidance for employers on how they can support employees with mental health problems. The modifications to Access to Work mark a significant step in recognising and responding to the specific needs of individuals with mental health problems.

Outcomes

Take-up by people with mental health problems has been very low. In 2012, only 3% of participants in the programme cited mental health problems as their primary disability. Another criticism levelled at the programme is that few employers are aware of it. To address low take-up and awareness, the government announced an extra GBP 15 million for the programme and launched a 12-month targeted marketing campaign to raise awareness of the scheme amongst under-represented groups and employers. The measures are welcome as Access to Work could be a major boost in support for employees struggling with mental ill-health in the workplace. However, it will be important to monitor the impact of the measures on take-up and further invest in the scheme if individuals with mental health conditions continue to be underrepresented.

Further reading

Gifford, G. (2013), *Access to Work: Official Statistics*, Department for Work and Pensions, London.

OECD (2013), *Mental Health and Work: United Kingdom*, OECD Publishing, Paris, http://dx.doi.org/10.1787/9789264204997-en.

Work and Pensions Committee (2009), *The Equality Bill: How Disability Equality Fits Within a Single Equality Act*, Third Report.

Factsheet 4.11
Switzerland: Individual case management by private health and daily allowance insurers

Context

In order to prevent long-term sickness absence, employers should be encouraged to address an employee's work problems at an early stage. They should ideally do so in collaboration with treating physicians, occupational doctors, or return-to-work case managers.

Programme

In Switzerland, most private health and daily allowance insurers have implemented a range of prevention measures (such as health promotion, risk assessment, and absence management systems in enterprises) and reintegration services (case management in particular). Sickness-related case management starts early, often after around 30 days of sickness absence, depending on the contract between the enterprise and the insurance. The case manager assesses whether case management might be useful for a reported sickness absence – for mental ill-health it is often assumed to be so. He or she then contacts: i) the treating physician for information about the health-related work incapacities; ii) the employer; and iii) the employee to discuss the situation and support the return-to-work process.

Case managers are usually non-specialists with, for example, a human resources management background and substantial professional experience. They have a key role in sampling the information gathered from the different actors and in establishing a co-ordinated return-to-work plan. In the event of possibly long-term sickness absence and/or severe mental health problems, the case manager often also contacts the invalidity insurance provider – in principle, after one month of sick leave. The case manager normally has an established relationship with the insured enterprise.

Outcomes

The outcomes of case management provided by insurers have not been evaluated so far. Practice shows, however, that clients suffering from a mental health problem are not only increasing sharply in number. They are also especially challenging for case managers, who are seldom familiar with mental disorders. A further difficulty that case managers face is their often problematic relationship with treating physicians. In response, the Swiss association of private insurance companies and the federal association of treating psychiatrists very recently drafted a letter of agreement which should give guidelines to case managers and psychiatrists on how to collaborate.

Further reading

OECD (2014), *Mental Health and Work: Switzerland*, OECD Publishing, Paris, http://dx.doi.org/10.1787/9789264204973-en.

Factsheet 4.12
Austria: One-stop shop to tackle longer-term sickness absence

Context

An active return-to-work management process is crucial for workers with a mental illness who often face long-term absences. Many OECD countries have developed strategies to support the return-to-work process through, for example, early-intervention services that provide initial counselling and timely referrals for treatment for sick-listed workers who need further care.

Programme

Sickness absence due to mental health problems has steadily increased in Austria (albeit from a very low level). Austria is among the OECD countries where the relatively fewest firms routinely analyse causes of sick leave and take measures to follow up on employees on long-term sick leave. This creates a special problem for sickness absences related to poor mental health and which are often long term. Sickness absences in Austria follow an all-or-nothing principle: the lack of a gradual return-to-work process is a barrier to sick employees resuming employment.

In order to provide greater return-to-work support for people on long-term sick leave, the Austrian Government – together with the social partners and social insurance providers – has initiated a new low-threshold information, counselling and support service for sick-listed employees and jobseekers as well as enterprises. The new "Fit2work" service, fully implemented in 2013, seeks to avert job losses and long-term unemployment. Health insurance contacts sick-listed employees after around 40 days of absence, offering general information (on possible treatment, for example) and – if necessary – counselling and return-to-work support, provided by a network of counselling firms. Psychotherapy is not provided but access to psychotherapists is facilitated in the event of mental health problems.

Outcomes

Initial evaluations show that only around one-quarter of all sick-listed people who were contacted and given information, considered to be counselled by a Fit2work service provider. Of all workers who had been on sick leave for more than 40 days and were contacted by the health insurers, only about 10% responded. To date, the Fit2work service has been used chiefly for workers and jobseekers suffering from mental disorders.

Fit2work's rationale of increasing sick workers' job retention and reintegrating unemployed people with health problems is valuable in view of Austria's weak focus on sickness absence. A number of critiques may nevertheless be made: i) Fit2work does not link with the health system; ii) it chiefly provides general information instead of direct and workplace-focused counselling, which is often needed more urgently; iii) employers are also a Fit2work target group, yet it has not reached out to them yet; and iv) counselled employees generally do not want any contact between the Fit2work service and their treating physician.

Further reading

Egger-Subotitsch, A. and M. Stark (2013), *Fit2work Implementierungsevaluierung, Bericht II* [Evaluation of the implementation of fit2work], Bundessozialamt, Vienna.

OECD (forthcoming 2015), *Mental Health and Work: Austria*, OECD Publishing, Paris.

Factsheet 4.13
United Kingdom: Fit for work services offering support to sick employees

Context

Sickness absence rates are relatively high among workers with mental health problems. Early intervention and support for those on sickness benefit due to a mental disorder are crucial in preventing long-term sickness absence, disability and early labour market exit. Return-to-work case management support has proven to be a successful approach.

Programme

The Fit for Work Service (FFWS) was piloted in several regions in the United Kingdom from April 2010 to March 2013. Its chief aim was to provide personalised back-to-work support for people in the early stages of sickness absence (4 to12 weeks of absence) and reduce the drift into welfare benefits.

The pilots brought together health, employment and local community organisations and offered biopsychosocial assessments of need and case-managed support to aid quick return-to-work. The service targeted people in work with a health condition, including those on sick leave and those at risk of sickness absence. Case managers offered support with goal setting, progress monitoring, confidence-building, motivation, and other forms of assistance. Individuals could access FFWS either by being referred by their general practitioner (GP) or other health service providers, or by contacting the pilot themselves after seeing the publicity or being told about it by their GP or employer.

Outcomes

Over the first year, take-up was significantly lower than expected. In addition, nearly all FFWS clients were employed, with only one-third on sick leave, even though they were the original policy target group. Among the clients on sick leave, fewer than 30% had been off work for 4-12 weeks. In most pilots, mental health conditions were the most commonly reported condition and many clients had more than one health condition. Those with a musculoskeletal disorder, for example, also widely suffered from common stress, depression, or anxiety-related mental health conditions. The average length of time people stayed with the service was four months. Most respondents said they would not have benefited from interventions had it not been for the support of the FFWS.

All services had difficulties securing the volume of referrals expected from GPs and from small businesses. Some pilots specifically sought to engage with employers, using a range of marketing and awareness-raising activities. As with GPs, direct approaches – such as tele-marketing and targeting specific employers – appeared to work best, but most had trouble sparking interest among smaller businesses.

The full Fit for Work Service, implemented in 2014, builds upon the pilot schemes. The new service will provide a work-focused biopsychosocial assessment to employees earlier in sickness absence – from around four weeks of absence onwards. It also offers advice to employers and employees on needs for rehabilitation and return-to-work support for both workers on sick leave and those still at work. It will thus continue the role previously played by the Occupational Health Advice Services (see Factsheet 4.15).

Further reading

Hillage, J. et al. (2012), "Evaluation of the Fit for Work Service Pilots: First Year Report", *DWP Research Report*, No. 792, London

OECD (2013), *Mental Health and Work: United Kingdom*, OECD Publishing, Paris, http://dx.doi.org/10.1787/9789264204997-en.

Factsheet 4.14
Netherlands: Occupational physicians in every company

Context

Integrating occupational health knowledge into the workplace is of paramount importance in the light of research findings that i) good health improves employment outcomes and ii) work contributes to good health. One way to bring occupational health expertise into companies is by ensuring they all have an occupational health professional available to them.

Programme

In the Netherlands, occupational physicians (OPs) are very much a part of company life, as the law obliges employers to consult an OP in sickness management. Most OPs are employed by occupational health services, but they can also work independently. One of OPs' most important functions is to carry out problem analyses and provide advice in the form of a reintegration action plan within six weeks of an employee calling in sick. The OP is also responsible for writing a reintegration report for the employee insurance agency after the 90th week of sickness absence (before the worker can file a disability benefit claim).

Outcomes

A national survey among employers showed that 81% have arranged for an OP to support sickness management. A comparable survey among employees showed that only 64% are aware that they can consult an OP. However, 35% had seen an OP because of their health at some point during their working life – a large minority given that sickness absence rates range between 2% and 6% in most Dutch companies.

An important drawback is that OPs are funded by employers, prompting questions over their neutrality. Research among 541 OPs showed that 21% of them were not able to conduct their work independently due to interference by employers and 52% thought workers did not trust their formally neutral position. Among 220 surveyed workers, 29% felt the OP defended the employers' interests rather than the employees'.

Further reading

de Zwart, B., R. Prins and J. Van der Gulden (2011), Onderzoek naar de positie van de bedrijfsarts: Eindrapport, Astri Beleidsonderzoek- en advies, Leiden.

Koppes, L. et al. (2013), Nationale enquête arbeidsomstandigheden 2012. Methodologie en golbale resultaten, TNO, Hoofddorp.

OECD (2014), *Mental Health and Work: Netherlands*, OECD Publishing, Paris, http://dx.doi.org/10.1787/9789264223301-en.

Oeij, P. et al. (2013), Werkgevers enquête arbeid 2012: Methodologie en beschrijvende resultaten, TNO, Hoofddorp.

van der Helm, I. (2013), "The Privacy Protection of the Sick Employee: The Dutch Case from a Comparative Perspective", *European Journal of Social Security*, Vol. 15, No. 3, pp. 273-296.

Factsheet 4.15
United Kingdom: Occupational health advice for smaller enterprises

Context

Companies with fewer than 250 employees generally have little or no access to occupational health support to help them deal with sickness absence or to tackle mental health issues at work. This is problematic because early intervention is central to vocational rehabilitation; the greater the length of absence from work, the more difficult the return to work becomes.

Programme

The Occupational Health Advice Lines pilots were launched in the United Kingdom in late 2009 to provide small and medium-sized enterprises with easy access to high-quality professional advice on all health conditions with a specific focus on mental health. The service was designed to provide practical advice to both employers and employees about health conditions affecting a staff member. Important policy objectives were to provide managers with better information in order to aid them in reducing sickness absence, retaining a productive workforce and, where appropriate, assisting employees back into the workplace as soon as possible following a period of sickness absence.

The service was delivered and managed by different teams in England, Scotland and Wales, with separate budgets in each region and a separate initial telephone number to ensure access. It was decided that a local angle to the service would make better use of existing services and infrastructure (and thereby ensure value for money). Local partnerships would have better know-how about businesses in their area and thereby be more effective at targeted marketing and offering advice on local services.

Outcomes

An evaluation of the Advice Lines service pilots found that users considered it extremely useful. They particularly appreciated access to "instant" advice and the one-stop-shop nature of the service. Most service users were, in line with policy aims, small companies dealing reactively with an employee who was either off work or struggling to stay in work due to a health condition. Employers often sought reassurance for actions they had taken or were about to take, with the service able to offer confirmation for those considering a range of different options. A few weeks after using the service, the vast majority of users had taken action as a result of using either Advice Lines or a service which an Advice Lines advisor had signposted. The measures taken by employers generally reflected good practice in absence management – e.g. communicating with the employee, conducting return-to-work plans, or changing the employee's role.

While most employers would probably have taken action in the absence of the service, one of its major advantages was that it reduced the amount of management time required to search for and implement solutions. As a result, employers using the service are likely to have been able to intervene more quickly, an important factor in effective absence management. Take-up in the period between December 2009 and March 2011 was lower than expected, but has improved considerably since then.

Further reading

OECD (2013), *Mental Health and Work: United Kingdom*, OECD Publishing, Paris, http://dx.doi.org/10.1787/9789264204997-en.

Sinclair, A., R. Martin and C. Tyers (2012), "Occupational Health Advice Lines Evaluation: Final Report", *DWP Research Report*, No. 793, London.

Chapter 5

Improving benefit systems and employment services for jobseekers with mental ill-health

The ability of benefit systems to identify clients' mental illness is crucial to helping them back into the labour market quickly and sustainably. Mental ill-health is highly prevalent not only among disability benefit recipients, but also among unemployment and social assistance recipients. Across OECD countries, between one-third and one-half of all benefit recipients suffer from mental ill-health. Activation policies can assure fast return to work for those people and prevent high caseloads in the disability benefit scheme.

Policy conclusions:

- *Prevent disability benefit claims with mental ill-health.*
- *Identify and support jobseekers with mental health problems.*
- *Invest in mental health competence for all benefit actors.*
- *Develop integrated health and work services in the employment sector.*

When people are about to lose or have just lost their job, benefit systems and employment services become critical. Benefits secure income and employment services deploy activation strategies to help people back into the labour market. This chapter discusses how the two – referred to here as the "employment sector" – can make a difference to people suffering from mental ill-health.

Across the OECD, mental ill-health has become the main driver of new disability benefit claims (OECD, 2010; OECD, 2012). However, mental ill-health is also highly prevalent among beneficiaries of all other types of income-replacement benefits. And causality runs in both directions: people with mental ill-health are at a higher risk of job loss and inactivity, while unemployment and (involuntary) non-employment themselves worsen people's mental health.

Population survey data suggest that across the OECD, between one-third and one-half of all benefit recipients suffer from poor mental health (Figure 5.1), with some cross-country variation. The share is highest among long-term sick, long-term unemployed and long-term inactive people who also frequently suffer from severe mental disorders. The share of people affected by mild-to-moderate mental ill-health is very much the same in most countries, regardless of the benefits they claim.

Time is a critical factor in helping people go back to work after economic or health-driven absence, job loss, and inactivity. The longer people are away from their job and from work in general, the less likely they are ever to return (OECD, 2010). That pattern is particularly true of people who suffer from mental illness, which is often chronic or recurrent. For them, work can be a key factor in recovering their well-being and self-esteem (OECD, 2012).

Sickness absence and unemployment are critical times. Activation policy must respond accordingly to ensure that people with a mental health condition return to work fast and durably and to prevent disability benefit claims. To those ends, systems should focus on identifying the mental health problems of their clients and developing the means to address the barriers arising therefrom.

This chapter discusses those barriers while focusing particularly on:

- Disability schemes that are better adapted to the peculiarities of mental ill-health,
- Early identification and action in the unemployment system,
- General understanding of mental health in benefit systems,
- More closely integrated health- and work-related services and interventions.

Adapting disability benefit schemes to claimants with mental ill-health

Mental ill-health accounts for the bulk of new disability benefit claims. Although the trend is universal and structural, it is not irreversible and has a range of causes. First, greater awareness of mental ill-health has led to shifts in diagnosed causes of the incapacity to work. It is more frequently identified as the root cause of work problems among people with co-morbid physical and mental illness. Second, work has become psychologically more demanding. As a result it is now more difficult to remain in work with a mental health problem. Third, the assessment tools and support measures used in disability systems are often inadequate when it comes to mental ill-health. Fourth, poor knowledge of mental ill-health tends to lead to underestimates of the capacity to work of people with mental illness reflected, for example, in fewer benefit denials, more frequent grants of full rather than partial benefits and less benefit outflows. The inference is that structural reform in some countries has succeeded in curbing all kinds of benefit claims except those for mental illness (OECD, 2012).

Figure 5.1. **The prevalence of mental ill-health is high on all working-age benefits**

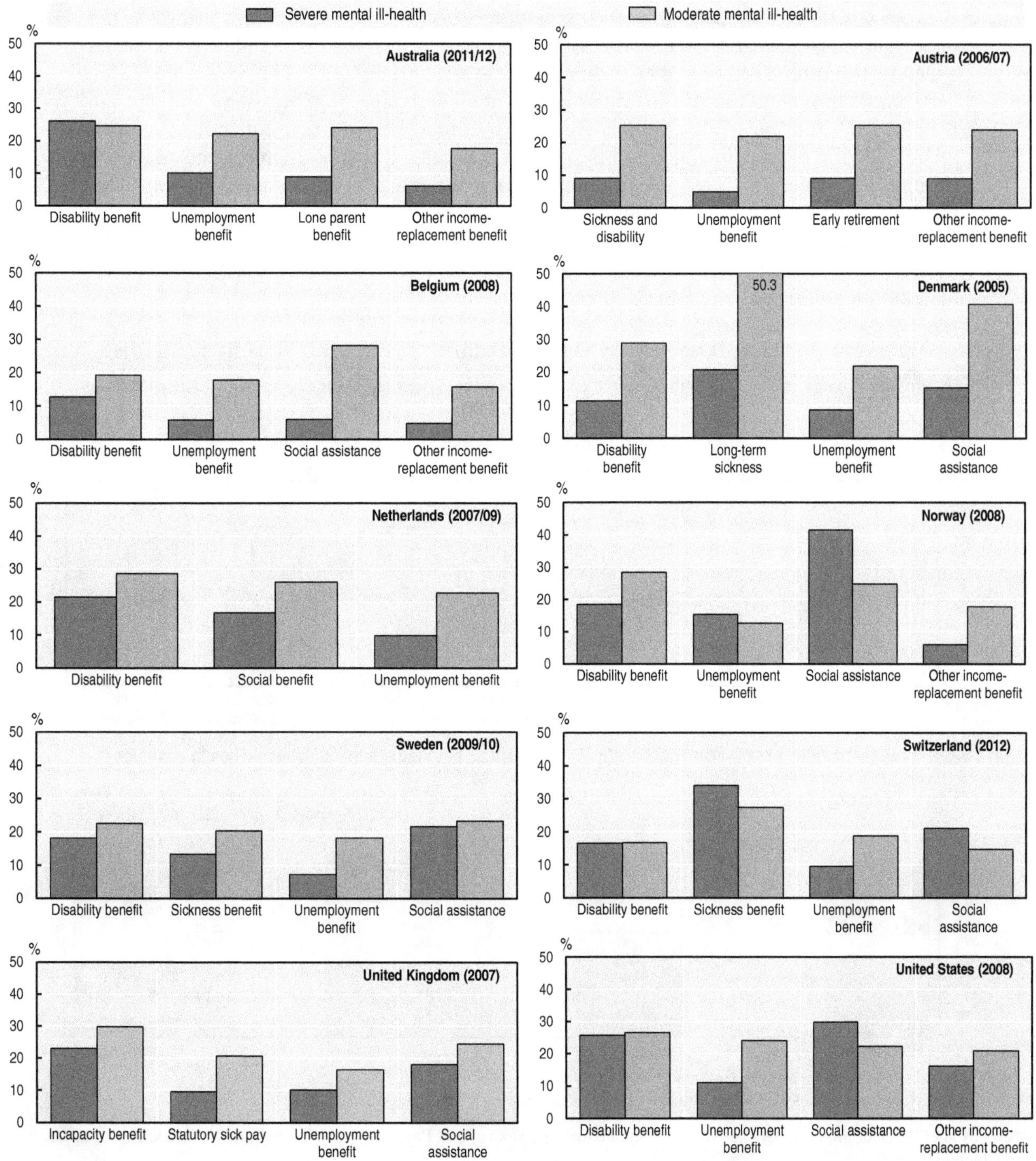

Note: Austria refers to the age group 50-64 only, the unemployment benefit in the Netherlands refers to unemployed people and data for the United Kingdom cover all persons with a mental disorder.

Source: National health surveys. Australia: National Health Survey 2011/12; Austria: Health Interview Survey 2006/07; Belgium: Health Interview Survey 2008; Denmark: National Health Interview Survey 2005; Netherlands: POLS Health Survey 2007/09; Norway: Level of Living and Health Survey 2008; Sweden: Living Conditions Survey 2009/10; Switzerland: Health Survey 2012; United Kingdom: Adult Psychiatric Morbidity Survey 2007; United States: National Health Interview Survey 2008.

StatLink http://dx.doi.org/10.1787/888933184218

Claimants with mental disorders are furthest removed from the labour market

The greater recognition of mental ill-health in disability benefit claims affords a fine opportunity for addressing the issue appropriately. Claimants with mental ill-health are different from most of those who suffer from physical complaints. The reason lies in the very nature of mental illness – its onset comes at an early age, it is persistent and chronic, it has high recurrence rates, and is frequently comorbid. The consequence is a much greater labour market distance, with frequent periods of unemployment and inactivity (Figure 5.2, Panel A). Most benefit applications for reasons of mental ill-health come from claimants going through long-term unemployment or long-term sickness. Few are from people with job contracts. In other words, the people with mental ill-health are already at a considerable distance from the labour market even before they enter the benefit system (Figure 5.2, Panel B).

Figure 5.2. **The large labour market distance of disability benefit claimants**

A. Proportion employed and not employed in the five years prior to a disability benefit claim, by health condition, Denmark, 2009

B. Distribution of new disability benefit claims by status before the benefit claim and health condition, Austria, 2012

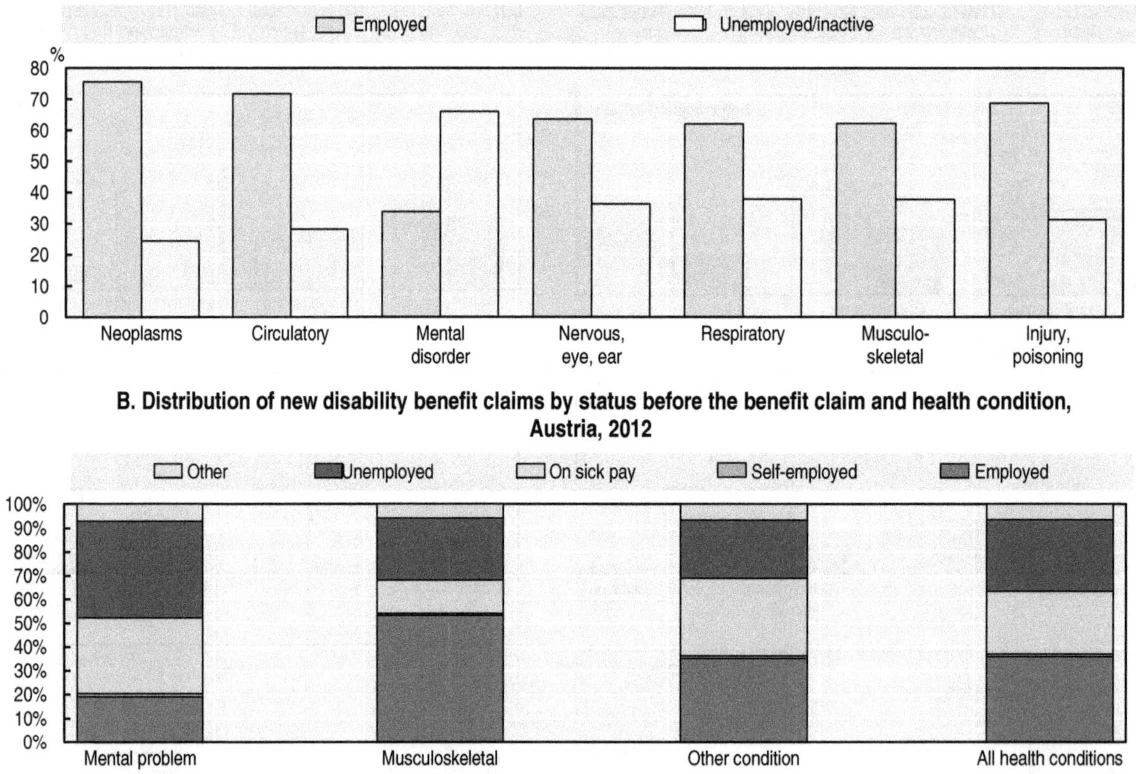

Note: "Inactive" refers to all persons who are not classified as employed or unemployed.

Source: Panel A: Data provided by the National Social Appeals Board; and Panel B: Austrian Ministry of Labour, Social Affairs and Consumer Protection, www.sozialministerium.

StatLink http://dx.doi.org/10.1787/888933184220

Strengthening the labour market focus of the disability system for mental ill-health

Disability benefit systems have to respond to the recent changes. Many OECD countries have successfully implemented structural reform to tackle the general increase in benefit claims over the past decades (OECD, 2010). But reforms have not been able to stop the rise in claims due to mental ill-health. Effective disability reform components have yet to be adapted to respond to the needs of claimants with mental ill-health.

Successful structural reform often includes one or more of the following measures: i) earlier intervention and faster decisions to curb disability claims; ii) better incentives to make work pay and stronger obligations on employers and public authorities to make disregard for health issues more costly; and iii) restricting disability benefits to only those who are fully and permanently unable to work.

Towards earlier action

Early identification and quicker intervention is particularly important for people with mental ill-health. The Swedish Work Introduction Programme is an intensive three-month scheme to reconnect people on long-term sick leave with the labour market. It involves psychologists and job coaches who motivate them, give them work experience, and provide them with counselling. Yet even schemes of its kind have limited impact when they are offered too late: in the Swedish case, only after someone has been sick for 914 days (OECD, 2013c).

Switzerland acts earliest in identifying health-related work problems: the disability insurance system gets involved, lending employers advice and support, while people still have a job. Intervening so far upstream is essential in that workers with mental ill-health are much better able to hold on to a job than to go back to one. Switzerland has also introduced new low-threshold measures for workers at risk of developing problems – particularly mental health ones – that could make them eligible for disability benefit (Factsheet 5.1).

Several other countries have also introduced policies to ensure earlier intervention when health problems surface, mostly through sickness benefit (see earlier chapters of the report). Nordic countries in particular focus strongly on partial sick leave as a means of speeding up gradual returns to work and pre-empting later disability benefit claims (OECD, 2013a).

Towards stronger incentives

The thinking behind such approaches is promising. But implementation often lags behind regulation because countries are poor at defining what is required of the different actors, monitoring existing obligations, and enforcing sanctions for non-compliance. The best way to make employers and employees meet stiffer obligations is by matching them with financial incentives. The Netherlands has gone furthest in this regard, making it attractive for workers with health problems to use their (partial) work capability in the job market and costly for employers not co-operate in seeking quick returns to work for sick employees (see Factsheet 4.7).

Also important are the roles and responsibilities of the bodies that administer benefits. Several countries – e.g. Austria, Denmark and Switzerland – have introduced and gradually tightened a rehabilitation-before-benefit principle which requires benefit bodies to explore all rehabilitation avenues before granting disability benefit (OECD, 2013b; OECD, 2014; OECD 2015). Again, however, implementation has proven challenging.

Denmark, for its part, has made considerable effort to strengthen incentives for the government departments and local authorities that administer benefits so that they deliver better services. It has put in place an online database to facilitate the benchmarking of the processes used and outcomes achieved by all municipal job centres. It also seeks to stimulate and steer their action by varying its rates of funding. The government thus requires municipal authorities to foot much of the bill for long-term benefit payments, but offers them strong incentives through reimbursement of the costs to provide rehabilitation and other labour market services (Factsheet 5.2). These are promising mainstream measures, but they can be effective for groups like people with mental ill-health only if they factor in their particularities.

Towards better assessments

Work capacity assessment is a critical factor in reforming the disability system. Many OECD countries are shifting towards identifying capacity and ability rather than incapacity and disability. Although it is a necessary structural change, acceptance is limited. Countries which spend relatively little on rehabilitation and reintegration services for people with disability face particular challenges when reforming assessment. In the United Kingdom, for example, the government has repeatedly had to adjust its new *Work Capability Assessment* in response to the many successful appeals against assessments and criticisms of the way in which people struggling with mental health issues have been deemed fit to work.

Reassessments of the capability to work are even more politically controversial. Most reforms apply to new disability claims only, leaving the rights of those already on benefit unchanged (Prinz and Tompson, 2009). Recently, however, more countries have started to apply new, more stringent criteria to recent benefit claimants, with the Netherlands and United Kingdom going so far as to reassess almost their entire caseloads of entitlements. Such policies can be helpful in bringing people with mental health problems into the labour market if they are matched with appropriate reintegration support.

Restricting the disability benefit entitlements of people who are still partially able to work has cut new benefit claims in some countries, e.g. Australia and Switzerland. Again, though, the policy's success depends on the extent to which other benefit schemes, particularly unemployment, can step in and properly serve the needs of those with partial work capacity due to mental health problems.

Very recent developments in some countries show the direction in which policy will have to move. Both Denmark and Austria have significantly restricted access to disability benefit, replacing it by schemes that are far more geared to bring people back into the labour market. In Denmark, the number of benefit claims dropped by almost half in 2013. The denied claimants are now undergoing new multidisciplinary, case-managed rehabilitation courses that the country's municipalities have developed (Factsheet 5.3). In Austria, many people will no longer be entitled to disability benefit. Instead, they will have to rely on either rehabilitation benefit (administered by the health insurance system) or retraining allowances, which are the responsibility of the labour market service (Factsheet 5.4). The impact of such reforms will depend on how they are implemented and the quality and adequacy of the rehabilitation and retraining that is provided.

Key messages

Countries struggle to make their disability benefit schemes more labour market-oriented. Although activation policies have proven effective for most groups of unemployed and inactive people, they have not had the same success with people with a disability, particularly those with mental health complaints (OECD, 2010; Martin, 2014). The main reason for this limited effectiveness is the poor timing of measures. Comprehensive programmes which kick in only after people have been away from the labour market for years are often ineffective. By then they have long given up on employment. Another challenge is striking the right balance between entitlements and responsibilities and implementing reciprocal obligations for claimants, workers, employers, and the health, employment and social security agencies and the employment service providers.

Effective measures to control the disability benefit claims of people grappling with mental ill-health include:

- Focusing on the early identification of people in need of support and intervening early with medical and vocational rehabilitation measures that target those with mental illness.
- Better recognising the work capability of those with mental illness and limiting disability benefits to all those who are *permanently* unable to work.
- Spelling out fair, clear reciprocal responsibilities and financial incentives for benefit administration bodies and employment service providers.

Identifying and supporting unemployed people with mental health problems

The strengthening of the activation agenda over the past two decades has prompted the public employment services (PESs) in many countries to focus on work-ready jobseekers and contributed to pushing people with health problems onto disability benefit. Recent structural reforms to disability benefit systems have tried to rectify that mistake by also activating jobseekers with poor physical and mental health. As a result, PES clienteles have changed. It is thought, for example, that the United Kingdom's employment service providers (who are private) will cater chiefly to groups of hard-to-place jobseekers and that 78% of all clients will have some current or previous connection to the disability system (Heap, 2012). This fact has yet to be understood by mainstream service providers.

Jobseekers with mental illness attend employment programmes but have poor outcomes

Statistics on the prevalence of mental ill-health among jobseekers in mainstream employment services are scarce, as PES and unemployment systems in most countries do no measure health. However, some do have information on numbers of jobseekers with diagnosed disabilities. Australia is an interesting case because it operates two parallel systems of job-seeking services: one for those with a disability and a mainstream one for the rest. Yet most people with identified mental disorders are in mainstream employment services (Figure 5.3, Panel A), where they are more likely to be found in streams 3 or 4, which provide high-intensity support, than in streams 1 and 2 (Figure 5.3, Panel B). Were all people with common mental illnesses to be identified in job-seeking statistics, the message would be even clearer: poor mental health is a key issue in employment services.

Figure 5.3. **Programme participation and employment outcomes for participants with mental ill-health**

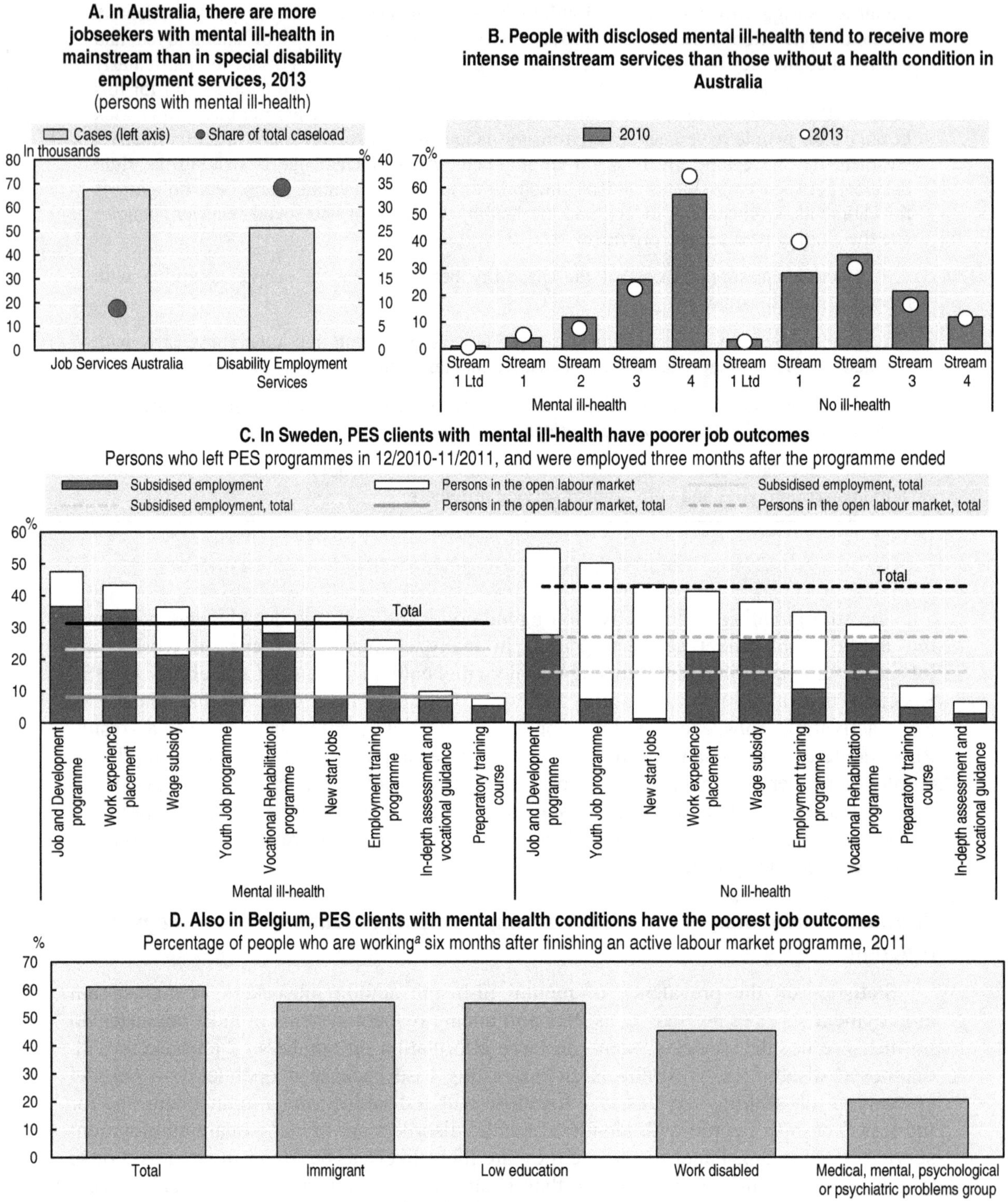

a. Employment includes sheltered employment and employment care.

Source: Panel A: Australia Department of Employment ESAt data; Panel B: OECD estimates based on administrative data from the Australian Department of Social Services; Panel C: the Swedish Public Employment Service; and Panel D: the Flemish Public Employment and Vocational Training Service.

StatLink http://dx.doi.org/10.1787/888933184231

PES clients with mental health conditions also have poorer job outcomes. In Sweden, three months after programme termination, only about 8% had moved into the open labour market and 23% into subsidised employment in 2010 and 2011. The figures for other PES clients were 27% and 16%, respectively (Figure 5.3, Panel C). In Belgium, six months after completing an employment scheme, 60% of all PES clients had found a job, in contrast to only 20% of those with recognised "medical, mental, psychological and psychiatric" problems (Figure 5.3, Panel D).

Identifying jobseekers' mental ill-health in the unemployment benefit system

Activation schemes start with an intake phase, where jobseekers are profiled to assign them to the appropriate target group. Yet only rarely is their mental health assessed – a wasted opportunity for early action. That being said, a few countries, such as Norway and Australia, do gather some health information during intake. Australia's *Jobseeker Classification Instrument* is a good example of a tool that efficiently matches client needs to services and refers them to in-depth assessment if necessary (Factsheet 5.5). In its current form, it cannot systematically spot labour market barriers related to mental ill-health, although it could easily be expanded to that effect.

Maybe the strongest focus on mental health in the intake phase is in Flanders, the Flemish-speaking part of Belgium. Jobseekers are systematically screened for reintegration barriers, which include mental health issues. Whenever problems are suspected, an interview can be requested and a referral can be made to an in-house psychologist or an external centre specialised in multidisciplinary screening (Factsheet 5.6). The PES in Belgium takes a special interest in screening jobseekers for health barriers because unemployment benefit is payable for an unlimited duration. There is thus a strong money-saving incentive for providing extra support to people who struggle with mental ill-health and run a high risk of long-term unemployment.

There are several ways to screen for mental ill-health in jobseeker populations. One is through validated instruments (Liwowsky et al., 2009) either for all clients or only when a caseworker suspects a problem. In that event, caseworkers should have clear guidelines on when to use the instrument, what to do when a mental health issue arises, and how to handle confidentiality. Another approach is to send clients to a psychologist for in-depth clinical screening or interviews.

The trend towards the computerisation of PESs in many of the countries reviewed by the OECD clears the way for mental health screening during initial registration and intake procedures. The Dutch PES's new *Work Explorer* too, for example, has great potential. It is a fully digitalised support system that can identify barriers to work – including those related to mental ill-health (Factsheet 5.7). Early digital screening also opens up new opportunities for the provision of web-based mental health therapy.

Many of the reviewed countries use PES performance management processes to support groups who are particularly exposed to long-term unemployment. The Danish Ministry of Employment, for example, sets three targets every year that municipal jobcentres have to meet. They may include a certain employment level or an improved placement rate for a particular group of jobseekers. Such a priority group could be jobseekers with mental health problems.

Earlier intervention for jobseekers with mental ill-health

The identification of jobseekers' poor mental health is meaningful only in combination with appropriate follow-up procedures and services, such as regular meetings with caseworkers. In this respect, Sweden's *Job Coach Programme* is a good illustration. A coach works closely with the jobseeker and the new employer, focusing strongly on the work environment (Factsheet 5.8).

A PES provision of follow-up services for registered jobseekers with health problems is essential to preventing them from slipping into reliance on disability benefit and suffering from long delays in employment support. Often such claimants will be sent back and forth between different agencies, losing their employability and motivation and becoming more prone to long-term unemployment. Shifts between benefit schemes are costly and unproductive for society and the person concerned.

Austria has sought to address the issue through a scheme called *Health Road* under which its unemployment and disability benefit systems share information to get agreed early assessments of claimants' work capacity. Knowing that a disability benefit application has no chance of success, the PES has a much stronger incentive for assisting the client (Factsheet 5.9). Another interesting approach to addressing both incentives and co-operation between benefit systems is the Swiss *Inter-Institutional Co-operation* scheme. It builds on information sharing and case management to achieve better outcomes for clients with complex problems and prevent them from being shuttled between institutions (Factsheet 5.10).

Key messages

It is important to spot mental ill-health and any labour market barriers as early as possible – ideally, on a jobseeker's first contact with the employment service, or soon after. Where a problem is identified or suspected, there should be a swift referral for counselling. The aim is, if necessary, to provide psychological support, advise the patient to seek help from the health care system and develop an adequate reintegration strategy with the PES caseworker.

Helping jobseekers with mental health conditions should be achieved by:

- Using adequate tools to identify mental health problems and how they compromise labour market access. Problems should be identified at the first interview with the job service or very soon after.
- Implementing clear guidelines for caseworkers on what to do when problems arise.
- Putting in place a strong follow-up process with frequent interviews with caseworkers and ensuring access to mainstream or special services for jobseekers with mental illness.
- Avoiding, as far as possible, exemptions from job-search and participation requirements.
- Making adjustments to the employment service's performance management process so that jobseekers who suffer from mental ill-health get proper attention.

Develop mental health competencies and support in the employment sector

To enable unemployment benefit systems, public employment services, and local welfare offices to cater to their clients' mental health needs, changes are required to: i) develop the mental health competencies of those institutions and ii) help people access adequate mental health support.

Research has shown that, typically, none of the systems address highly prevalent mental illness. German data found that among the older long-term unemployed who struggle with poor mental health only 10% had received adequate treatment and most no treatment at all (Bühler et al., 2013). Similarly, Norwegian data suggest that one-third of claimants who receive disability benefit for mental illness have never been treated in any way (Øverland et al., 2007).

Addressing mental health needs early on through better mental health awareness and competence by employment services is a key factor in preventing long-term unemployment and permanent inactivity. In Austria, it has been found that anyone who once tried to claim a disability benefit, even unsuccessfully, hardly ever joins the labour market again (Fuchs, 2013).

Mental health training and guidelines for caseworkers

The reviewed countries have developed a range of strategies to develop mental health competence in their employment services and local welfare offices. Sweden is a case in point. Country-wide the PES has about 330 psychologists, 200 occupational therapists and 30 psychotherapists providing specialist support. Yet the high caseload they face is a considerable strain on their ability to provide adequate support. Significant investment will be needed to develop this into a fully functional support structure.

PES caseworkers need training and guidelines to enable them to work with jobseekers suffering from mental ill-health and to identify situations which call for specialised employment or mental health interventions. In that regard, the University of Leipzig has devised a scheme for tackling high levels of under-treatment. It combines one-day mental health training for PES caseworkers with the provision of psychosocial coaching. Coaching involves an initial diagnostic interview, advice on treatment, mental health first aid and short-term therapy (Pfeil et al., 2013). The university's scheme has helped to significantly improve both treatment rates and overall motivation.

Another possibility is to work with specialised employment service providers that have mental health expertise. The return-to-work programme of the Danish Mental Health Foundation (a private non-profit provider) is a good example. Psychologically trained caseworkers work with low caseloads of no more than 10-20 jobseekers, which allows close contact with and better outcomes for clients all of whom suffer from common mental illness (Factsheet 5.11).

The Swedish national social insurance system, which administers sickness and disability benefit, meets treatment needs by purchasing care from the health sector for clients at risk of long-term absence. Treatment consists mostly, but not only, of short-term cognitive behavioural therapy that lasts between 8 and 20 sessions. This approach, known as the *Rehabilitation Guarantee,* has been effective for clients who still have links with their employer. Those who do not, however, require additional support (Factsheet 5.12).

Key messages

Across the OECD, mental health competencies and psychological expertise in the employment sector are still underdeveloped and not commensurate with the high prevalence of mental illness among jobseekers and welfare clients. The sector will come under extra strain as a result of recent policy changes in many countries that will increase the number of clients with partially reduced work capability in mainstream employment services. Better mental health competencies have to be developed to make early identification and quick intervention possible in all systems. Efforts in that direction should come, first and foremost, in the unemployment system because better job retention and reintegration at this early stage can prevent people with poor mental health from slipping into welfare and disability.

Improving the mental health competencies in the employment sector is facilitated by the provision of:

- Mental health training for caseworkers in the PES, welfare counsellors and social workers.
- An available, quickly accessible, psychological coaching capacity in employment services and local welfare offices.

Integrated work and health action to activate jobseekers with mental ill-health

Employment and health needs are rarely addressed together. Even where jobseekers' mental health issues are recognised, the approach of employment services in most reviewed countries is usually to exempt them from job-search and availability requirements, expect – but not request – them to seek treatment, and hope that they return fit and healthy to seek work. Exemptions are granted on the basis of a medical certificate or, at least initially, the caseworker's judgement.

Ignoring health often accounts for failed labour market reintegration

The passive approach of employment services in the event of ill-health – be it mental or physical – emerges clearly in comparisons between outcomes for sick people who are unemployed and those who have a job. In Austria, for example, the incidence of sickness among unemployed people is more than double that of their employed peers, a disparity that has gradually widened during the past 20 years (Figure 5.4, Panel A). Long spells of sickness absence are more frequent among jobseekers. Swedish data on unemployed people returning from long-term sickness further confirm that those who struggle with mental ill-health have the lowest chance of finding work (Figure 5.4, Panel B).

Data for the Netherlands are particularly illuminating because the entire system hinges on strongly enforced employer obligations. People who do not have an employer responsible for their swift return to work – i.e. unemployed people and temporary workers whose contract has ended – receive much less support in resuming work. Publicly funded support can compensate only partially (Figure 5.4, Panel C). The lack of employer support may account in part for work resumption rates among the sick unemployed being much lower: two years after a long-term (nine-month) sick leave, only about one in four unemployed people had found a job in 2012, compared to more than 80% of their peers who were in work when they fell ill (Figure 5.4, Panel D). Support for the sick unemployed obviously falls short of their health and employment needs.

Figure 5.4. **Longer sickness durations and poorer labour market outcomes for sick unemployed people**

A. Sickness absence rate of Austrian employed and unemployed workers

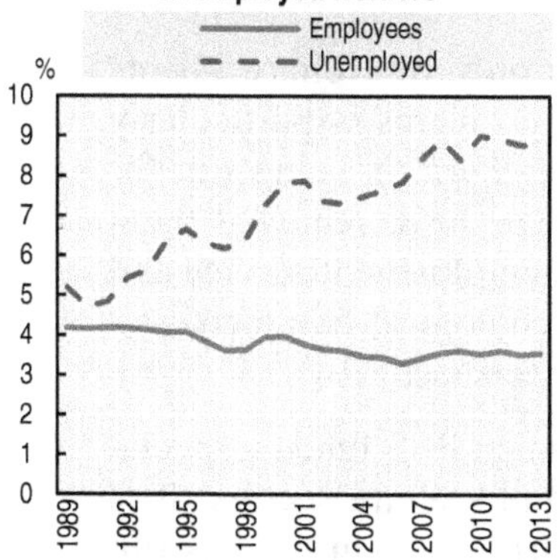

B. Unemployed sick in Sweden move back into employment less often
Share of individuals ending a sickness spell during 2011, by destination (percentage)

	Starting new sickness spell		Registered with employment service		Into disability		Other (mostly into employment)	
	Mental ill-health	Other illness	Mental ill-health	Other illness	Mental ill-health	Other illness	Mental ill-health	Other illness
Employed	17.8	16.9	3.5	1.8	1.1	0.7	77.6	80.6
Unemployed	19.4	19.9	4.4	2.8	4.8	2.3	71.5	75.0

C. In the Netherlands, sick unemployed people receive less reintegration support than sick employees...
Supporting actors in the work resumption process, 2012

D. ...and they resume work less often
Work resumption after 10, 18 and 27 months by the unemployed and employees on long-term (9 months) sick leave

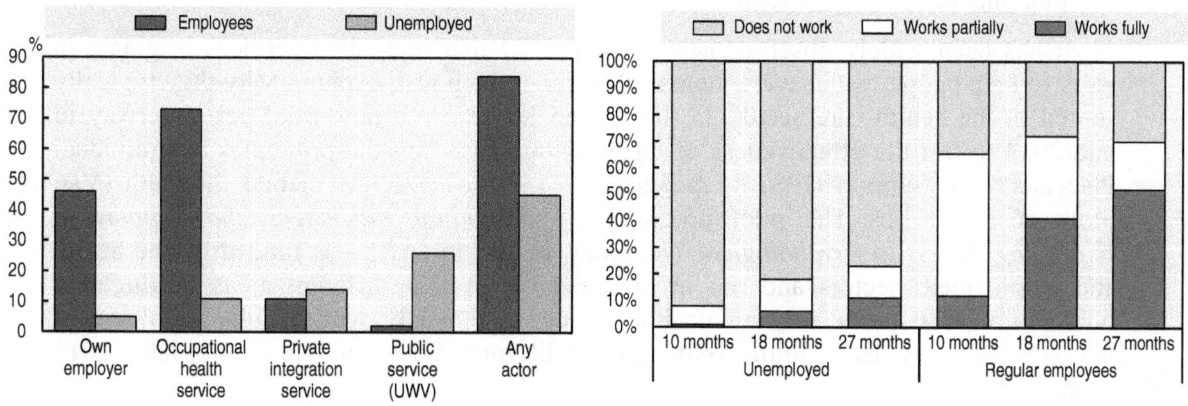

Note: In Panel C several answers are possible; the bars do not sum up to 100%.

Source: Panel A: WIFO-update based on Leoni, T. (2010), "Differences in Sick Leave Between Employed and Unemployed Workers", *WIFO Working Paper No. 372/2010*; Panel B: Swedish Social Insurance Agency data used in Van der Burg, C. et al. (2013); Panel C: Weg naar de WIA: Langdurig zieken 2012 [Road to the WIA: Long-term sick 2012], AStri Beleidsonderzoek en -advies, Leiden; and Panel D: de Jong, P. et al. (2010), "Nederland is niet meer ziek: Van WAO-debakel naar WIA mirakel" [The Netherlands is no longer sick: From WAO-debacle to WIA-miracle], APE/AStri Beleidsonderzoek en –advies.

StatLink http://dx.doi.org/10.1787/888933184242

Developing integrated health and work services in the employment sector

A PES can address clients' health needs either by co-ordinating its services with the health care system or providing integrated services itself. One approach is to pool resources with other sectors to facilitate provision in line with clients' multiple needs. Sweden has taken that line of action to good effect through local associations that co-ordinate funding from the national employment service, the regional health authority, municipal welfare offices, and the national social insurance system (Factsheet 5.13). The multidisciplinary rehabilitation services thus cater for long-term sick or unemployed people.

The new Danish rehabilitation model (described above) steers many potential claimants away from disability benefit. It takes an integrated approach to rehabilitation that brings together labour market services, health care, social services, and education. All municipal job centres are required to develop such arrangements, with each sector covering its own costs (see Factsheet 5.3).

In most other OECD countries, municipalities take charge only of welfare clients among whom the prevalence of mental ill-health and multiple problems is particularly high. In five big Dutch municipalities a new pilot project, *Fit-4-Work*, is being run for welfare recipients whose many psychological and social problems have removed them from the labour market. The scheme is co-funded by the national employment service and local social and mental health offices. Key features include psychological treatment and quick job placement with follow-up coaching in the workplace (Factsheet 5.14).

Belgium (Flanders) uses a similar approach in which the Flemish PES funds a special programme developed in co-operation with the mental health and welfare sectors. It is designed for jobseekers with severe psychological and psychiatric problems and is run through an institution that specialises in combining care and employment support. Three coaches bring their expertise to bear: a job coach (who is also the overall co-ordinator), a health coach, and an empowerment coach from the welfare sector (Factsheet 5.15). The scheme could be expanded to reach many more of the large number of people with common mental health problems.

It has been widely observed across the OECD that integrated services originate in work to help people with severe mental ill-health, which also explains why they typically started in the health care sector. In the United Kingdom, a new pilot got underway in mid-2014 to test the effectiveness of interventions based on the principles of Individual Placement and Support (IPS) for people with mild-to-moderate mental ill-health (Van Stolk et al., 2014). The pilot programme – *Individual Placement and Support in Improving Access to Psychological Therapies*, or IPS in IAPT – is funded by the health and employment sectors and run in different versions in different areas of England, linking up partly with existing health services and partly with regular employment intervention providers. Initial outcomes will not be available until late 2015 (Factsheet 5.16).

Key messages

Evidence from across OECD countries suggests that they struggle to deliver co-ordinated, integrated health and employment services because of the lack of coherent incentives, obligations and guidelines for stakeholders and participating professionals (Arends et al., 2014). Integrating services requires a PES to address clients' health and employment needs at the same time, be it through internal mental health expertise or new structures that provide integrated services.

Ways to develop integrated health and work services in the employment sector include:

- Pooling resources with, or purchasing services from, the health sector in order to deliver a multidisciplinary, integrated rehabilitation provision.
- Developing programmes targeted at jobseekers and welfare clients with common mental illness. Such programmes should combine psychological counselling with job-placement services or work experience programmes.

REFERENCES

Arends, I., N. Baer, V. Miranda, C. Prinz and S. Singh (2014), "Mental Health and Work: Achieving Well-Integrated Policies and Service Delivery", *OECD Social, Employment and Migration Working Papers No. 161*, OECD Publishing, Paris, http://dx/doi/org/10.1787/5jxsvvn6pq6g-en.

Bühler, B., R. Kocalevent, R. Berger, A. Mahler, B. Preiß, I. Liwowsky, P. Carl and U. Hegerl (2013), "Versorgungssituation von Langzeitarbeitslosen mit psychischen Störungen" [Treatment of the long-term unemployed with psychological disorders], *Der Nervenarzt*, Vol. 84: pp. 603-607.

de Jong, P. et al. (2010), "Nederland is niet meer ziek: Van WAO-debakel naar WIA mirakel" [The Netherlands is no longer sick: From WAO-debacle to WIA-miracle], APE/AStri Beleidsonderzoek en –advies.

Fuchs, M. (2013), "Die weitere Erwerbsbiographie von Arbeitern und Angestellten deren Antrag auf Invaliditätspension abgelehnt wurde", *Soziale Sicherheit*, Vol. 5/2013, pp. 256-265.

Heap, D. (2012), "Integrating and Mainstreaming Sick and Disabled Benefit Claimants in the 'Active' UK Welfare State", Department of Social Policy, University of Edinburgh.

Leoni, T. (2010), "Differences in Sick Leave Between Employed and Unemployed Workers", *WIFO Working Paper No. 372/2010.*

Liwowsky, I., D. Kramer, R. Mergl, A. Bramesfeld, A.-K. Allgaier, E. Pöppel and U. Hegerl (2009), "Screening for Depression in the Older Long-term Unemployed", *Social Psychiatry & Psychiatric Epidemiology*, Vol. 44, pp. 622-627.

Martin, J. (2014), "Activation and Active Labour Market Policies in OECD Countries: Stylized Facts and Evidence on their Effectiveness", *IZA Policy Paper*, No. 84, IZA, Bonn.

OECD (forthcoming 2015), *Mental Health and Work: Austria*, OECD Publishing, Paris.

OECD (2014), *Mental Health and Work: Switzerland*, OECD Publishing, Paris, http://dx.doi.org/10.1787/9789264204973-en.

http://dx/doi/org/10.1787/9789264178984-en.

OECD (2013a), *Mental Health and Work: Norway*, OECD Publishing, Paris,

OECD (2013b), *Mental Health and Work: Denmark*, OECD Publishing, Paris, http://dx/doi/org/10.1787/9789264188631-en.

OECD (2013c), *Mental Health and Work: Sweden,* OECD Publishing, Paris, http://dx.doi.org/10.1787/9789264188730-en.

OECD (2012), *Sick on the Job? Myths and Realities about Mental Health and Work*, OECD Publishing, Paris, http://dx.doi.org/10.1787/9789264124523-en.

OECD (2010), *Sickness, Disability and Work: Breaking the Barriers,* OECD Publishing, Paris, http://dx.doi.org/10.1787/9789264090606-en.

Øverland, S., N. Glozier, S. Krokstad and A. Mykletun (2007), "Undertreatment Before the Award of a Disability Pension for Mental Illness", *Psychiatric Services*, Vol. 58/11, pp. 1479-1482.

Pfeil, S., K. Holtz, J. Tiefensee, T. Bresner, A. Kästner, A. Kopf and U. Hegerl (2010), "Hilfe für psychisch kranke Langzeitarbeitslose: Das Leipziger Modellprojekt" [Help for long-term unemployed with mental disorders: the Leipzig model project], *Nervenheilkunde*, Vol. 32/8, pp. 592-594.

Prinz, C. and D. Tompson (2009), "Sickness and Disability Programmes: What is Driving Policy Convergence?", *International Social Security Review*, Vol. 62/4, pp. 41-46.

Van der Burg, C. et al. (2013); Panel C: Weg naar de WIA: Langdurig zieken 2012 [Road to the WIA: Long-term sick 2012], AStri Beleidsonderzoek en -advies, Leiden.

Van Stolk, C., J. Hofmann, M. Hafner and B. Janta (2014), "Psychological Wellbeing and Work: Improving Service Provision and Outcomes", RR-407, Department of Work and Pensions/Department of Health/UK Cabinet Office, London.

FACTSHEETS 5.1 to 5.16

Factsheet 5.1
Switzerland: Early intervention by invalidity insurance

Context

Different OECD countries have introduced structural reforms to tackle the steep increase in disability benefit caseloads in recent decades. Countries are moving away from merely compensating work disability towards activating claimants to return them to the world of work.

Programme

The increase in invalidity claimants since the 1990s led to several revisions of the Swiss Invalidity Insurance Act. The 5th revision, in 2008, switched the strong focus on invalidity benefit to the ability to work. The reform reinforced the emphasis on vocational rehabilitation, added a new focus on job retention, and implemented a paradigm shift in the invalidity insurance's focus to early identification and activation of potential claimants. The main measures introduced by the reform and primarily targeting claimants with a mental illness were:

- Early identification through early notification of problems to invalidity insurance, by the employer, employee, the treating doctor, or any other stakeholder.

- A set of early intervention measures to secure job retention or to help claimants find a new job. Measures included: i) workplace adaptations; ii) educational courses; iii) active job placement; iv) vocational counselling; v) social-vocational rehabilitation; and vi) activation. These measures require an assessment and binding rehabilitation plan.

- Substantial wage subsidies for employers hiring a claimant. Subsidies may be paid for half a year at up to 100% of the salary if the claimant has not regained full work capacity. Moreover, if a hired claimant is again absent through sickness, any increase in the employer's premium to sickness benefit insurance is reimbursed.

Outcomes

A recent evaluation of the effects of new and early intervention measures showed that, before the reform, 40% of all claimants were back in employment roughly 18 months after initial contact with the cantonal invalidity office. After the reform, the rate rose slightly to 44%. Claimants who were employed when they first contacted the cantonal invalidity insurance office had a much higher employment rate 18 months afterwards than unemployed claimants, both before and after the reform. Of those employed at the time of uptake, 55% were employed 18 months later compared to 30% among initially unemployed claimants. It has to be seen whether early intervention will deliver a more significant improvement of the employment outcome in the future (the first evaluation came at a rather early stage).

Further reading

Bolliger, C. et al. (2012), "Eingliederung vor Rente. Evaluation der Früherfassung und der Integrationsmassnahmen in der Invalidenversicherung" [Rehabilitation Before Pension. Evaluation of Early Detection and Integration Measures in the Disability Insurance], *FoP-IV Forschungsbericht*, Bundesamt für Sozialversicherungen (BSV), Bern.

OECD (2014), *Mental Health and Work: Switzerland*, OECD Publishing, Paris, http://dx.doi.org/10.1787/9789264204973-en.

Factsheet 5.2
Denmark: Incentives for municipalities through variable funding rates

Context

Without the right incentives, benefit and employment services can be reluctant to actively help claimants back into work. Financial incentives, together with systematic monitoring and benchmarking, can be effective mechanisms for strengthening the activation policies of benefit and employment departments.

Programme

The Danish benefit system has differential reimbursement rates that vary according to state and municipal budgets (responsible for benefit and employment services) and the type of benefit or intervention that claimants receive. The main idea behind this stimulus scheme is to give incentives to municipalities for offering measures that help a person back into the labour market and prevent long-term benefit pay-outs. Accordingly, the state reimburses 65% of the costs of rehabilitation and wage subsidies, but only 35% of disability benefit costs, 30% of the costs of social assistance and unemployment exceeding eight weeks, and none of the costs of sickness benefit payments that exceed one year. Reimbursement rates are also set at 0% whenever insufficient documentation is provided or active measures are unduly delayed.

At the same time, the government moved towards stronger, more systematic monitoring and benchmarking of claimants' benefit and employment outcomes, so giving poorer-performing municipal job centres the opportunity to learn from good practices. The work of job centres is measured more stringently against a comprehensive benchmarking tool that monitors the use of programmes for different clients (Jobindsats) and another tool that measures the cost-effectiveness of those programmes (Effektivindsats). Jobindsats data are available online to everyone and allow comparisons by municipal job centre or employment region.

Outcomes

There is little information available on the impact that the differential reimbursement rates and municipal practices have on different groups of clients, including those who suffer from mental ill-health. While the stimulus scheme has significant potential, it has also been shown to allow "tactical" behaviour – i.e. providing too few services to clients with complex mental health and social problems. There is also a great risk that municipalities' reactions to the differential reimbursement scheme are driven by short- rather than long-term considerations.

In general, benchmarking and "naming and shaming" are considered more appropriate and administratively more efficient than sanctions. With no information being collected on the mental health problems of job centre clients (or health problems more generally), none of the monitoring mechanisms target mental disorders. Additional municipal targets with regard to jobseekers with a mental disorder, however, would be possible – and could lead to a more systematic, transparent approach to that group. Sufficiently accurate instruments which enable the early detection of mental health issues are available.

Further reading

OECD (2013), *Mental Health and Work: Denmark*, OECD Publishing, Paris, http://dx/doi/org/10.1787/9789264188631-en.

Factsheet 5.3
Denmark: Integrated rehabilitation services to prevent disability claims

Context

When people start claiming disability benefit they are at risk of permanent inactivity. That trend is especially problematic for young people with little work experience, as it shunts them away from the labour market altogether. Early vocational rehabilitation that integrates health and employment support can help to bring people with health problems into jobs.

Programme

In response to the large and growing number of young adults under the age of 25 moving to claim disability benefit (in most cases due to mental ill-health), the Danish Government has made a major reform to the disability scheme. The intention is to largely abolish disability benefit for the under-40s (unless they are totally unable to work), replacing it with a new rehabilitation model whose chief features are that:

- The health sector, labour market institutions, social services and the education sector are involved, with responsibility lying with the municipal job centre.
- An interdisciplinary rehabilitation team is established in every municipality to ensure the integrated approach will work in practice.
- The rehabilitation team discusses needs, makes recommendations, and co-ordinates actions, although decisions are taken jointly by every institution towards an agreed goal.
- It lasts for up to five years depending on the client's needs.
- It involves a co-ordinator, whose role is to co-ordinate action and steer clients through the system.
- During rehabilitation, people continue to receive whatever benefit they are on or, if not entitled to any, a minimum income at the social assistance level.

The new model aims to ensure treatment where necessary, with work seen as part of the solution. It is focused neither on assessing the degree of illness (the health sector view) nor the work capability (the job centre view), but on integrating those approaches.

Outcomes

The success of the reform will depend on the way it is implemented. The new approach is promising, although it is too early to tell how well it will work in practice and what its longer-term outcomes might be. Initial data for 2013 suggest there is a chance that the reform may achieve at least some of its aims – it has already more than halved the number of new disability benefit allowances. Those people no longer entitled to disability benefit (especially young people and those with mental illness) are now engaged in the new rehabilitation process. It is too early to tell whether they will be reintegrated into the labour market in a sustainable manner.

Further reading

OECD (2013), *Mental Health and Work: Denmark*, OECD Publishing, Paris, http://dx/doi/org/10.1787/9789264188631-en.

The Danish Government (2013), *The National Reform Programme Denmark 2013*, Copenhagen.

The Danish Government (2012), *The National Reform Programme Denmark 2012*, Copenhagen.

Factsheet 5.4
Austria: Focus on rehabilitation and retraining to prevent disability

Context

Limiting disability benefits to people permanently unable to work can be a solution to large, steep increases in the disability benefit caseload. Mental illness is often not permanent, though often chronic and recurrent. Temporary disability benefits have shown little positive impact for people with mental ill-health. A much stronger focus on retraining and rehabilitation instead of granting a temporary disability benefit could be a way forward.

Programme

In late 2012, the Austrian Government agreed on a comprehensive reform to reduce the number of disability benefit claims by improving the labour market integration of people with chronic health problems or disabilities, but who had the capacity to work. Only people permanently unable to work, can now access disability benefit. For those who are no longer entitled, two new benefits were introduced – rehabilitation and retraining benefit.

People who are temporarily too sick to work and in need of treatment will now be entitled to rehabilitation benefit. They had previously to apply for a temporary disability benefit which was in reality a dead end and will now be abolished. Health insurance pays the rehabilitation benefit. Although it is not a temporary benefit, the health status of recipients will be reassessed regularly (at least once a year). The amount is identical to sickness benefit – normally 60% of the last wage.

People who are fit enough to work but unable to exercise their profession will now be entitled to a retraining benefit (a special unemployment benefit with a 22% top-up) and receive retraining in a comparable profession.

Moreover, people on either rehabilitation or retraining benefit are legally entitled to medical rehabilitation if it is necessary to their reinstatement in the workplace.

Outcomes

The new rules, applicable since January 2014, will be phased in gradually and apply to everyone who was under 50 years old at the time they came into force. The expectation is that between 2014 and 2018, around 15 000 people will receive retraining benefit and some 23 000 rehabilitation benefit. It is estimated that the cuts in disability benefit spending will yield savings in the order of EUR 700 million by 2018. Initially, however, data for the first months of the first year suggest that the real figure could be much lower.

In the coming 15 years, the changes will gradually be extended to the entire working-age population. One downside, however, is that the reform will apply only to blue- and white-collar workers: civil servants, farmers, and the self-employed (who all have their own pension and disability benefit systems) are not included. This remains an important policy gap, particularly as farmers and civil servants have comparatively easier access to disability benefits.

Further reading

OECD (forthcoming 2015), *Mental Health and Work: Austria*, OECD Publishing, Paris.

Factsheet 5.5
Australia: Unemployment profiling tool ensures quick referral

Context

Mental illness is often a considerable barrier to labour market re-entry for the unemployed. When the public employment service identifies poor mental health early, it can help improve jobseeker activation and prevent long-term unemployment and disability benefit dependence. So far, however, most OECD employment support schemes do not assess the jobseekers' mental health status upon intake.

Programme

In Australia, the Job Seeker Classification Instrument (JSCI) is the primary profiling tool used for determining clients' labour market disadvantages and quickly referring them to an employment service or for more in-depth assessment. JSCI interviews are conducted during face-to-face or telephone interviews after jobseeker have registered for income support. It seeks to determine a person's labour market disadvantage and connect them quickly to an appropriate employment service. More importantly, for people with mental ill-health, diagnosed or not, the JSCI is the earliest opportunity in the system for identifying and assessing the impact of their health condition on their past and future participation in the labour market.

Outcomes

While the profiling tool could determine a client's labour market disadvantage more accurately, the actual identification of mental ill-health is not self-evident. The instrument does not seem to work well for people with mild-to-moderate mental illness, as the JSCI question relating to mental health is voluntary. If their condition is undiagnosed and/or they do not disclose their condition in the JSCI interview, then it is unlikely they will be quickly referred for a more intensive assessment conducted by an allied health professional. As a consequence, the person's underlying barrier to labour market reintegration can long go unidentified. And even if jobseekers disclose their mental health issues, it will only have a relatively small impact on the JSCI score measuring their level of disadvantage. Consequently, there is lots of room for improving a profiling tool that in principal has considerable potential.

Further reading

OECD (forthcoming 2015), *Mental Health and Work: Australia*, OECD Publishing, Paris.

Factsheet 5.6
Belgium: Assessing mental health problems at intake

Context

It is important that the public employment service identifies mental ill-health early if it is to prevent long-term unemployment and disability benefit dependence. Systematically assessing jobseekers for reintegration barriers can improve the employment outcomes of those who have mental health problems.

Programme

Since 2010, jobseekers estranged from the labour market are systematically assessed by the Flemish Public Employment Service (VDAB) for problems that hinder their re-employment. Such assessment used to take place within the first six months of unemployment, but not necessarily when jobseekers enrolled. The target group includes people with reduced psychological stability and those who are unable to deal with stress. Upon intake, caseworkers use an assessment form to map jobseekers' possibilities and inabilities. The caseworkers look out for employment-specific competencies and qualifications, job-search behaviour, social and communication skills, disabilities, secondary conditions (e.g. mobility, childcare, and the inactivity trap), and health problems. After the caseworker has completed the assessment form and proposed a follow-up programme, a VDAB psychologist has to approve the application.

The aim of the assessment is to quickly detect multiple problems in order to prevent long-term unemployment and offer the jobseeker a tailor-made activation programme. Assessment can be requested at any time during unemployment if there is any sign of a problem. When a caseworker believes there is a more severe mental health problem, he or she refers the client for diagnosis to a VDAB psychologist or an external employment research centre specialised in in-depth multidisciplinary screening.

Outcomes

In the first half of 2014, 7 676 jobseekers were registered for an assessment by the VDAB. Of those 8% were referred for in-depth multidisciplinary screening. After following an activation programme, 35% were ready to work on the regular labour market. The rest need additional support and care.

Supervisors of the activation programmes are satisfied with the quality of the screening reports they receive from caseworkers. The reports contain sufficient information on jobseeker' possibilities and inabilities. The assessment form is more easily accessible than its predecessor and leaves plenty of scope for (qualitative) information sharing through the use of empty text boxes that jobseekers fill in. However, supervisors believe the screening process could be improved by adding objective facts about jobseekers (e.g. internships, previous employer references), in addition to self-assessment.

Further reading

OECD (2013), *Mental Health and Work: Belgium*, OECD Publishing, Paris, http://dx.doi.org/10.1787/9789264187566-en.

Factsheet 5.7
Netherlands: Digital support for people on unemployment benefit

Context

Public employment services do not always have the resources to provide their clients with personal support. Computerising support services – including evidence-based e-mental health programmes such as online cognitive behavioural therapy – could be fruitful.

Programme

Since 2013, the Dutch Employee Insurance Agency (UWV) has been using a digitalised system to support its clients. During the first three months of unemployment, all contact with UWV goes through the Internet: benefit administration, job search and applications, and online workshops and training. After three months, UWV conducts an evaluation to see whether or not the unemployment benefit recipient is eligible for intensive support.

In the future, eligibility for intensive support will be assessed through the use of a digital questionnaire, called "Work Explorer", which determines a jobseeker's chances of resuming work within a year. The outcome of the questionnaire will determine whether or not the jobseeker is entitled to intensive support as well as the kind of support that is necessary to increase his or her chances of finding a job. The questionnaire consists of a list of 20 questions on hard factors (e.g. age, job tenure and knowledge of the Dutch language) and soft factors like jobseekers' personal takes on their chances of resuming work, perception of their health, active job search behaviour, and physical and psychological work capability. Work Explorer's questions are drawn from an extensive review of the literature and an econometric analysis designed to select those with the highest predictive power.

Outcomes

UWV is still developing its digital support system on the basis of national and international experience in e-services in the health sector combined with strategies from the behavioural sciences to influence the behaviour and motivation of jobseekers. To jobseekers with mental health problems it would be particularly relevant if UWV would consider the inclusion of Internet-administered cognitive behavioural therapy for depression and anxiety as part of its support provision.

Further reading

Andrews, G. et al. (2010), "Computer Therapy for Anxiety and Depressive Disorders is Effective, Acceptable and Practical Care: A Meta-analysis", *PlOS One*, Vol. 5, No 10, e13196.

Bijlert, J., K. Bongers and H. Goossensen (2012), Gedragsbeïnvloeding in een online omgeving. Een verkennende literatuurstudie naar de mogelijkheden van online gedragsbeïnvloeding toegepast op UWV, Centrum voor Criminaliteitspreventie en Veiligheid, Utrecht.

OECD (2014), *Mental Health and Work: Netherlands*, OECD Publishing, Paris, http://dx.doi.org/10.1787/9789264223301-en.

Factsheet 5.8
Sweden: Job coaches for people moving in and out of employment

Context

Although employers could help considerably improve the employment levels of people with mental ill-health, they often lack knowledge of mental health issues. They need better tools to identify critical situations. Co-operation between the public employment service (PES) and employers could help to retain sick workers.

Programme

In 2012, the Swedish PES initiated a pilot project in collaboration with the Work Environment Authority. Known as the Job Coach Programme, the pilot was designed to enhance co-operation with employers by enlisting job coaches with special workplace-related competencies to: i) offer support to employers in understanding psychosocial issues in the workplace; ii) smooth the return to work for jobseekers who have been out of the workplace for long periods; and iii) help employers retain jobseekers who resume work.

The main target groups of the programme are the long-term unemployed and people with records of disrupted employment and PES programme participation. Although sickness benefit recipients and people with mental ill-health are not targeted explicitly, many of them match the target groups.

The job coach can be a psychologist, social worker, or a workplace specialist with a minimum experience of one year in the psychosocial side of work. The programme lasts for three months during which time the employer, the jobseeker, and the PES have a minimum of four meetings. In the first meeting, the job coach meets solely with the jobseeker to understand his or her needs and what prevents the return to work. The second meeting brings in the employer and seeks to draft an initial plan for securing entry into the workplace. The last two meetings are used to evaluate the plan and action of employers and to develop recommendations for further improvement.

Outcomes

So far, there is no evidence available as to the success of the programme. Evidence from other labour market programmes targeted at harder-to-place client groups shows that co-operation of the kind in the Job Coach Programme can facilitate job retention and early returns to work.

Further reading

OECD (2013), *Mental Health and Work: Sweden*, OECD Publishing, Paris, http://dx.doi.org/10.1787/9789264188730-en.

Factsheet 5.9
Austria: Health road to improve the unemployment-disability interface

Context

Unemployed people who suffer from mental ill-health are often sent back and forth between different agencies. They gradually lose their employability and motivation and become increasingly at risk of long-term unemployment. If the unemployment and disability benefit systems shared information, they could prevent long delays in support provision.

Programme

The Gesundheitsstraße, or Health Road, is a project that Austria first launched as pilots in some regions in 2009 before recently rolling it out nationwide. Health Road seeks to replace multiple assessments by putting in place a central assessment authority which can take decisions that are binding both on the disability benefit agency (PVA) and the public employment service (PES). If a PES caseworker has doubts about a client's ability to take up employment, he or she can be referred for an early assessment at the PVA to determine whether or not he or she is able to work or at least benefit from rehabilitation. The PVA also needs to clarify whether the client should stay with the PES or be handed over to the PVA. In this way, the PES gains some insight into PVA know-how at an earlier stage. If the client refuses the PVA assessment, his or her unemployment benefit is suspended.

Administratively, the new assessment authority is based in the PVA but the costs of early assessments are covered by the PES (because at this stage the client is a customer of the PES). If assessed as "able to work", the client will be served by the PES. If not, an application for a disability benefit is recommended – but eligibility will be tested more carefully. Although the assessment has to include a decision on the person's ability to work, it should also go into further detail about reasonable job requirements and, where applicable, recommend medical and/or vocational rehabilitation.

Outcomes

The advantages of the new approach include: an acceleration of the work ability assessment process (the medical report has to be prepared within three weeks and is valid for six months); no more contradictory assessments; greater legal certainty since decisions are binding on both agencies; more transparency for the client and agencies; considerable savings; and earlier rehabilitation and better reintegration chances.

From the evaluation period to late 2011, more than 5 000 clients were assessed (85% within one month). Of those, 22% were deemed temporarily unable to work. About 40% of all clients had mental health problems and their chance of being assessed as temporarily unable to work was higher – 35%. However, one year after the assessments very few clients were working, even among those assessed as able to do so, which points to the importance of rehabilitation measures for clients with mental health problems. Qualitative interviews also showed that clients following the Health Road generally believed they could work and were more interested in the support provided than those who applied directly for disability benefit.

Further reading

Hausegger, T., C. Reidl and C. Scharinger (2012), "Begleitende Evaluierung der Gesundheitsstraße", Endbericht, Prospect Research & Solution [Report for the Federal Ministry of Labour, Social Affairs and Consumer Protection], Vienna.

OECD (forthcoming 2015), *Mental Health and Work: Austria*, OECD Publishing, Paris.

Factsheet 5.10
Switzerland: Interinstitutional co-operation to improve work outcomes

Context

Clients with complex problems, often involving mental health, tend to be shifted around between different social protection systems. They face service gaps and service duplication as well as poor labour market outcomes. The situation is neither efficient nor cost-effective and demands greater inter-institutional co-operation.

Programme

Inter-institutional co-operation (IIZ) was launched in Switzerland in the early 2000s. IIZ's objectives include bringing clients with complex needs to the right institution faster; improving co-operation across institutions to increase clients' chances of reintegrating into employment; clarifying funding responsibilities for complex cases; and identifying and addressing (mental) health problems which hinder fast labour market reintegration.

A recent inventory of existing IIZ initiatives identified four major types of IIZ: i) multilateral co-operation concentrated on the integration of the young and young adults; ii) bilateral co-operation between two institutions, most frequently unemployment insurance and local social welfare; iii) multilateral co-operation for people with complex problems, generally involving case management; and iv) structural co-operation, which includes, for example, training provided jointly by two or more institutions.

IIZ MAMAC, a special project launched in 2006, aimed at making IIZ work better through: i) joint assessments of a person's work capacity that is binding on all institutions involved; ii) reintegration measures jointly agreed by all IIZ partners; and iii) making one institution responsible for managing a particular case throughout the entire process. IIZ MAMAC clients had to fulfil two criteria: i) suffer from health problems and face social difficulties but have been enrolled for less than six months with identified reintegration potential, and ii) be clients of at least three institutions (typically cantonal disability insurance, cantonal unemployment insurance, and municipal social assistance).

Outcomes

Evaluating the effect of IIZ is difficult because it is a highly decentralised initiative – with most forms of co-operation taking place on a regional and often local level – and a process that is constantly expanding. The only evaluation available concerns IIZ MAMAC. The project was well received by clients and adopted in most cantons, but has neither improved labour market outcomes nor reduced costs. Insufficient financial incentives to engage and the voluntary nature of IIZ explain to a considerable degree why implementation was very slow. Anecdotal evidence suggests that, despite all efforts to expand co-operation, it takes maybe half a year on average for a client to be referred to an IIZ team. People then typically stay between one and one-and-a-half years in co-operative schemes, during which time their employability gradually increases. Between one-third and one-half of clients might eventually find a job, which might not be sustainable, however. IIZ still reaches too few people and comes too late in most cases, thereby losing impact significantly. Meanwhile, the focus of all the institutions involved continues to be on their own cost containment rather than service efficiency and effectiveness for society as a whole.

Further reading

Bieri, O., E. Nadai and E. Flamand-Lew (2014), "IIZ – ein Label, unterschiedliche Formen der Zusammenarbeit", *Soziale Sicherheit CHSS*, No. 2, pp. 111-115.

Egger, M., V. Merckx and A. Wüthrich (2010), "Evaluation des nationalen Projekts IIZ-MAMAC", Beiträge zur Sozialen Sicherheit, Forschungsbericht 9/10, Bundesamt für Sozialversicherungen, Bern.

OECD (2014), *Mental Health and Work: Switzerland,* OECD Publishing, Paris, http://dx.doi.org/10.1787/9789264204973-en.

SECO (2004), Handbuch zur Interinstitutionellen Zusammenarbeit (IIZ), SECO, Bern.

Factsheet 5.11
Denmark: Return-to-work with caseworkers trained in psychology

Context

Employment services deal with many clients who suffer from mild-to-moderate mental ill-health. They need support in addressing their mental health, workplace, and employment issues. Since employment services are rarely in a position to offer them much face-to-face time, specialist providers take over.

Programme

The return-to-work programme of the Danish Mental Health Foundation (a non-profit organisation) targets clients with mild-to-moderate mental health conditions who have considerable labour market experience but have been on sick leave for at least six months. Because the programme deems motivation essential, clients must agree to interventions and be ready to be helped. Client commitment is determined in a preparatory meeting with the municipal job centre, which makes all referrals. Any client judged not to be job ready will be refused.

Interventions are structured, educating clients on their mental illness while tackling workplace issues and providing short-term treatment through cognitive behavioural therapy. After initial clarification, intervention typically last 19 weeks: 6 weeks of (group) courses to help understand the illness and teach coping mechanisms, followed by 13 weeks of trial employment or apprenticeships of a few hours per week.

Interventions are essentially specialised casework with a particularly low caseload (of between 10 and 20 clients) and are run by people specialised in working with clients suffering from mild-to-moderate mental ill-health. Most counsellors are psychologists who talk to clients as recovery counsellors, not therapists. The counsellor's focus in the weekly one-to-one meetings with a client is on education and employment, not the client's personality. Talking about resuming work (often in a new workplace), psychological counselling and helping to access mental health treatment are key aspects of the meetings.

Outcomes

The Foundation only acts in the Greater Copenhagen area (representing a population of approximately 1.5 million people), and solely as a knowledge, research, education and coaching centre for civil servants at the municipal job centers who run the programme.

There is no evaluation of the programme available. Anecdotal evidence suggests that most clients end up in employment, but there is no longer-term follow-up. Immediate outcomes after the 19-week interventions are as follows: 34% are ready to move into education or employment; 42% start treatment with a psychologist or a psychiatrist; and 24% stop the course or move onto benefits.

Further reading

OECD (2013), *Mental Health and Work: Denmark*, OECD Publishing, Paris, http://dx/doi/org/10.1787/9789264188631-en.

Danish speakers may want to have a look at www.psykiatrifonden.dk/.

Factsheet 5.12
Sweden: Ensuring psychological treatment for people on sick leave

Context

It is important to intervene quickly when employees are absent from work for reasons of mental ill-health. Both the health and the employment sector have major roles to play in averting long-term sickness, but they often undertake their policies in isolation. Collaboration could provide people with poor mental health with the multiple supports they need.

Programme

In 2008, the Swedish Ministry of Health and Social Affairs introduced its Rehabilitation Guarantee for people on sick leave or at risk of longer-term leave as a result of long-standing psychological problems such as anxiety, depression or stress. Through the scheme, county councils may receive direct payment from the Social Insurance Agency (which grants and pays sickness and disability benefits) for each medical intervention. The Rehabilitation Guarantee offers rehabilitation measures in the form of cognitive behavioural therapy (CBT) and interpersonal psychotherapy for relatively short periods (typically between 8 and 20 sessions). Those working with CBT must be qualified, and assessment and treatment can take place either individually or in groups.

Outcomes

Evaluation studies show mixed outcomes. On the one hand, the Rehabilitation Guarantee reduces the risk of absence among employees who are still at work compared to those who have not benefitted from it. On the other hand, no positive effect on sickness absence has been found among people who undergo interventions under the scheme while on sick leave without a valid job contract. They do, however, show improvements in self-reported health. While the programme is still in its early stages of delivery, important lessons can be learnt. For instance, one major challenge the Rehabilitation Guarantee is managing are the high drop-out rates before the end of treatment. A need for stronger incentives may be inferred to encourage people to take up, comply with, and complete courses of treatment. The lack of expertise in CBT was another problem that undermined the effectiveness of the programme.

Further reading

Karolinska Institutet (2011), "En nationell utvärdering av rehabiliteringsgarantins effekter på sjukfrånvaro och hälsa, Slutrapport del I", Stockholm.

OECD (2013), *Mental Health and Work: Sweden,* OECD Publishing, Paris, http://dx.doi.org/10.1787/9789264188730-en.

Factsheet 5.13
Sweden: Delta – Financial co-ordination to provide integrated services

Context

Medical and vocational rehabilitation requires the involvement of different policy sectors. The alignment and integration of health policies is still particularly weak in most countries. As a result, rehabilitation may be hampered by different and even contradicting priorities, poor communication, and inadequate joint planning leading to longer sickness absences and poor return-to-work outcomes.

Programme

DELTA is a local Swedish association that ensures financial co-ordination between the national employment service, the regional health authority, the municipal social service, and the national social insurance department. The four institutions supply the funding for DELTA. Established first in 1997 as a pilot project, it aims to improve cross-sector, inter-professional, and inter-organisational collaboration in order to meet rehabilitation needs in the working-age population more efficiently. Such needs are related mainly to mental ill-health, musculoskeletal disorders, complex social problems, or long-term work incapacity. The funds are pooled into a joint budget, which is allocated to the different rehabilitation services provided by the association.

Most of the activities under the aegis of DELTA operate with the objective of early, co-ordinated rehabilitation and may be divided into three main areas: i) social and medical activities included in treatment plans to shorten patient treatment, ii) occupational activities to speed up return-to-work, and iii) preventive activities that seek to avert sickness absence and social exclusion. These activities are carried out by multidisciplinary teams, consisting of professionals from the different sectors and institutions involved – e.g. physicians, nurses, physiotherapists, psychologists, economists, lawyers, and social workers. The teams are supervised by co-ordinators appointed by the association.

Outcomes

A number of evaluations have shown that DELTA has led to improved job-finding outcomes. Eight out of ten formerly unemployed people were able to maintain gainful employment, while two out of three were no longer sick-listed. Users also perceive services as well integrated and adapted to their needs. However, little is known about actual co-operation. One drawback of financial co-ordination is that it remains solely voluntary. It does not guarantee sustained collaboration in the long run or effective follow-up of individuals who need the greatest support. Improvements to programmes such as DELTA can also be made by involving employers in facilitating returns to work.

Further reading

Ahgren, B., S.B. Axelsson and R. Axelsson (2009), "Evaluating Intersectoral Collaboration: A Model for Assessment by Service Users", *International Journal of Integrated Care*, Vol. 9, January-March.

OECD (2013), *Mental Health and Work: Sweden*, OECD Publishing, Paris, http://dx.doi.org/10.1787/9789264188730-en.

Wollberg, P. (2006), *Integrated Service in Rehabilitation – On Co-ordination of Organisation and Financing*, Host Country Report, Peer Review and Assessment in Social Inclusion, European Commission.

Factsheet 5.14
Netherlands: Integrated Fit-4-Work services for municipal clients

Context

Mental ill-health is common among social assistance recipients, although they are not necessarily identified as having such a condition. Better identification of mental health problems and co-operation with the mental health sector would help provide recipients with appropriate support in returning to the labour market.

Programme

To better co-ordinate services across sectors for clients with multiple psychosocial problems, the Dutch employee insurance agency (UWV) and the social and mental health services of five large municipalities started a pilot project in 2013 called Fit-4-Work. The project's goal is to activate benefit recipients whose multiple psychosocial problems have disconnected them from the labour market and to help at least 50% of them find sustainable employment (longer than one year).

Fit-4-Work has seven component parts: i) diagnosis of the problem; ii) discussion in a multi-disciplinary team that brings together the social services, UWV, and the mental health sector; iii) integral service packages that include psychological treatment (without waiting time) and social interventions (such as debt relief, social activation and participation, and housing services); iv) care continuity; v) a fast problem-solving approach; vi) quick job placement; and vii) coaching for the client and employer during and after the placement.

Outcomes

Fit-4-Work is built on national and international experience in multidisciplinary integration approaches, including the ExIT project in Rotterdam and the WeCare project in New York. An evaluation of the ExIT approach showed a 40% outflow to work compared with 13% in a control group that followed a regular trajectory.

The pilot project is financed by the stakeholders and subsidised by the government. However, an *ex ante* cost-benefit analysis shows that the benefits should outweigh the costs for all stakeholders within four years. Actual reintegration is the work of a private provider (selected through a tender process), which is paid 75% of the budget after a client has held a job for more than one year. The remaining 25% is paid if at least 50% of the participants are still in employment after four years.

Further reading

Jagmohansingh, S. (2008), *Evaluatie ExIT Feijenoord* [Evaluation ExIT Feijenoord], Sociale Zaken en Werkgelegenheid, Rotterdam.

Kok, L. et al. (2011), "Fit-4-Work: een ex-ante kosten-baten analyse", *SEO Economisch Onderzoek*, Amsterdam.

OECD (2014), *Mental Health and Work: Netherlands*, OECD Publishing, Paris, http://dx.doi.org/10.1787/9789264223301-en.

van Dijk, K. and R. van Rijn (2013), "Fit4Work: Mensen met psychosociale klachten en multiproblematiek begeleiden naar werk", Contribution to SZW Experts Meeting on 30 January, Gezond aan het werk: Samenwerken aan gezondheidsbevordering en participatie van mensen in de bijstand, Ministerie van Sociale Zaken en Werkgelegenheid, The Hague.

Factsheet 5.15
Belgium: Activation team for jobseekers with mental health problems

Context

Efficient co-operation between public employment services and the mental health sector is crucial for reintegrating jobseekers with mental health problems into the workplace. The employment sector can address clients' health needs by co-ordinating its services with the health sector or providing integrated services within the sector. One way is to run a centre specialised in combining care and employment support.

Programme

In 2009, the Flemish Public Employment Service (VDAB) in Belgium developed a project in co-operation with the mental health and welfare sectors designed for jobseekers with severe medical, mental, psychological, or psychiatric problems. Under the scheme, they follow intensive activation programmes that combine care and employment support provided by a specialised non-profit centre (GTB). Recipients of disability benefits and social welfare were recently also allowed into the programmes. All services are financed by the Flemish Government and free of charge for jobseekers.

The activation team consists of three players: 1) a job coach; 2) a health coach; and 3) an empowerment coach. VDAB pays a fixed amount to each coach and requires them to work closely together in activation guidance and to meet on a regular basis.

The job coach – employed by GTB – puts in place an individual action plan together with the jobseeker and introduces him or her to the health coach and the empowerment coach who are responsible for identifying the right services in the health sector and welfare sector respectively. During the entire process, the job coach makes sure that the activation guidance keeps its focus firmly on work.

The health coach – typically a psychologist working in a centre for mental health – focuses on the health problems and provides rehabilitation and training in, for instance, self-confidence, coping with stress, assertiveness, and self-image. Individual or group therapies are provided in-house or by partner providers.

The empowerment coach from the welfare sector focuses on economic, psychosocial and social impediments and deals with issues such as mobility, personal budgeting, and housing (also either on an individual or group basis).

Outcomes

Co-operation between the three sectors delivers tailored services to long-term jobseekers who have grown remote from the labour market. Co-operation with a psychologist, the focus on case management, and the multidisciplinary team meetings are the major strengths of the programme.

In 2011, some 12% of the long-term unemployed in Flanders underwent in-depth multidisciplinary screening. Between 2007 and 2012, 11% of participants in the activation guidance programme found a job in the regular labour market and no longer receive unemployment benefits. Another 5.5% moved into sheltered employment and 2.8% into other forms of employment outside the regular labour market.

Further reading

OECD (2013), *Mental Health and Work: Belgium*, OECD Publishing, Paris, http://dx.doi.org/10.1787/9789264187566-en.

Factsheet 5.16
United Kingdom: Individual placement and support for common mental illness

Context

Integrated health and employment services for people with common mental illnesses are scarce. On the contrary, for people with severe mental illnesses evidence-based approaches exist with a strong focus (among other things) on fast job placement, integrated health intervention and post-placement follow-up. The evidence base on the cost and potential of such an approach for people with common mental illnesses is lacking.

Programme

Individual Placement and Support (IPS) for people with severe disability (and in particular, severe mental illness) works with a strict fidelity model and has a strong evidence base. England's National Health Service is now the first to test the potential of IPS for a much larger target group, i.e. people with common mental illnesses. The hope being that it will be less costly per person and therefore equally cost-effective for this group.

This pilot will test whether treatment within the Individual Access to Psychological Therapy (IAPT) programme together with employment support based on the IPS model, improves labour market outcomes compared to:

- Usual Jobcentre support (i.e. usual support by the employment sector)
- Usual IAPT support (i.e. usual support by the health sector).

The target group for the new pilot are disability benefit claimants (i.e. claimants of UK's Employment and Support Allowance) with common mental health problems.

Outcomes

The pilot began in June 2014 and runs across four Jobcentre districts. First outcomes will become available in mid-2015.

Further reading

OECD (2014), *Mental Health and Work: United Kingdom*, OECD Publishing, Paris, http://dx.doi.org/10.1787/9789264204997-en.

ORGANISATION FOR ECONOMIC CO-OPERATION AND DEVELOPMENT

The OECD is a unique forum where governments work together to address the economic, social and environmental challenges of globalisation. The OECD is also at the forefront of efforts to understand and to help governments respond to new developments and concerns, such as corporate governance, the information economy and the challenges of an ageing population. The Organisation provides a setting where governments can compare policy experiences, seek answers to common problems, identify good practice and work to co-ordinate domestic and international policies.

The OECD member countries are: Australia, Austria, Belgium, Canada, Chile, the Czech Republic, Denmark, Estonia, Finland, France, Germany, Greece, Hungary, Iceland, Ireland, Israel, Italy, Japan, Korea, Luxembourg, Mexico, the Netherlands, New Zealand, Norway, Poland, Portugal, the Slovak Republic, Slovenia, Spain, Sweden, Switzerland, Turkey, the United Kingdom and the United States. The European Commission takes part in the work of the OECD.

OECD Publishing disseminates widely the results of the Organisation's statistics gathering and research on economic, social and environmental issues, as well as the conventions, guidelines and standards agreed by its members.

OECD PUBLISHING, 2, rue André-Pascal, 75775 PARIS CEDEX 16
(81 2014 19 1 P) ISBN 978-92-64-22091-1 – 2015

www.ingramcontent.com/pod-product-compliance
Lightning Source LLC
Chambersburg PA
CBHW061214240926
51846CB00006B/1223
9789264220911